GRIMM UNIVERSE CREAT

JOE BRUSHA AND RALPH T

Grimm Fairy Tales

Wonderland

Clash of Queens

AGE OF DARKNESS

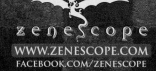

zenescope
WWW.ZENESCOPE.COM
FACEBOOK.COM/ZENESCOPE

GRIMM UNIVERSE

Wonderland
♠ ♥ Clash of Queens ♣ ♦
AGE OF DARKNESS

STORY
JOE BRUSHA
RALPH TEDESCO

WRITERS
RAVEN GREGORY
(ISSUES 1-2)
TROY BROWNFIELD
(ISSUES 3-5)

ARTWORK
MANUEL PREITANO

COLORS
DANIEL MORALES
(ISSUES 1-4)
BEN SAWYER
(ISSUE 5)

LETTERS
JIM CAMPBELL

ART DIRECTOR
ANTHONY SPAY

TRADE DESIGN
CHRISTOPHER COTE
STEPHEN SCHAFFER

EDITOR
PAT SHAND

THIS VOLUME REPRINTS THE COMIC
SERIES GRIMM FAIRY TALES PRESENTS:
WONDERLAND: CLASH OF QUEENS
#1-5 PUBLISHED BY ZENESCOPE
ENTERTAINMENT.

WWW.ZENESCOPE.COM

FIRST EDITION, JULY 2014
ISBN: 978-1-939683-71-7

ZENESCOPE ENTERTAINMENT, INC.

Joe Brusha • President & Chief Creative Officer
Ralph Tedesco • Editor-in-Chief
Jennifer Bermel • Director of Licensing & Business Development
Anthony Spay • Art Director
Christopher Cote • Senior Designer & Production Manager
Dave Franchini • Direct Market Sales & Customer Service

Grimm Fairy Tales presents

Wonderland

Clash of Queens

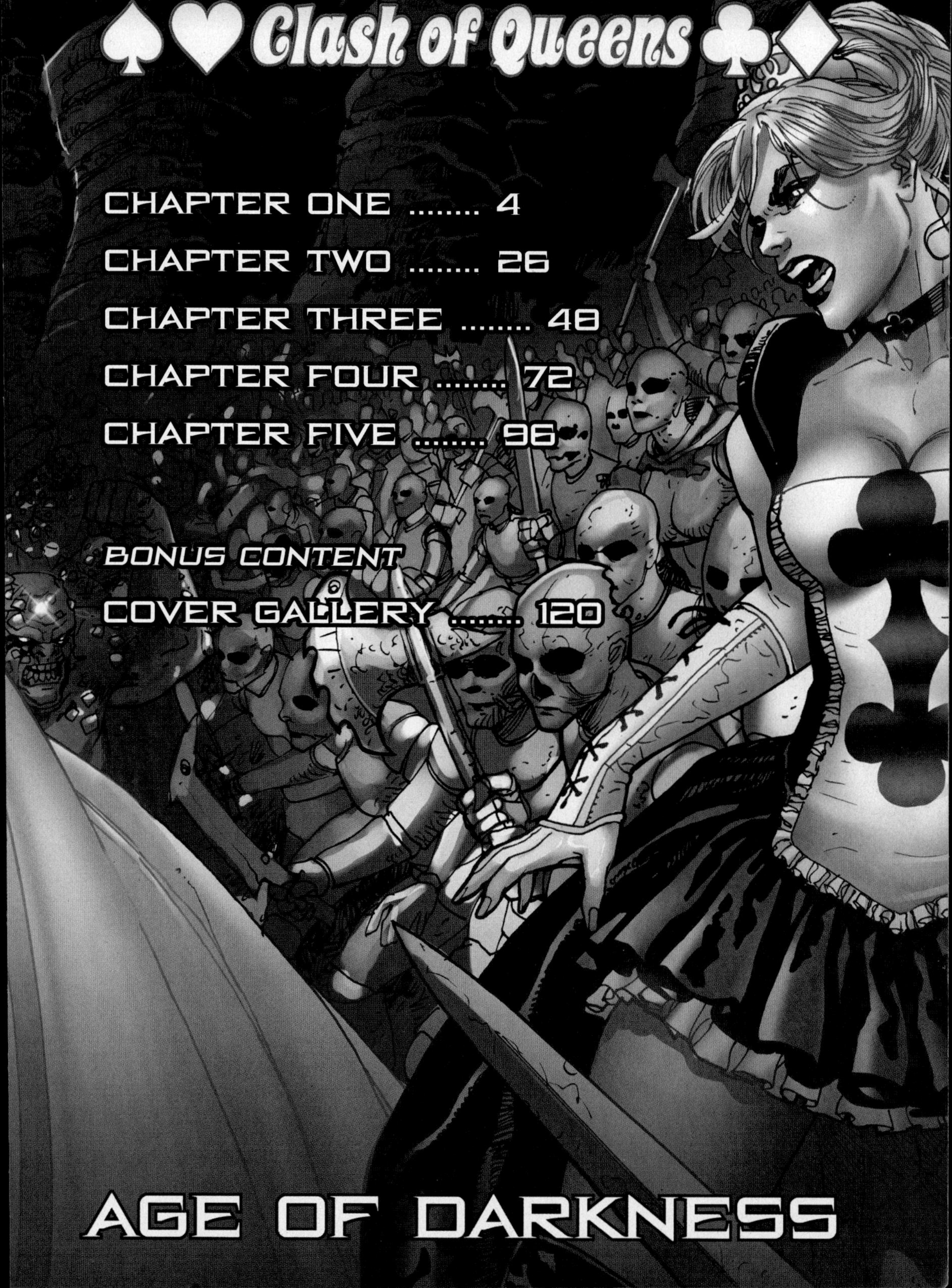

AGE OF DARKNESS

CHAPTER ONE

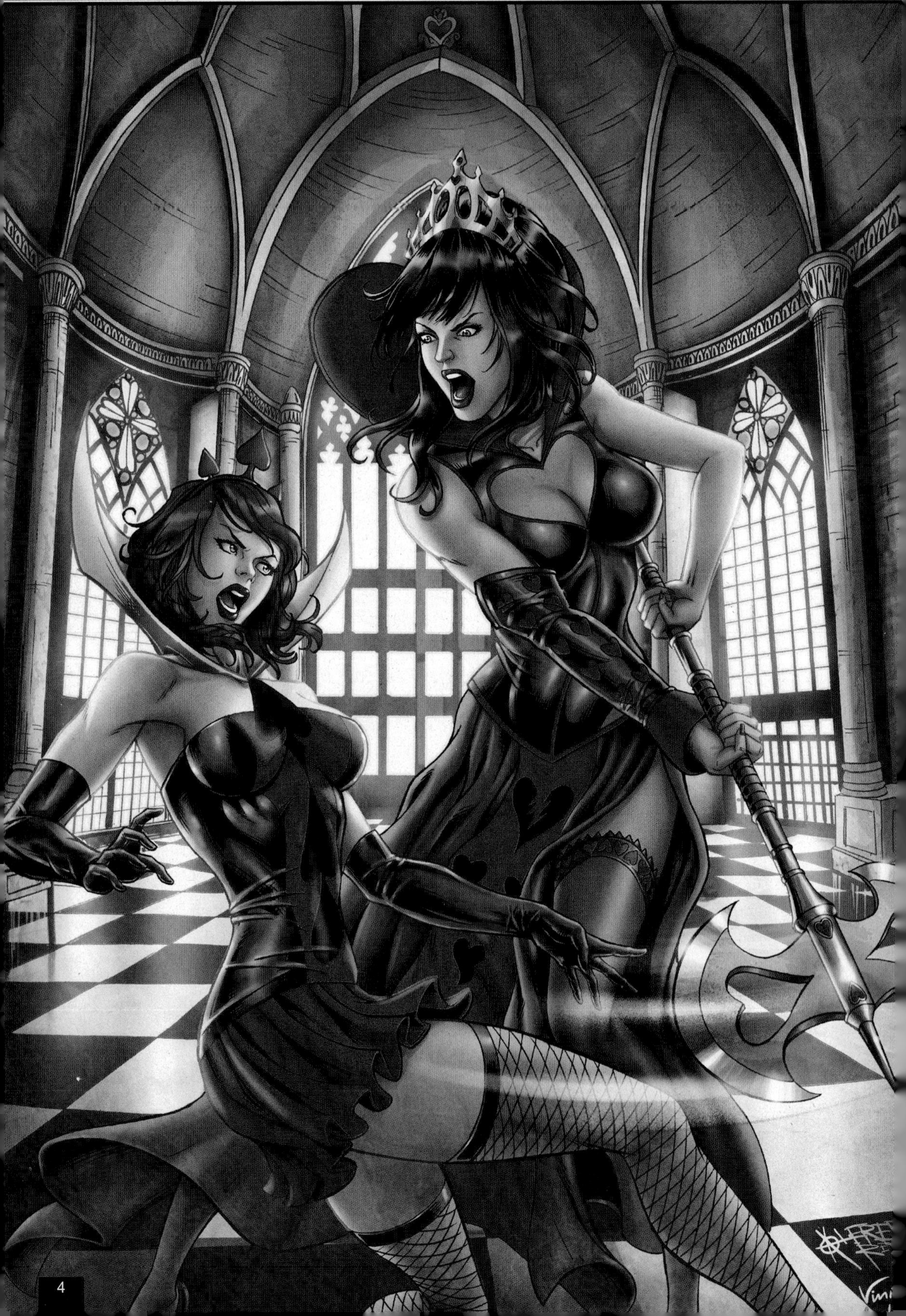

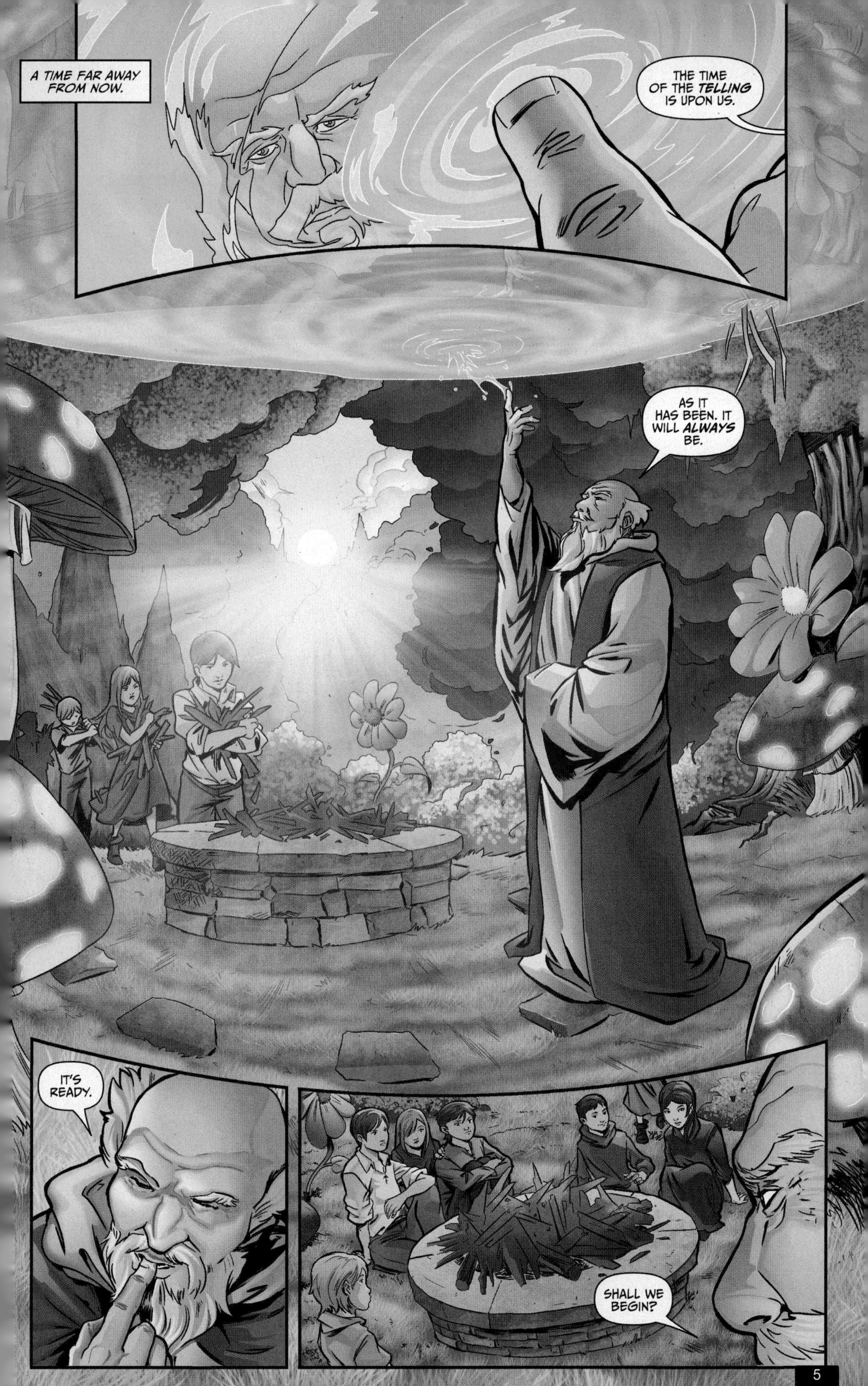
A TIME FAR AWAY FROM NOW.
THE TIME OF THE TELLING IS UPON US.
AS IT HAS BEEN. IT WILL ALWAYS BE.
IT'S READY.
SHALL WE BEGIN?

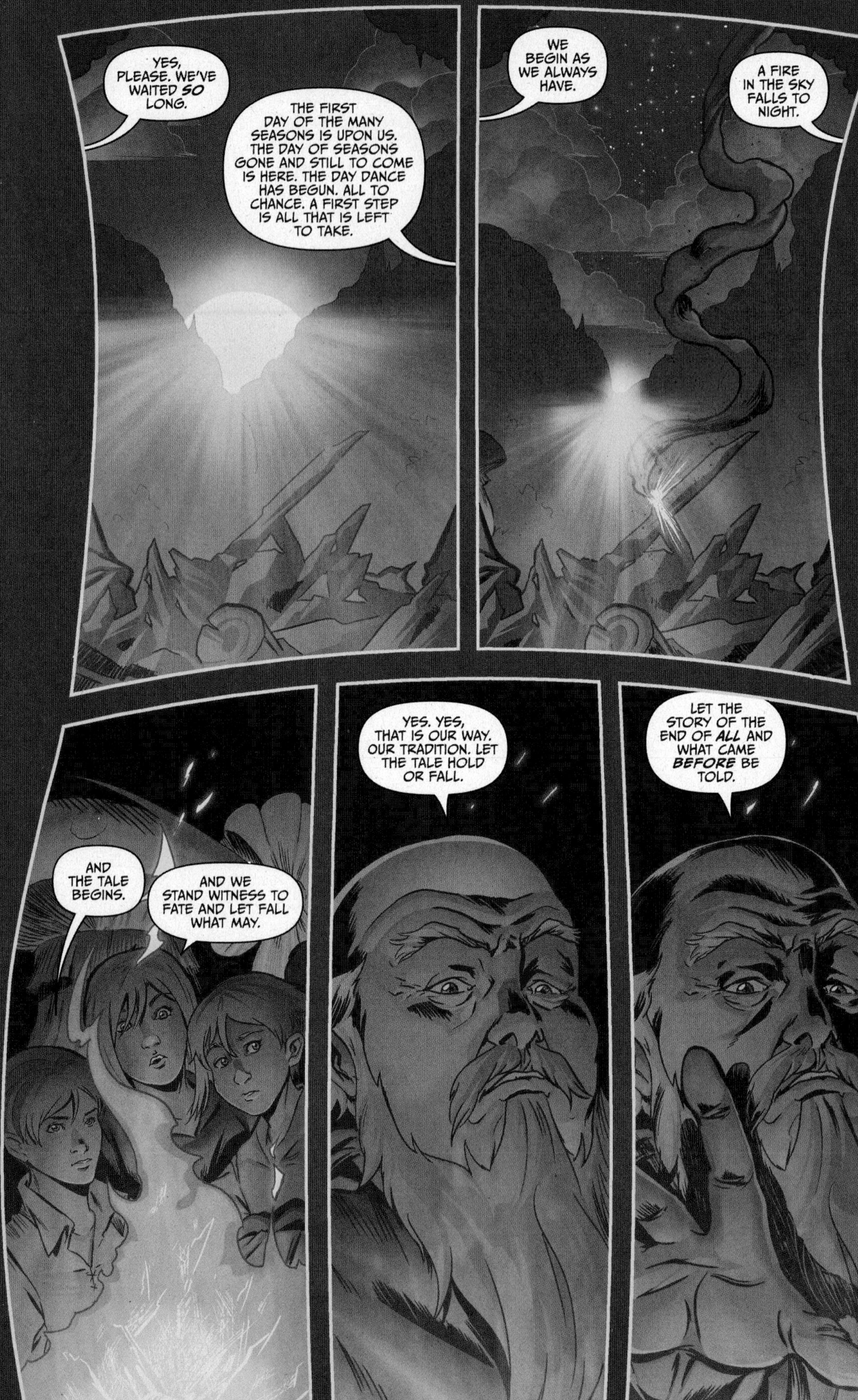
YES, PLEASE. WE'VE WAITED **SO** LONG.
THE FIRST DAY OF THE MANY SEASONS IS UPON US. THE DAY OF SEASONS GONE AND STILL TO COME IS HERE. THE DAY DANCE HAS BEGUN. ALL TO CHANCE. A FIRST STEP IS ALL THAT IS LEFT TO TAKE.
WE BEGIN AS WE ALWAYS HAVE.
A FIRE IN THE SKY FALLS TO NIGHT.
AND THE TALE BEGINS.
AND WE STAND WITNESS TO FATE AND LET FALL WHAT MAY.
YES. YES, THAT IS OUR WAY. OUR TRADITION. LET THE TALE HOLD OR FALL.
LET THE STORY OF THE END OF **ALL** AND WHAT CAME **BEFORE** BE TOLD.

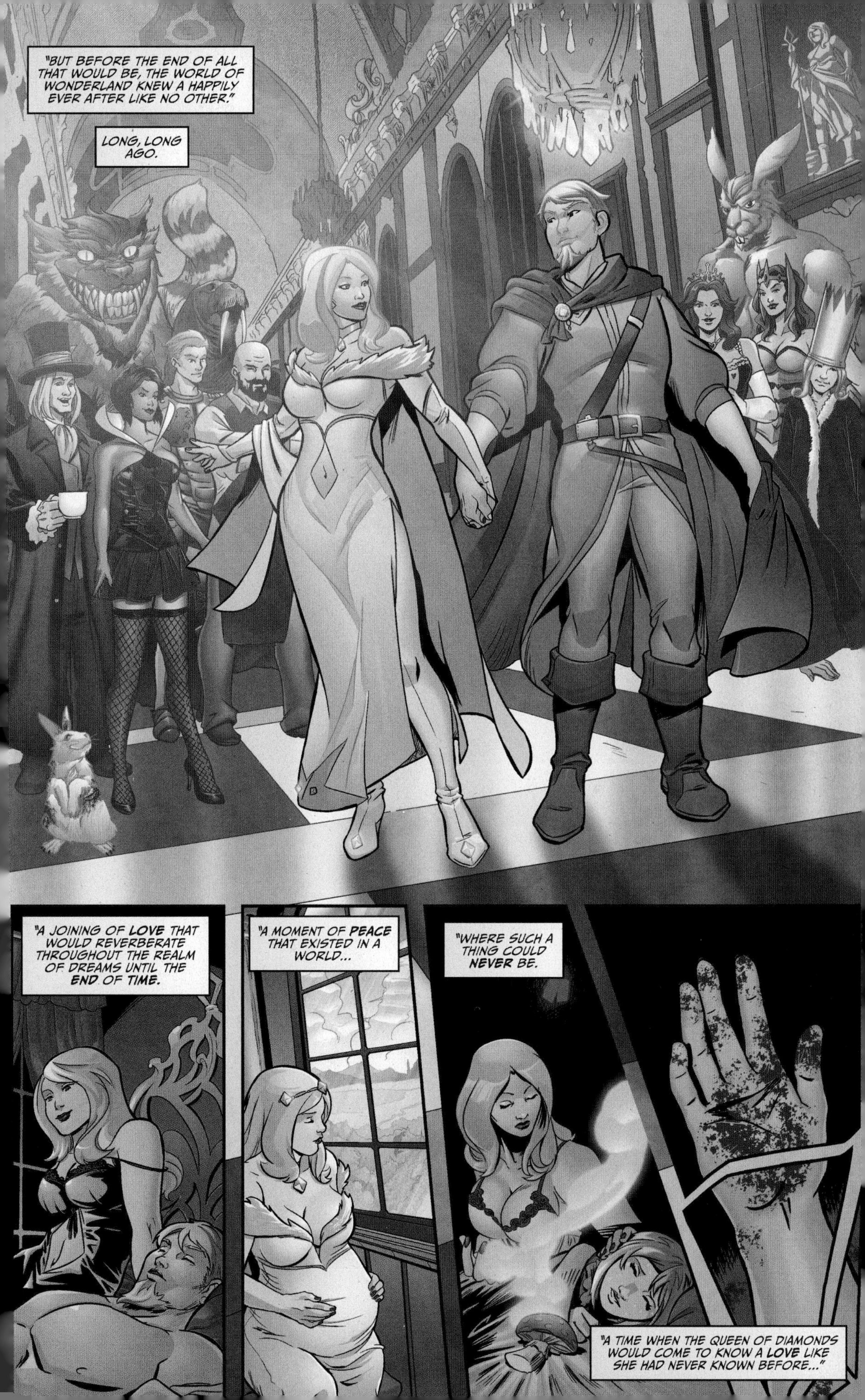
"BUT BEFORE THE END OF ALL THAT WOULD BE, THE WORLD OF WONDERLAND KNEW A HAPPILY EVER AFTER LIKE NO OTHER."
LONG, LONG AGO.
"A JOINING OF **LOVE** THAT WOULD REVERBERATE THROUGHOUT THE REALM OF DREAMS UNTIL THE **END** OF **TIME**.
"A MOMENT OF **PEACE** THAT EXISTED IN A WORLD...
"WHERE SUCH A THING COULD **NEVER** BE.
"A TIME WHEN THE QUEEN OF DIAMONDS WOULD COME TO KNOW A **LOVE** LIKE SHE HAD NEVER KNOWN BEFORE..."

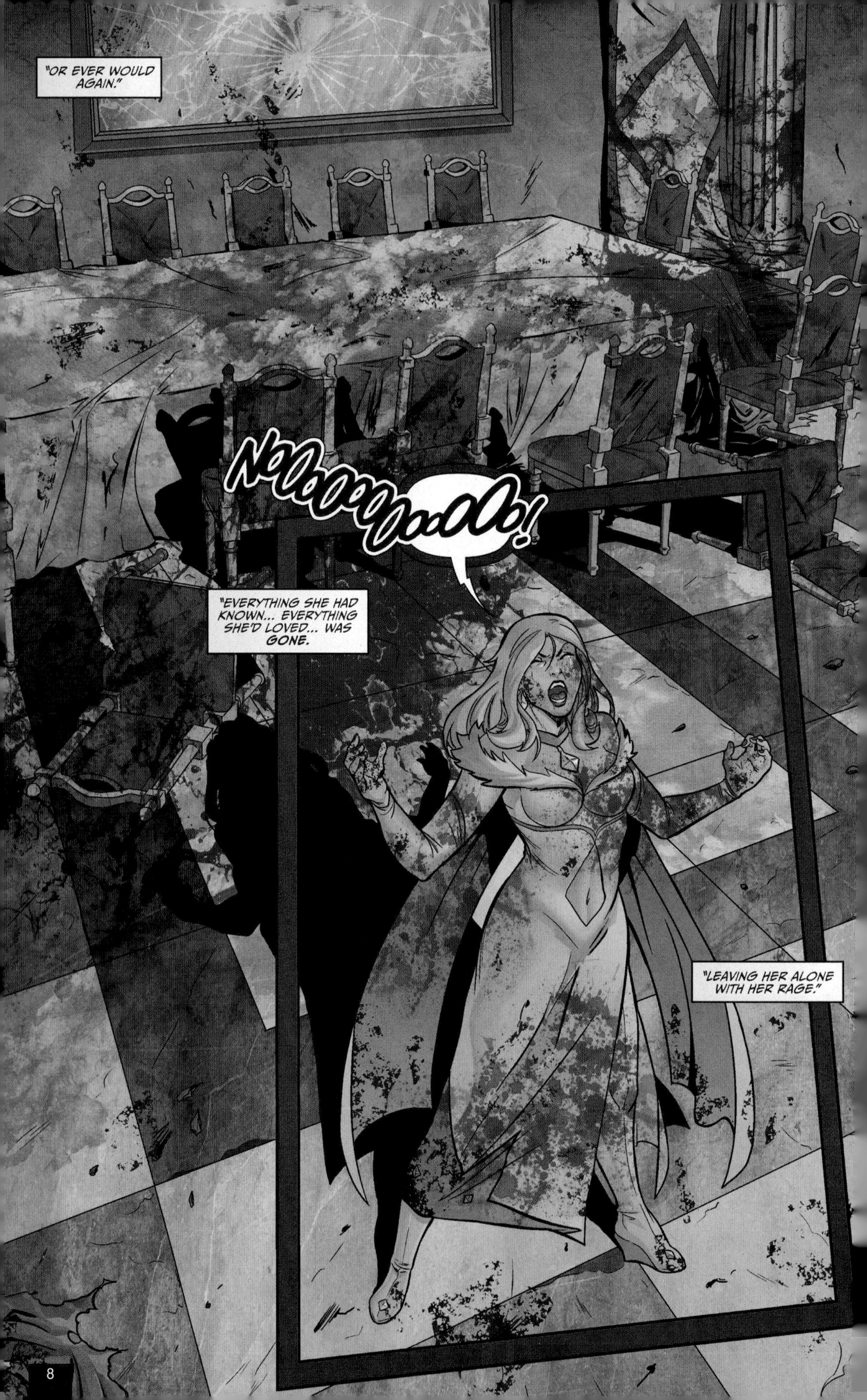
"OR EVER WOULD AGAIN."
NOOOOOOOOOOO!
"EVERYTHING SHE HAD KNOWN... EVERYTHING SHE'D LOVED... WAS GONE.
"LEAVING HER ALONE WITH HER RAGE."

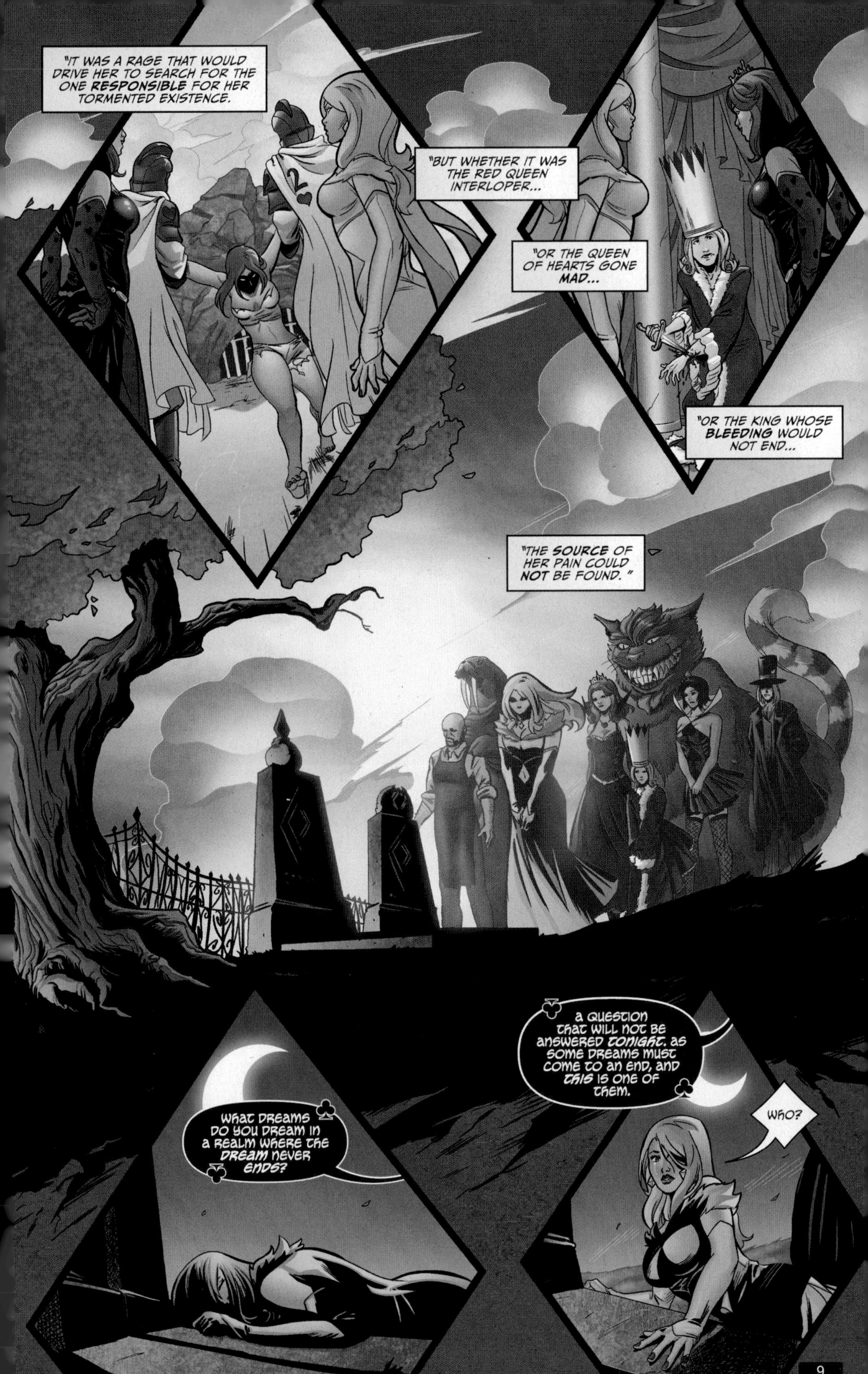
"IT WAS A RAGE THAT WOULD DRIVE HER TO SEARCH FOR THE ONE RESPONSIBLE FOR HER TORMENTED EXISTENCE.
"BUT WHETHER IT WAS THE RED QUEEN INTERLOPER...
"OR THE QUEEN OF HEARTS GONE MAD...
"OR THE KING WHOSE BLEEDING WOULD NOT END...
"THE SOURCE OF HER PAIN COULD NOT BE FOUND."
WHAT DREAMS DO YOU DREAM IN A REALM WHERE THE DREAM NEVER ENDS?
A QUESTION THAT WILL NOT BE ANSWERED TONIGHT. AS SOME DREAMS MUST COME TO AN END, AND THIS IS ONE OF THEM.
WHO?

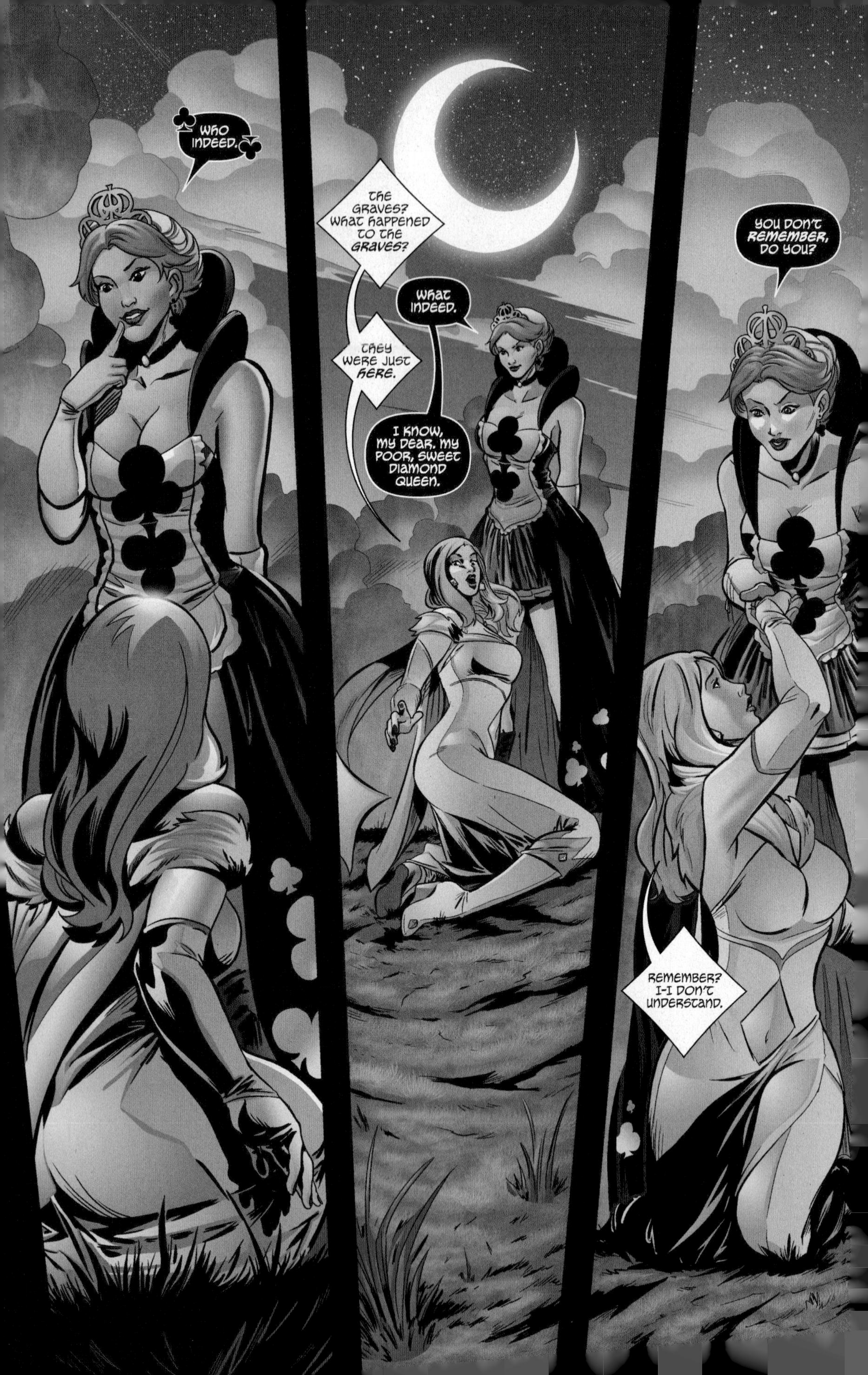
WHO INDEED.
THE GRAVES? WHAT HAPPENED TO THE GRAVES?
WHAT INDEED.
THEY WERE JUST HERE.
I KNOW, MY DEAR. MY POOR, SWEET DIAMOND QUEEN.
YOU DON'T REMEMBER, DO YOU?
REMEMBER? I-I DON'T UNDERSTAND.

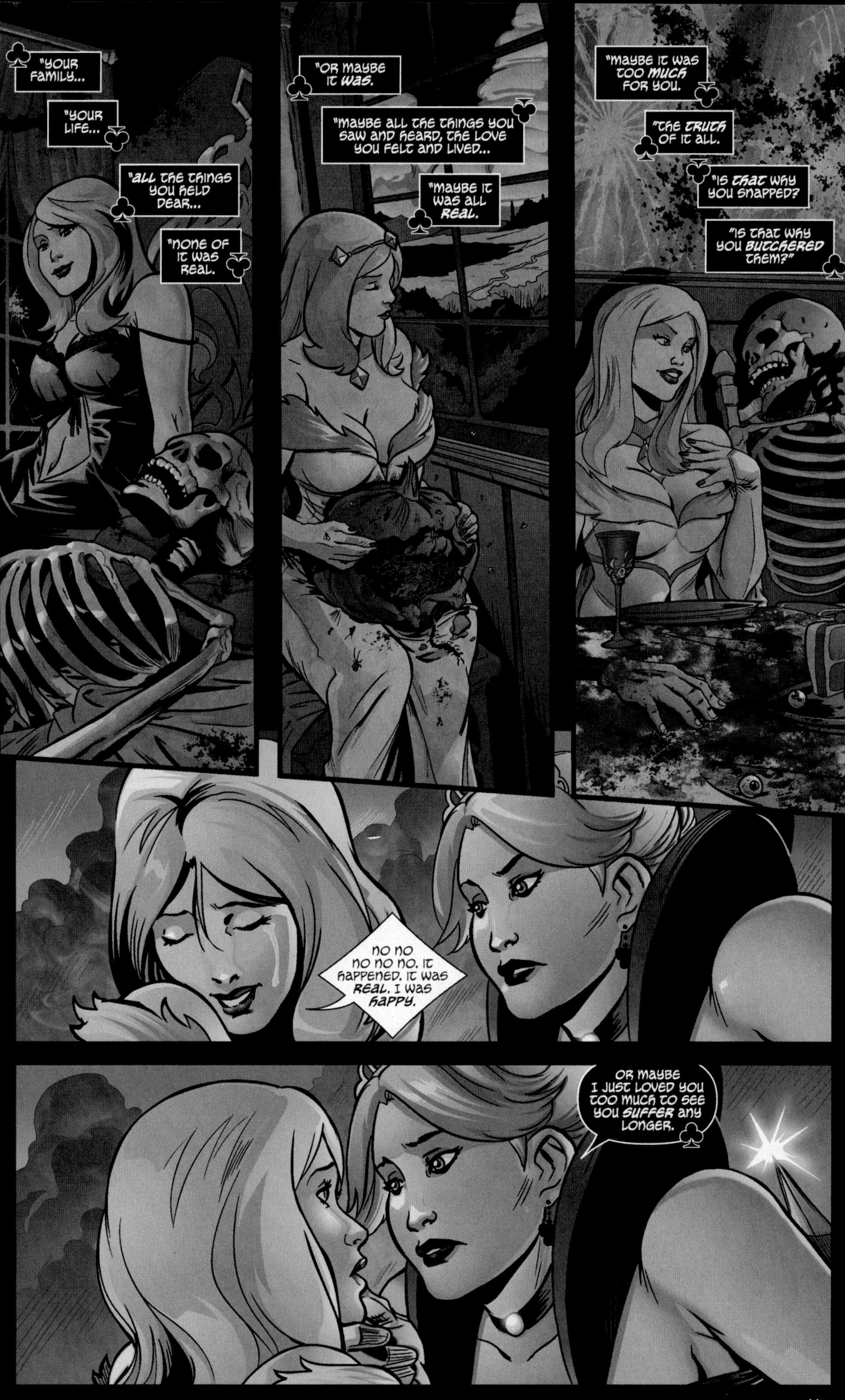
"YOUR FAMILY...
"YOUR LIFE...
"ALL THE THINGS YOU HELD DEAR...
"NONE OF IT WAS REAL.
"OR MAYBE IT WAS.
"MAYBE ALL THE THINGS YOU SAW AND HEARD, THE LOVE YOU FELT AND LIVED...
"MAYBE IT WAS ALL REAL.
"MAYBE IT WAS TOO MUCH FOR YOU.
"THE TRUTH OF IT ALL.
"IS THAT WHY YOU SNAPPED?
"IS THAT WHY YOU BUTCHERED THEM?"
NO NO NO NO NO. IT HAPPENED. IT WAS REAL. I WAS HAPPY.
OR MAYBE I JUST LOVED YOU TOO MUCH TO SEE YOU SUFFER ANY LONGER.

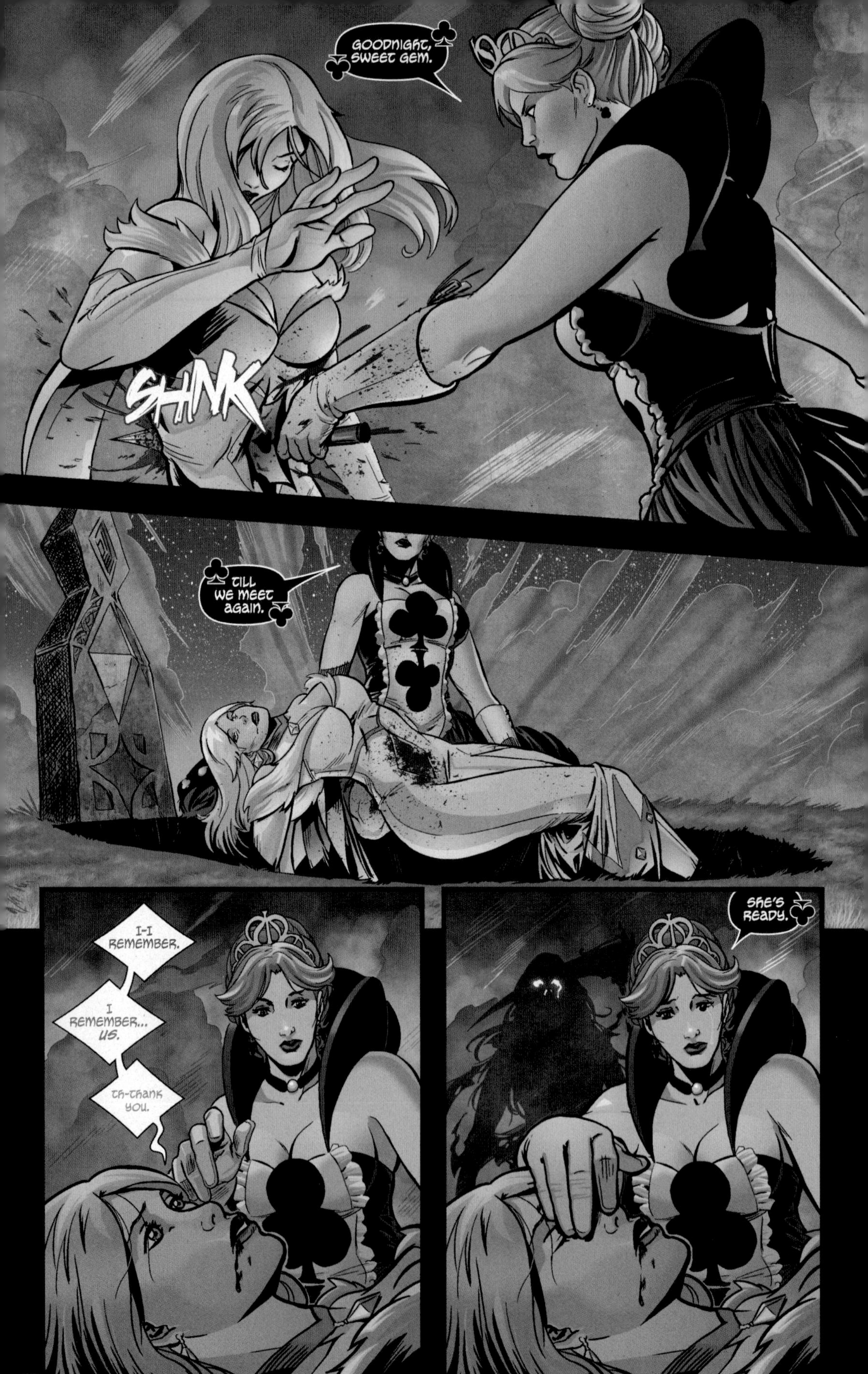
GOODNIGHT, SWEET GEM.
SHINK
TILL WE MEET AGAIN.
I-I REMEMBER.
I REMEMBER... US.
TH-THANK YOU.
SHE'S READY.

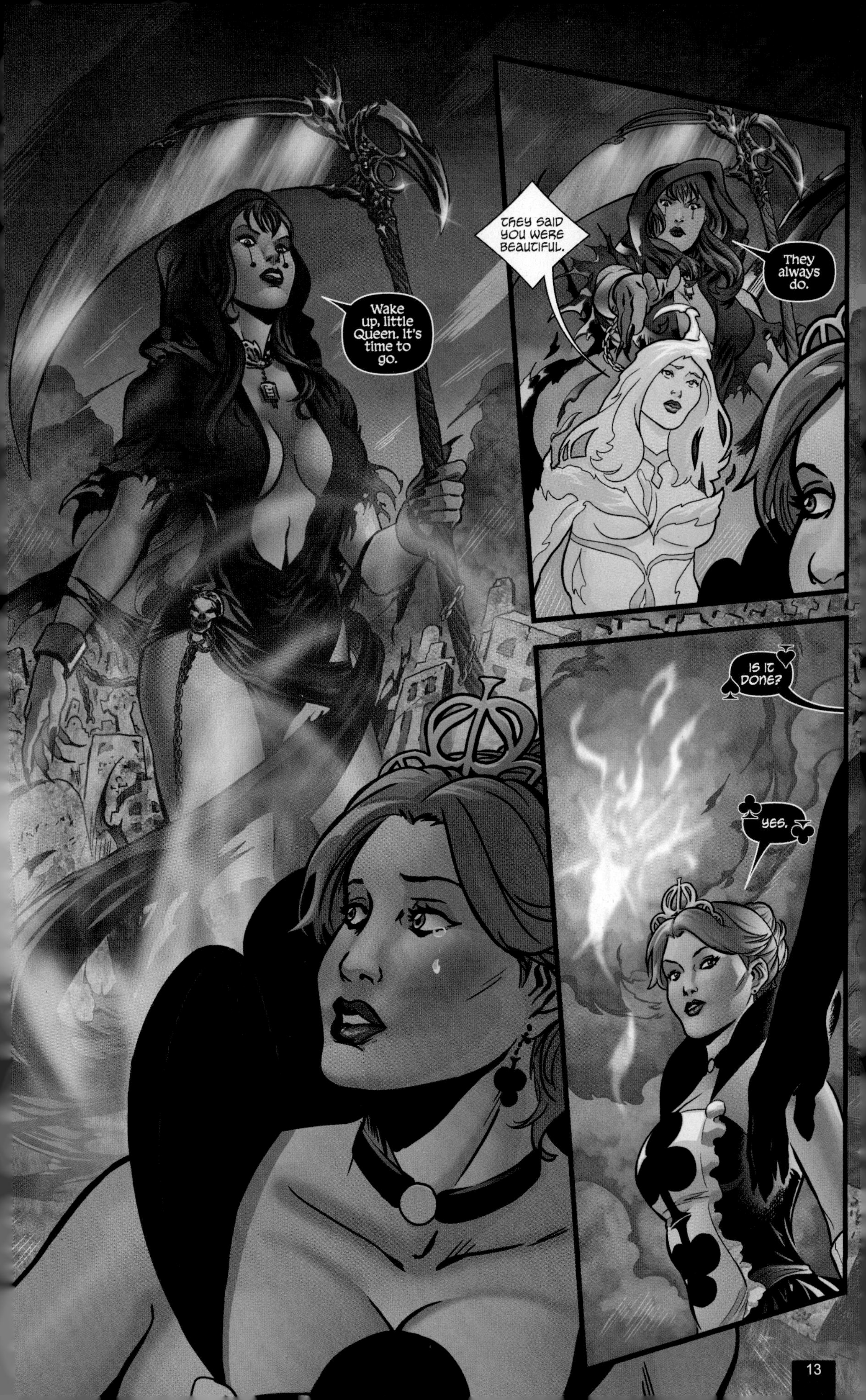
Wake up, little Queen. It's time to go.
THEY SAID YOU WERE BEAUTIFUL.
They always do.
IS IT DONE?
YES.

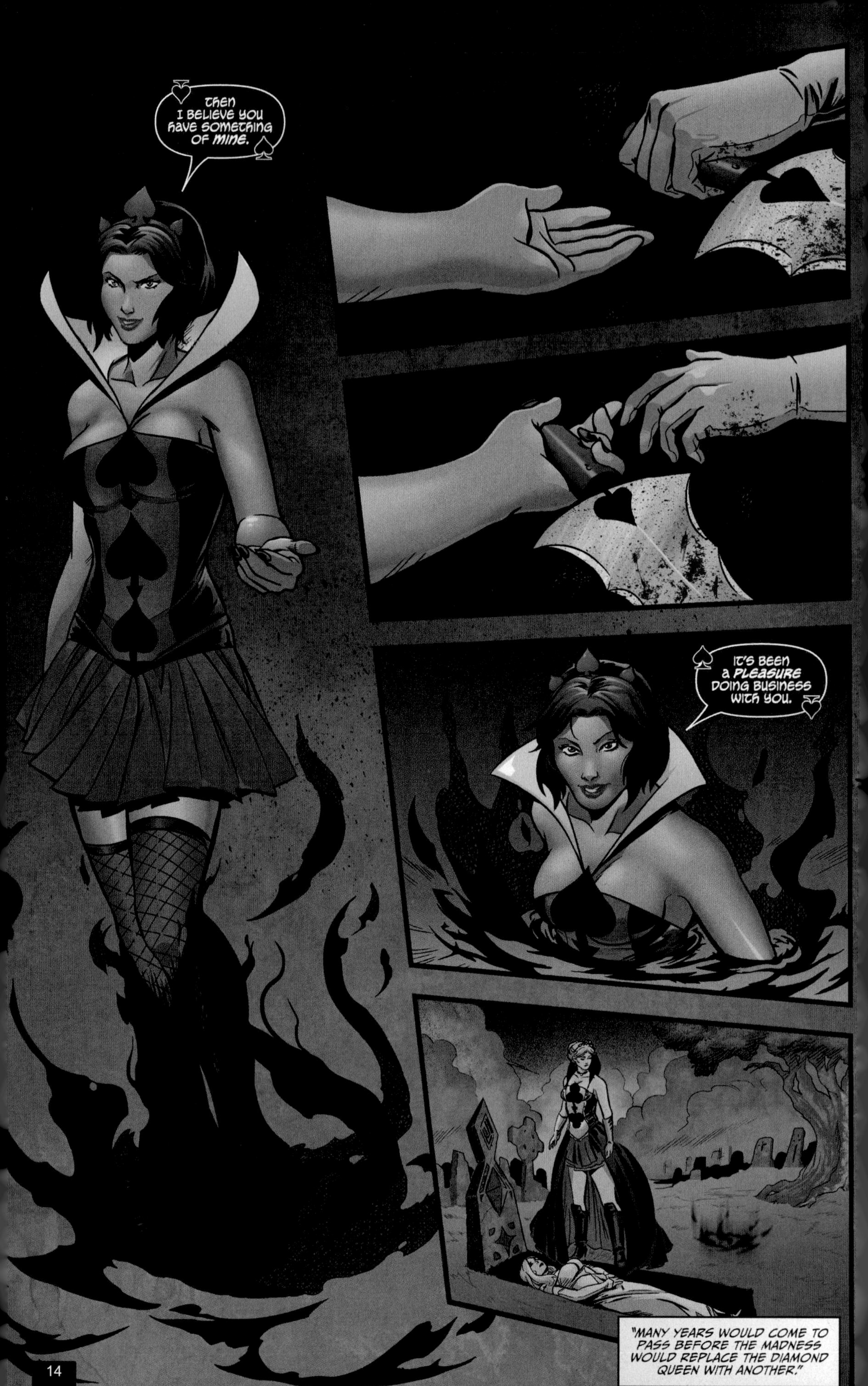
THEN I BELIEVE YOU HAVE SOMETHING OF MINE.
IT'S BEEN A PLEASURE DOING BUSINESS WITH YOU.
"MANY YEARS WOULD COME TO PASS BEFORE THE MADNESS WOULD REPLACE THE DIAMOND QUEEN WITH ANOTHER."

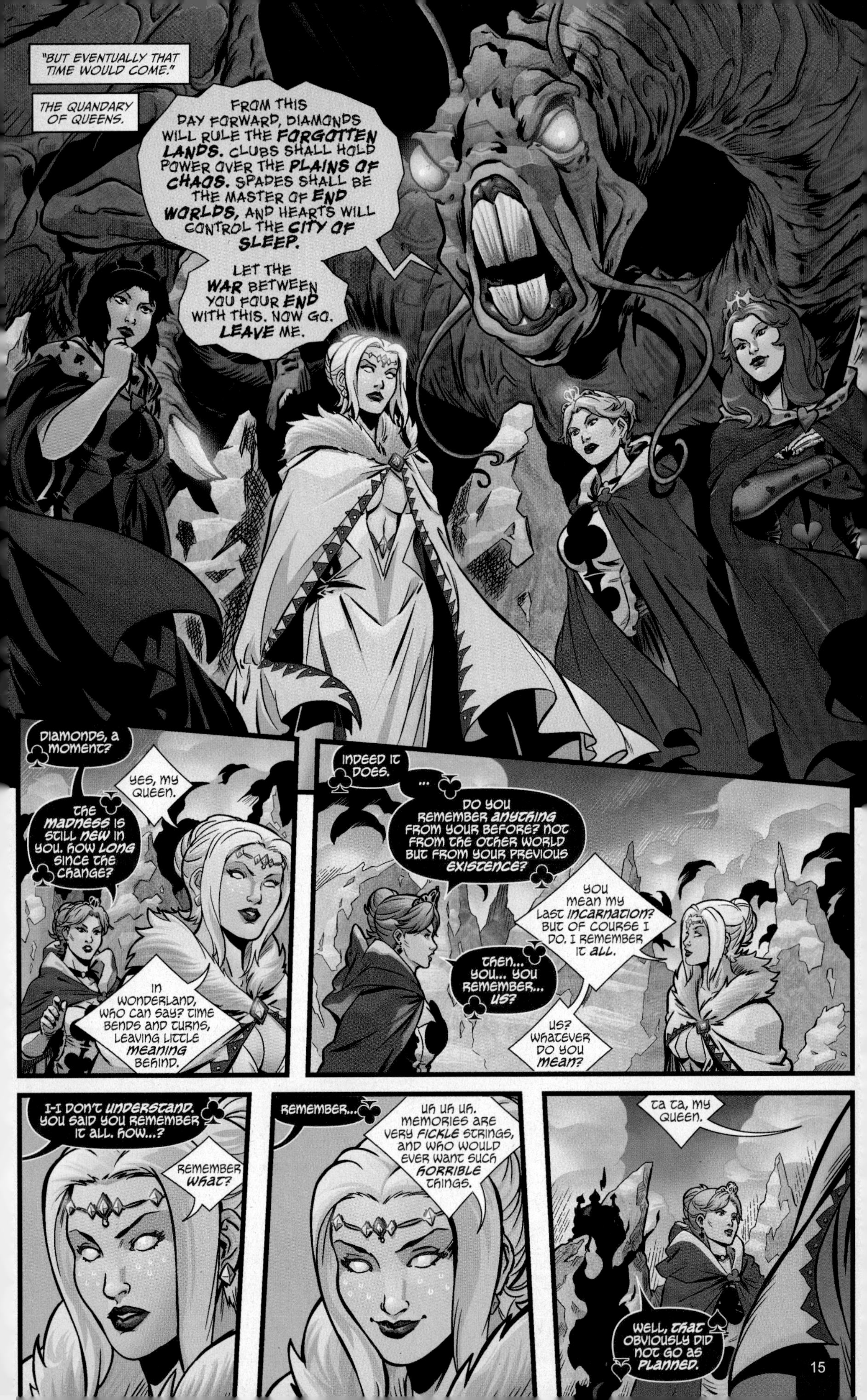

"BUT EVENTUALLY THAT TIME WOULD COME."
THE QUANDARY OF QUEENS.
FROM THIS DAY FORWARD, DIAMONDS WILL RULE THE FORGOTTEN LANDS. CLUBS SHALL HOLD POWER OVER THE PLAINS OF CHAOS. SPADES SHALL BE THE MASTER OF END WORLDS, AND HEARTS WILL CONTROL THE CITY OF SLEEP.
LET THE WAR BETWEEN YOU FOUR END WITH THIS. NOW GO. LEAVE ME.
DIAMONDS, A MOMENT?
YES, MY QUEEN.
THE MADNESS IS STILL NEW IN YOU. HOW LONG SINCE THE CHANGE?
IN WONDERLAND, WHO CAN SAY? TIME BENDS AND TURNS, LEAVING LITTLE MEANING BEHIND.
INDEED IT DOES.
...
DO YOU REMEMBER ANYTHING FROM YOUR BEFORE? NOT FROM THE OTHER WORLD BUT FROM YOUR PREVIOUS EXISTENCE?
YOU MEAN MY LAST INCARNATION? BUT OF COURSE I DO. I REMEMBER IT ALL.
THEN... YOU... YOU REMEMBER... US?
US? WHATEVER DO YOU MEAN?
I-I DON'T UNDERSTAND. YOU SAID YOU REMEMBER IT ALL. HOW...?
REMEMBER WHAT?
REMEMBER...
UH UH UH. MEMORIES ARE VERY FICKLE STRINGS, AND WHO WOULD EVER WANT SUCH HORRIBLE THINGS.
TA TA, MY QUEEN.
WELL, THAT OBVIOUSLY DID NOT GO AS PLANNED.

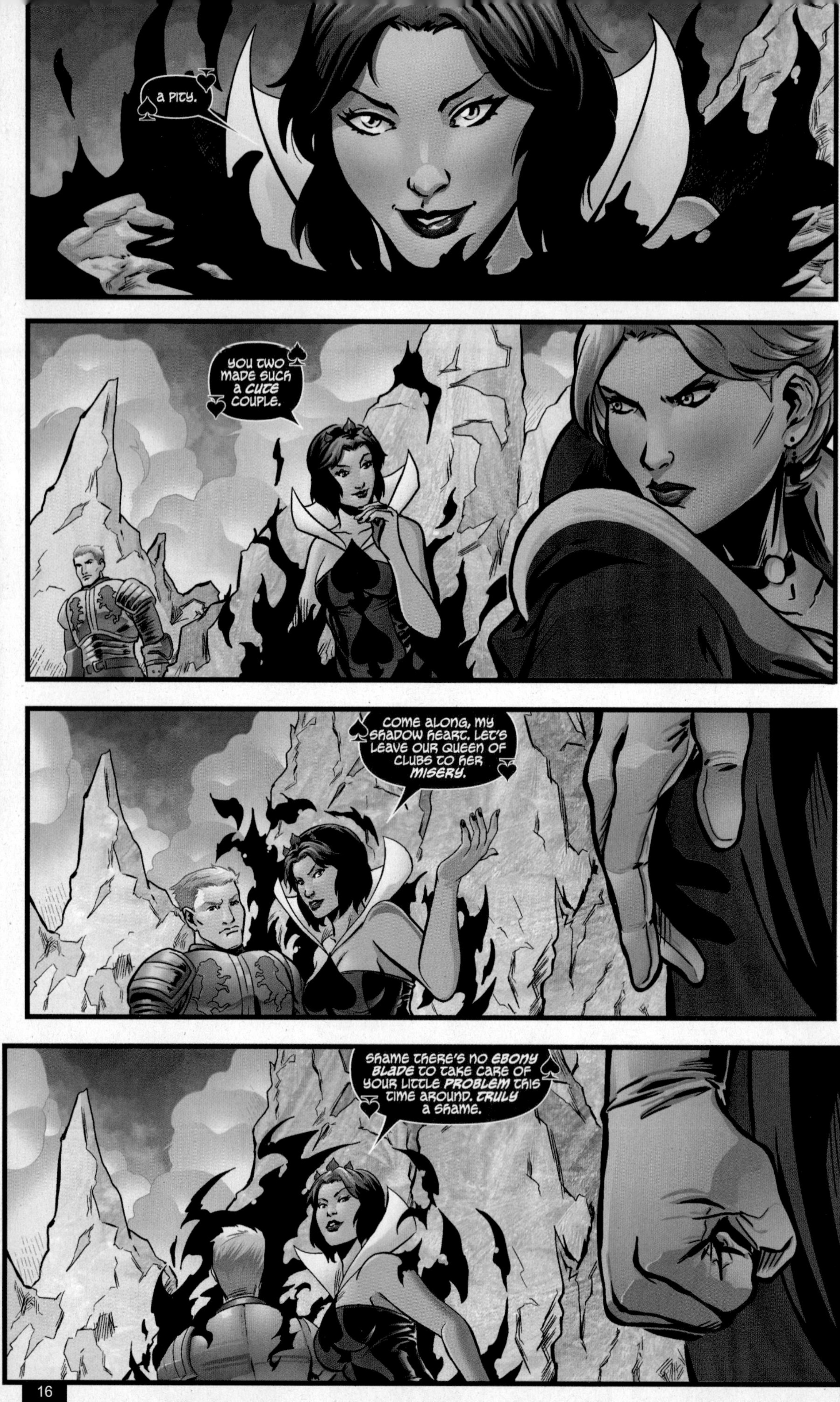
A PITY.
YOU TWO MADE SUCH A CUTE COUPLE.
COME ALONG, MY SHADOW HEART. LET'S LEAVE OUR QUEEN OF CLUBS TO HER MISERY.
SHAME THERE'S NO EBONY BLADE TO TAKE CARE OF YOUR LITTLE PROBLEM THIS TIME AROUND. TRULY A SHAME.

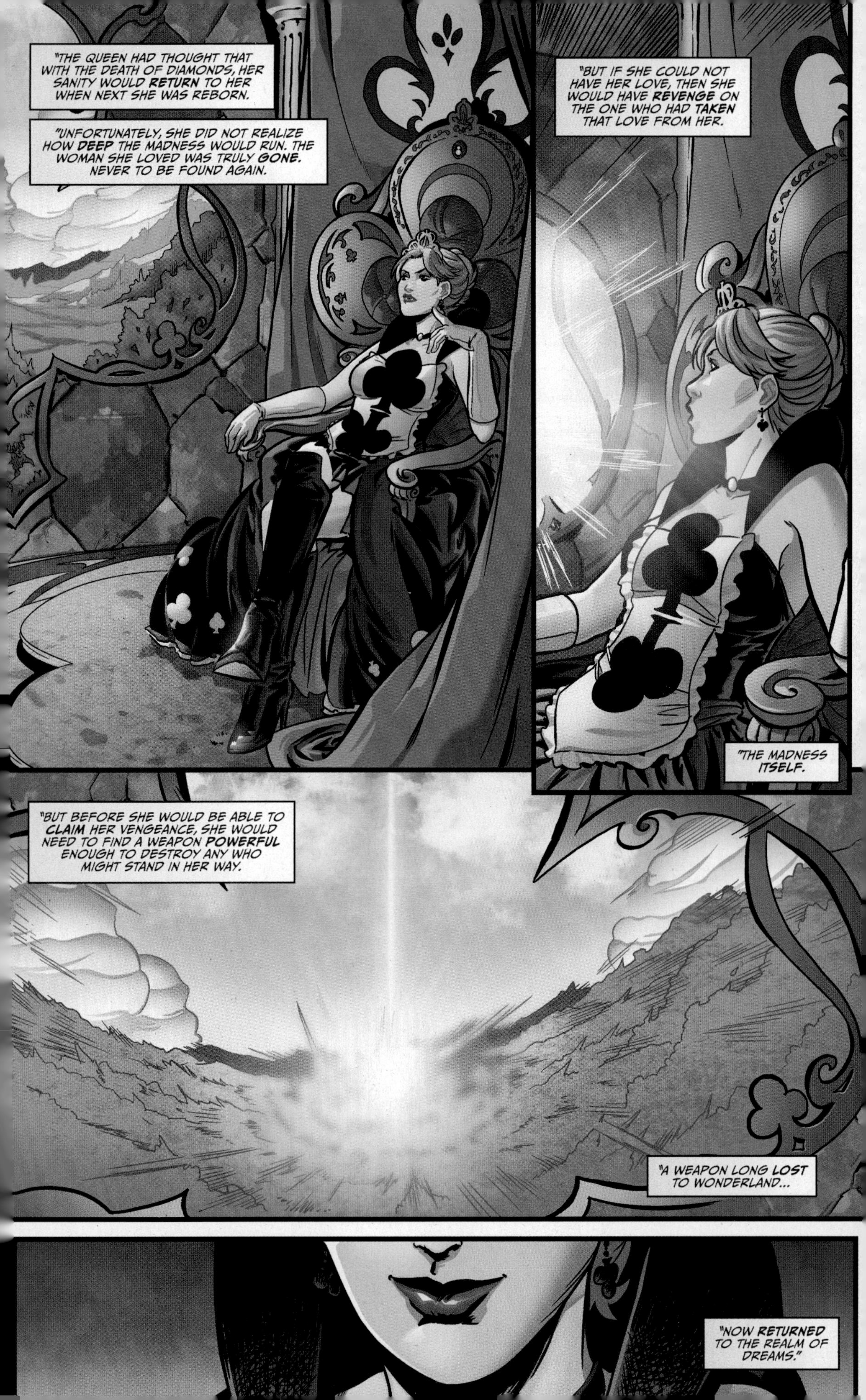
"THE QUEEN HAD THOUGHT THAT WITH THE DEATH OF DIAMONDS, HER SANITY WOULD RETURN TO HER WHEN NEXT SHE WAS REBORN.
"UNFORTUNATELY, SHE DID NOT REALIZE HOW DEEP THE MADNESS WOULD RUN. THE WOMAN SHE LOVED WAS TRULY GONE. NEVER TO BE FOUND AGAIN.
"BUT IF SHE COULD NOT HAVE HER LOVE, THEN SHE WOULD HAVE REVENGE ON THE ONE WHO HAD TAKEN THAT LOVE FROM HER.
"THE MADNESS ITSELF.
"BUT BEFORE SHE WOULD BE ABLE TO CLAIM HER VENGEANCE, SHE WOULD NEED TO FIND A WEAPON POWERFUL ENOUGH TO DESTROY ANY WHO MIGHT STAND IN HER WAY.
"A WEAPON LONG LOST TO WONDERLAND...
"NOW RETURNED TO THE REALM OF DREAMS."

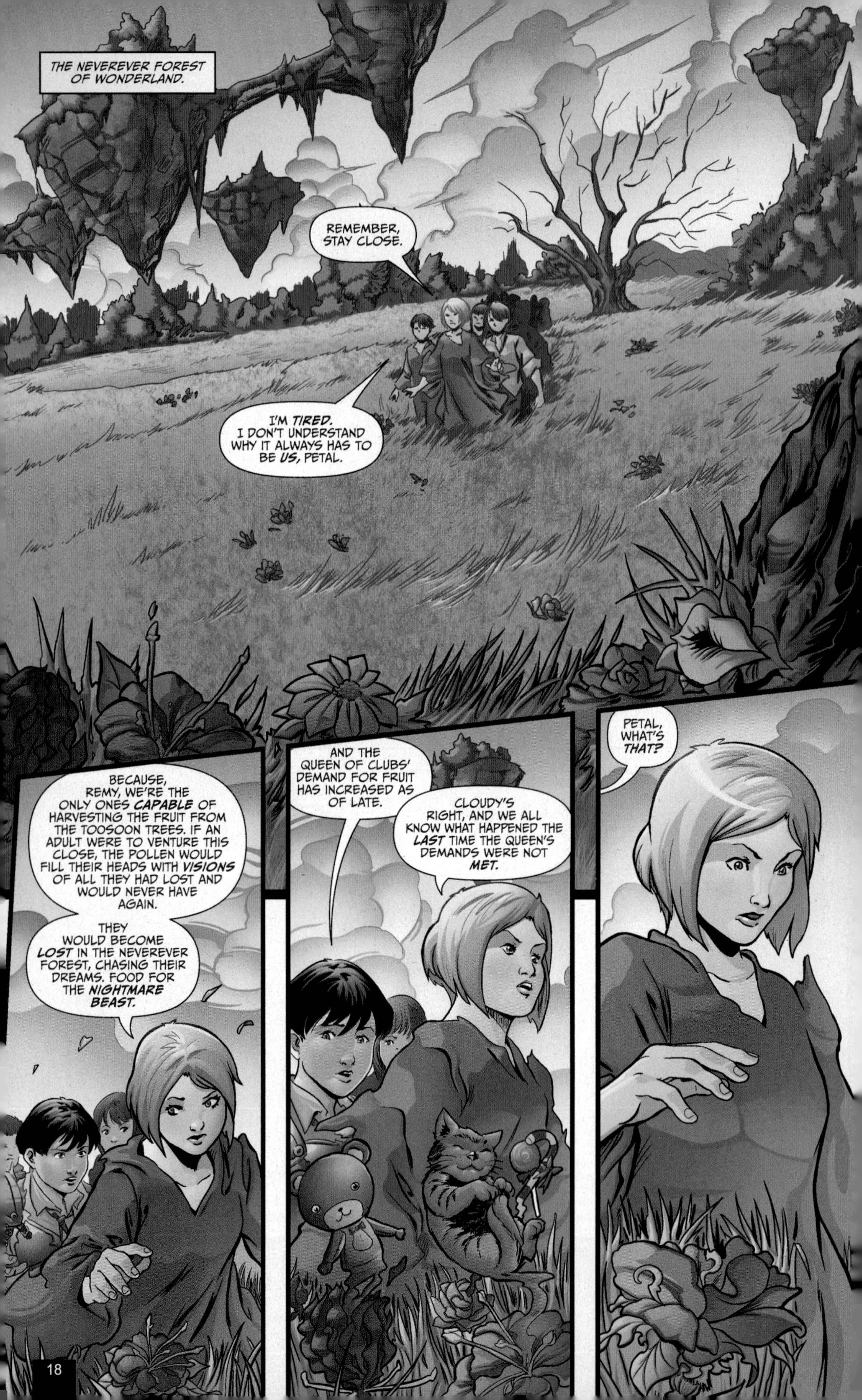
THE NEVEREVER FOREST OF WONDERLAND.
REMEMBER, STAY CLOSE.
I'M TIRED. I DON'T UNDERSTAND WHY IT ALWAYS HAS TO BE US, PETAL.
BECAUSE, REMY, WE'RE THE ONLY ONES CAPABLE OF HARVESTING THE FRUIT FROM THE TOOSOON TREES. IF AN ADULT WERE TO VENTURE THIS CLOSE, THE POLLEN WOULD FILL THEIR HEADS WITH VISIONS OF ALL THEY HAD LOST AND WOULD NEVER HAVE AGAIN.
THEY WOULD BECOME LOST IN THE NEVEREVER FOREST, CHASING THEIR DREAMS. FOOD FOR THE NIGHTMARE BEAST.
AND THE QUEEN OF CLUBS' DEMAND FOR FRUIT HAS INCREASED AS OF LATE.
CLOUDY'S RIGHT, AND WE ALL KNOW WHAT HAPPENED THE LAST TIME THE QUEEN'S DEMANDS WERE NOT MET.
PETAL, WHAT'S THAT?

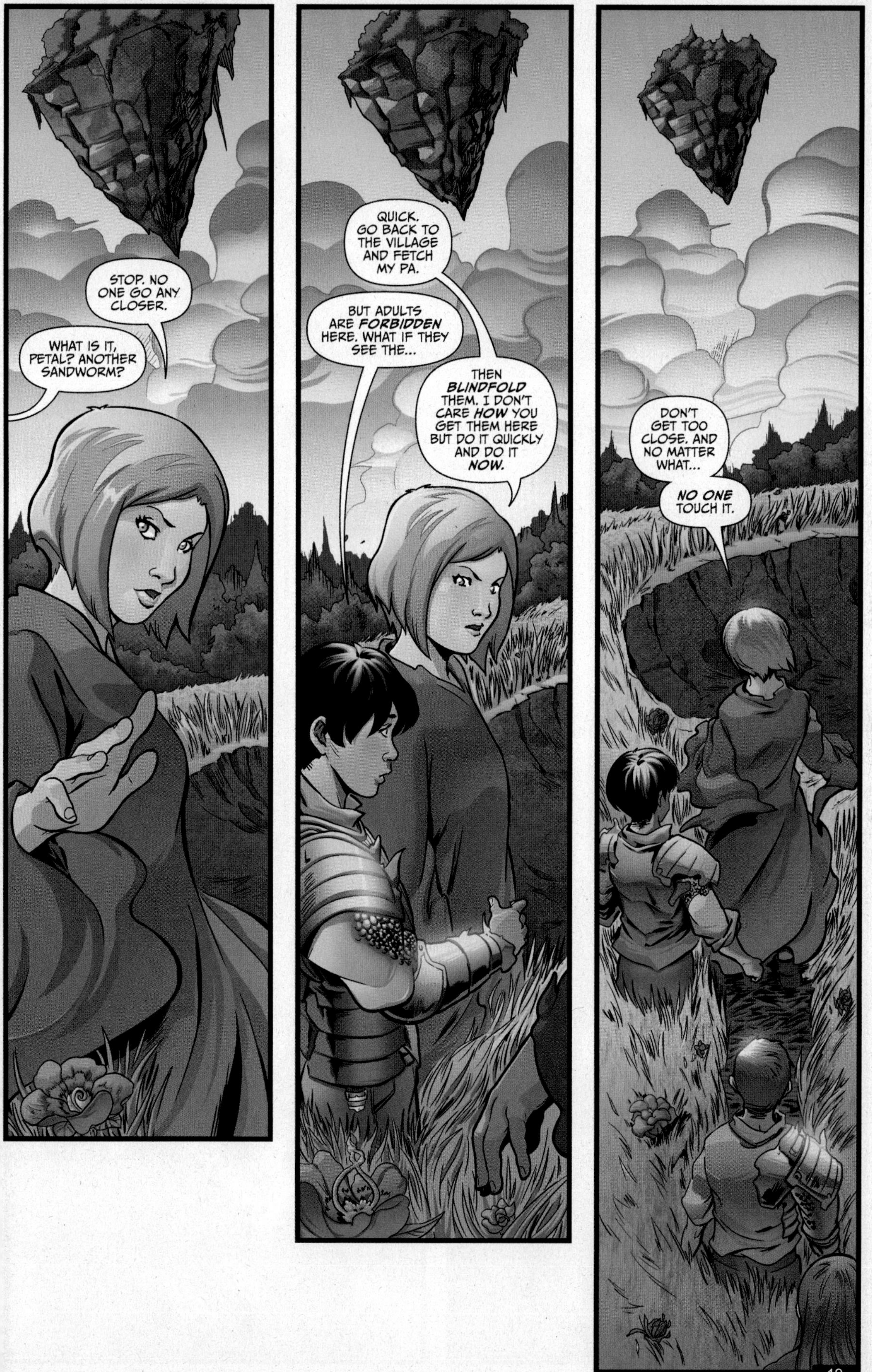
STOP. NO ONE GO ANY CLOSER.
WHAT IS IT, PETAL? ANOTHER SANDWORM?
QUICK. GO BACK TO THE VILLAGE AND FETCH MY PA.
BUT ADULTS ARE FORBIDDEN HERE. WHAT IF THEY SEE THE...
THEN BLINDFOLD THEM. I DON'T CARE HOW YOU GET THEM HERE BUT DO IT QUICKLY AND DO IT NOW.
DON'T GET TOO CLOSE. AND NO MATTER WHAT...
NO ONE TOUCH IT.

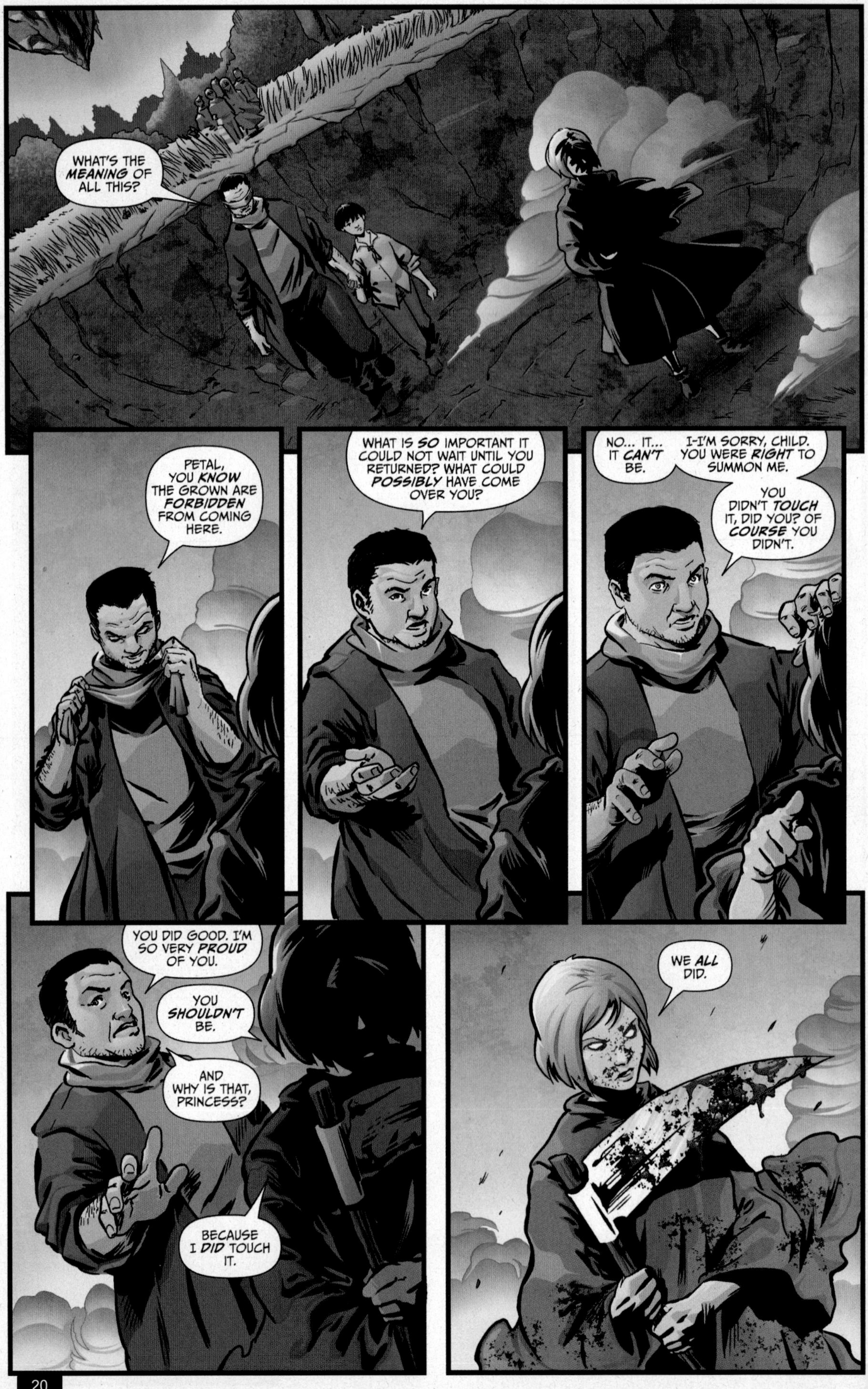
WHAT'S THE MEANING OF ALL THIS?
PETAL, YOU KNOW THE GROWN ARE FORBIDDEN FROM COMING HERE.
WHAT IS SO IMPORTANT IT COULD NOT WAIT UNTIL YOU RETURNED? WHAT COULD POSSIBLY HAVE COME OVER YOU?
NO... IT... IT CAN'T BE.
I-I'M SORRY, CHILD. YOU WERE RIGHT TO SUMMON ME.
YOU DIDN'T TOUCH IT, DID YOU? OF COURSE YOU DIDN'T.
YOU DID GOOD. I'M SO VERY PROUD OF YOU.
YOU SHOULDN'T BE.
AND WHY IS THAT, PRINCESS?
BECAUSE I DID TOUCH IT.
WE ALL DID.

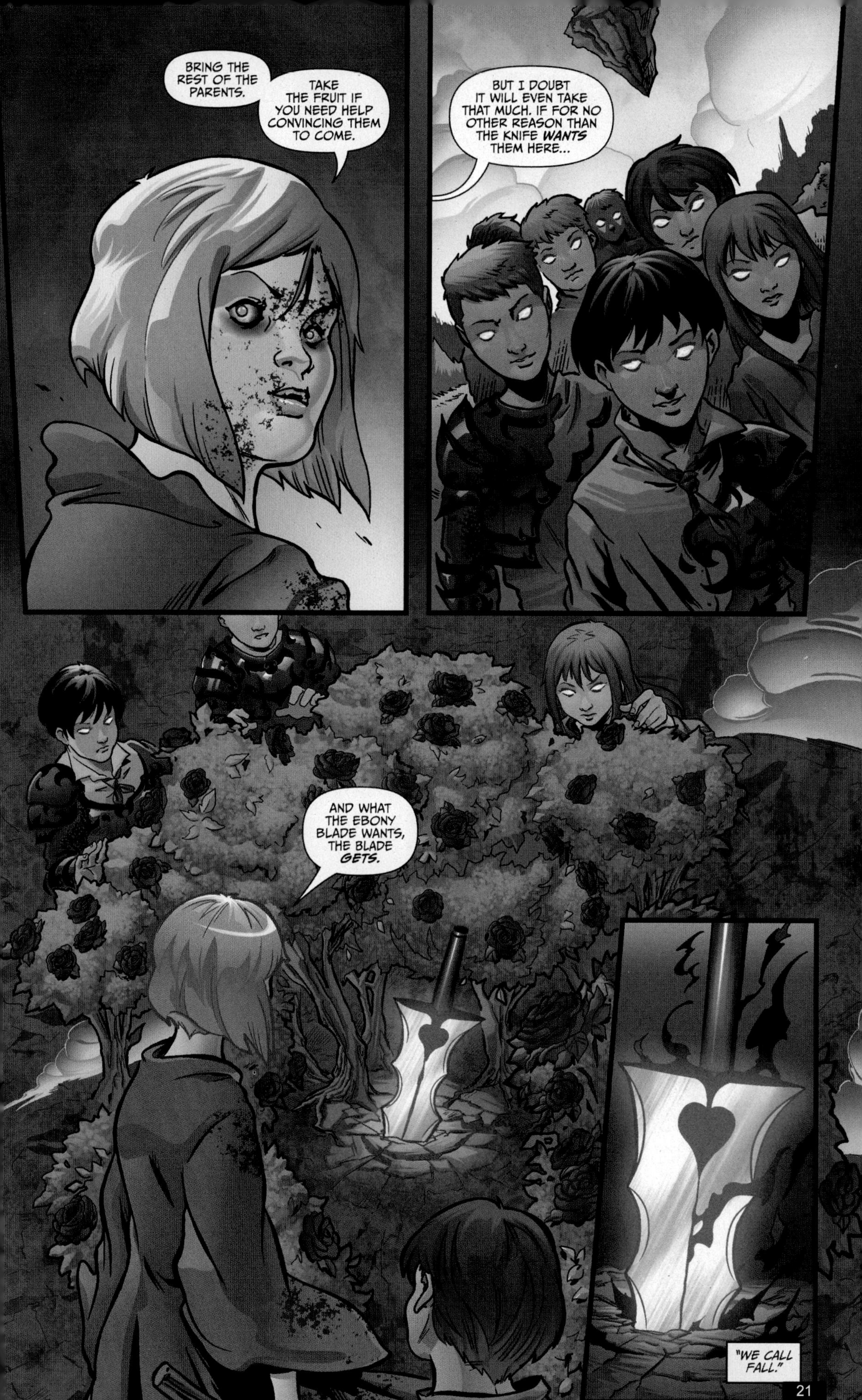
BRING THE REST OF THE PARENTS.
TAKE THE FRUIT IF YOU NEED HELP CONVINCING THEM TO COME.
BUT I DOUBT IT WILL EVEN TAKE THAT MUCH. IF FOR NO OTHER REASON THAN THE KNIFE *WANTS* THEM HERE...
AND WHAT THE EBONY BLADE WANTS, THE BLADE *GETS.*
"WE CALL FALL."

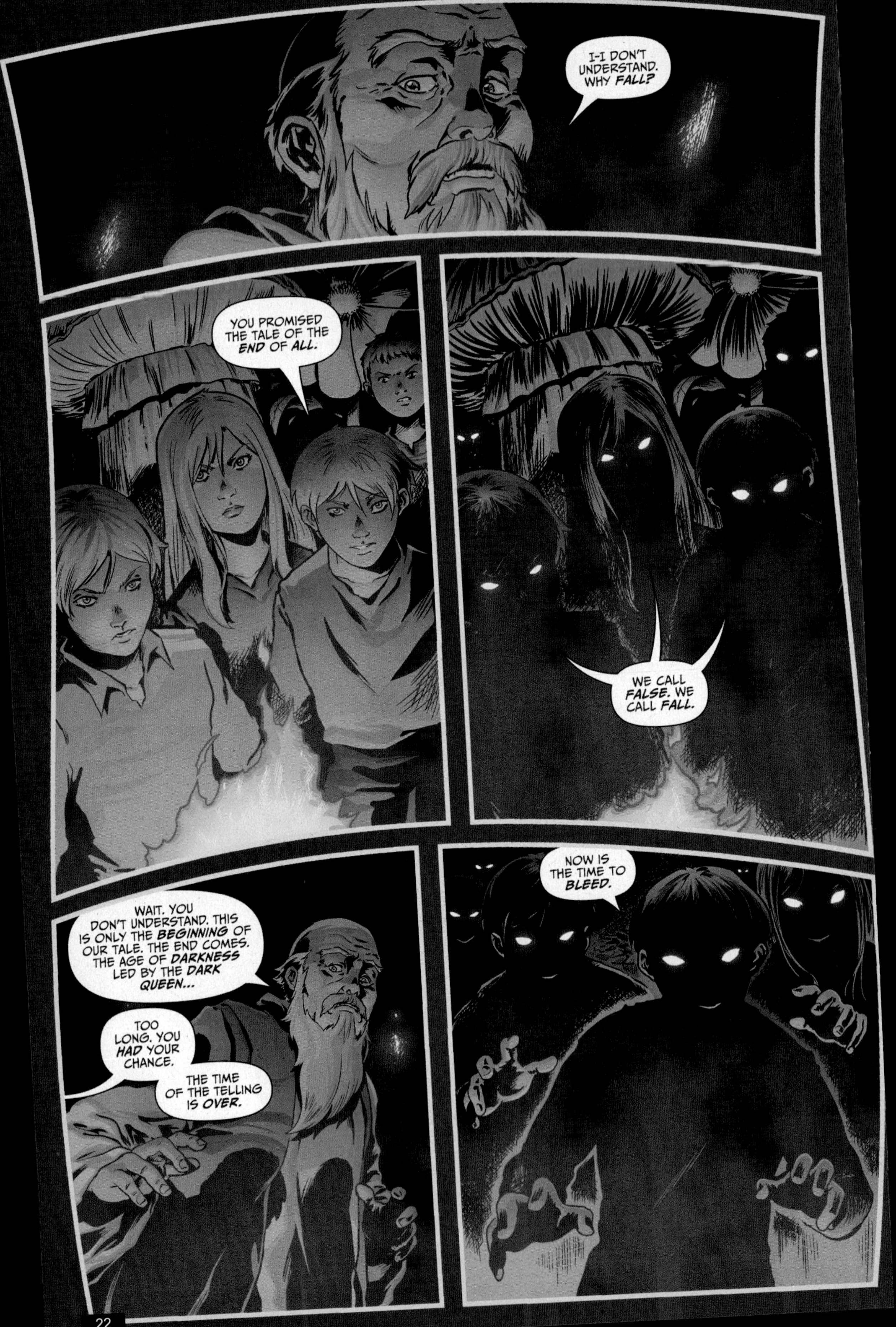
I-I DON'T UNDERSTAND. WHY FALL?
YOU PROMISED THE TALE OF THE END OF ALL.
WE CALL FALSE. WE CALL FALL.
WAIT. YOU DON'T UNDERSTAND. THIS IS ONLY THE BEGINNING OF OUR TALE. THE END COMES. THE AGE OF DARKNESS LED BY THE DARK QUEEN...
TOO LONG. YOU HAD YOUR CHANCE.
THE TIME OF THE TELLING IS OVER.
NOW IS THE TIME TO BLEED.

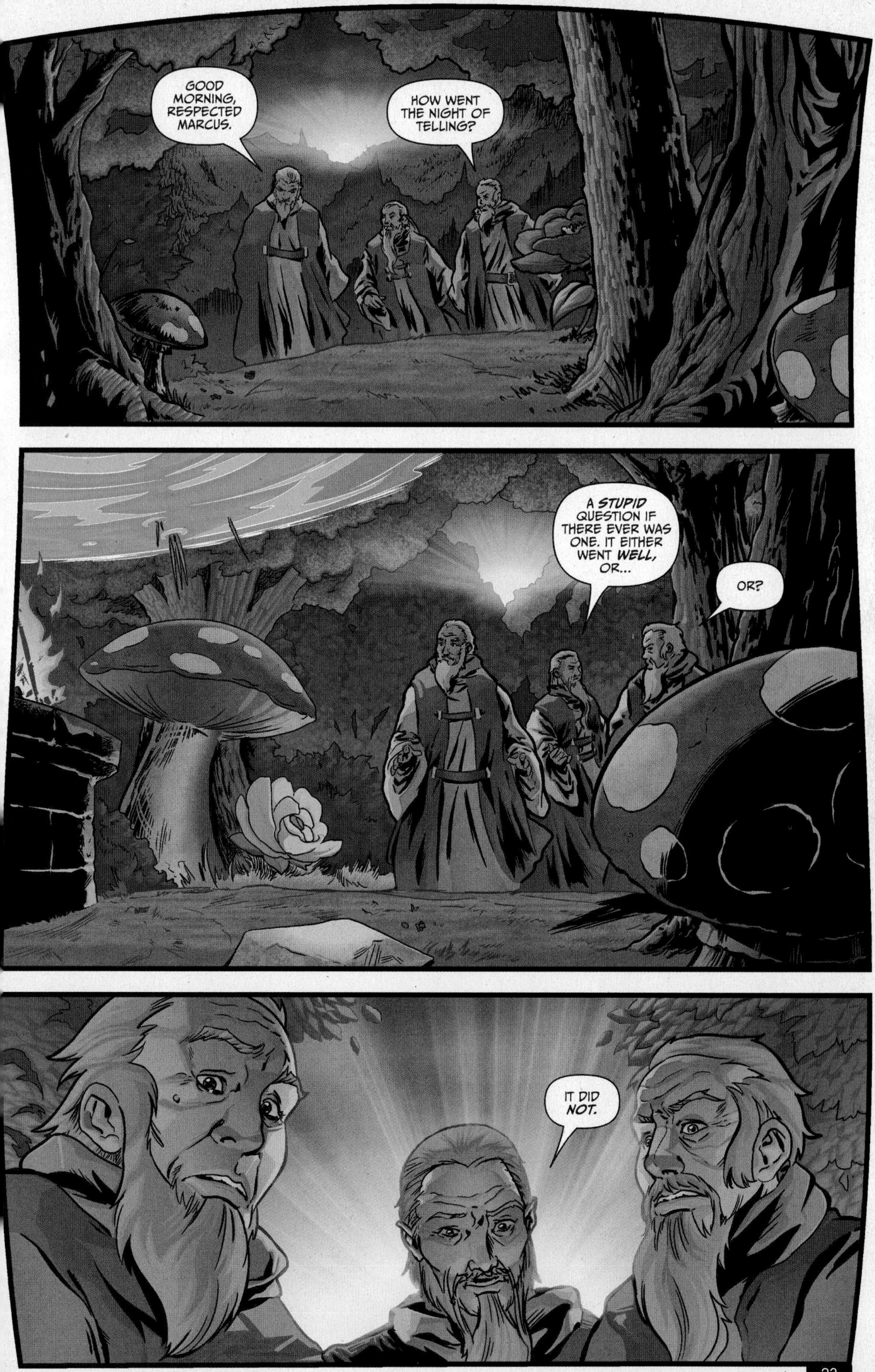
GOOD MORNING, RESPECTED MARCUS.
HOW WENT THE NIGHT OF TELLING?
A STUPID QUESTION IF THERE EVER WAS ONE. IT EITHER WENT WELL, OR...
OR?
IT DID NOT.

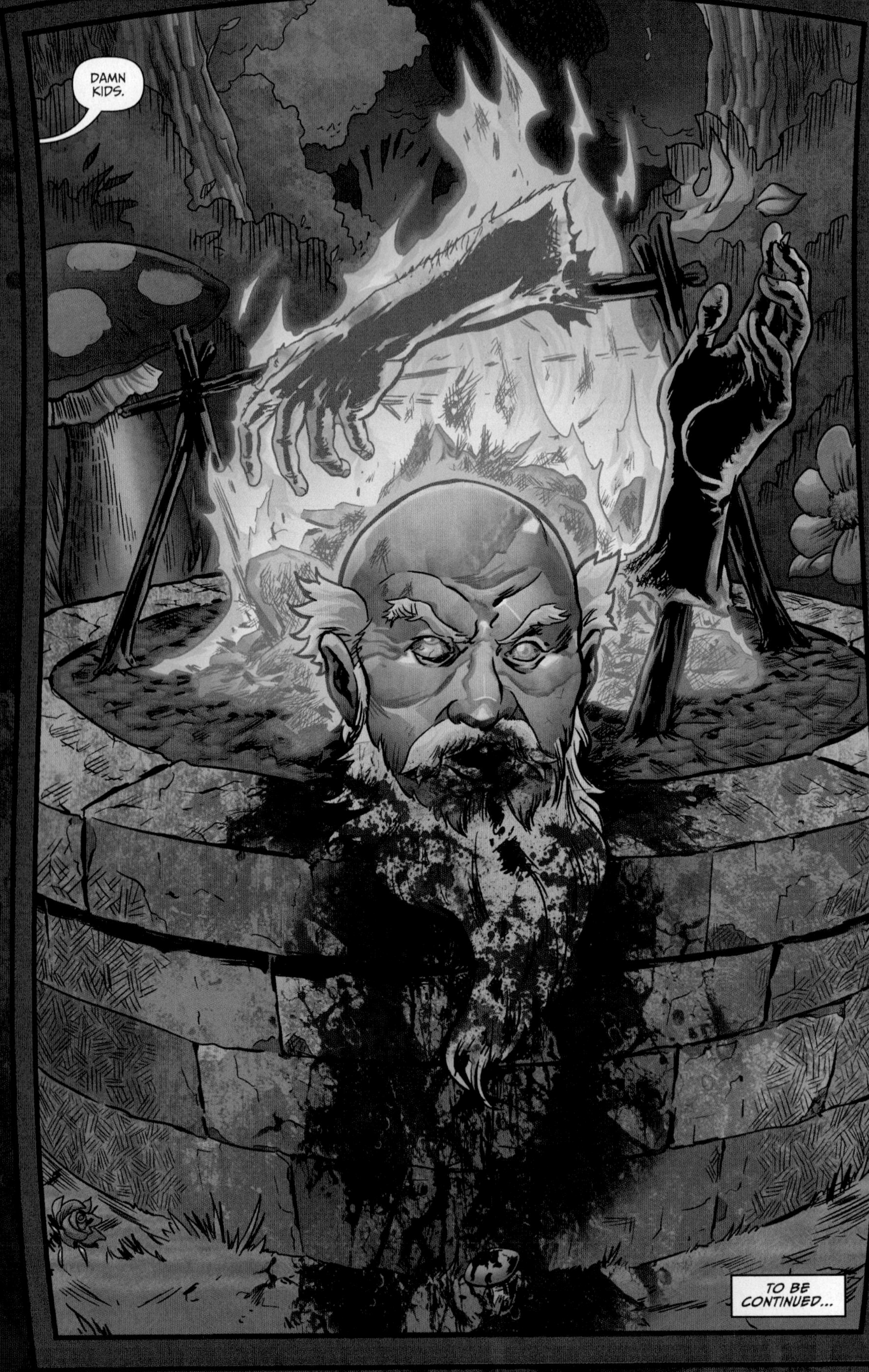
DAMN KIDS.
TO BE CONTINUED...

Grimm Fairy Tales

Wonderland

♠ ♥ *Clash of Queens* ♣ ♦

AGE OF DARKNESS

CHAPTER TWO

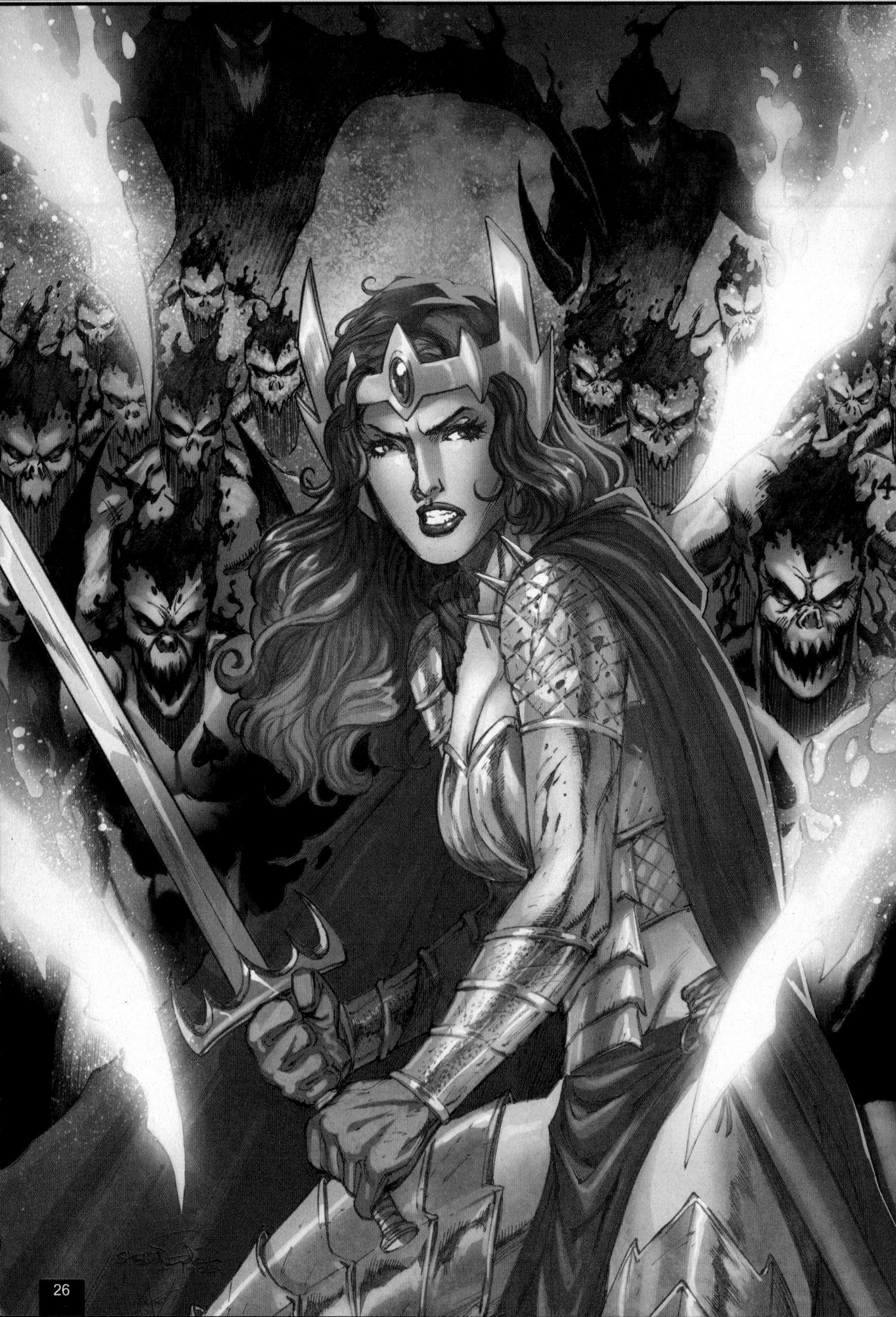

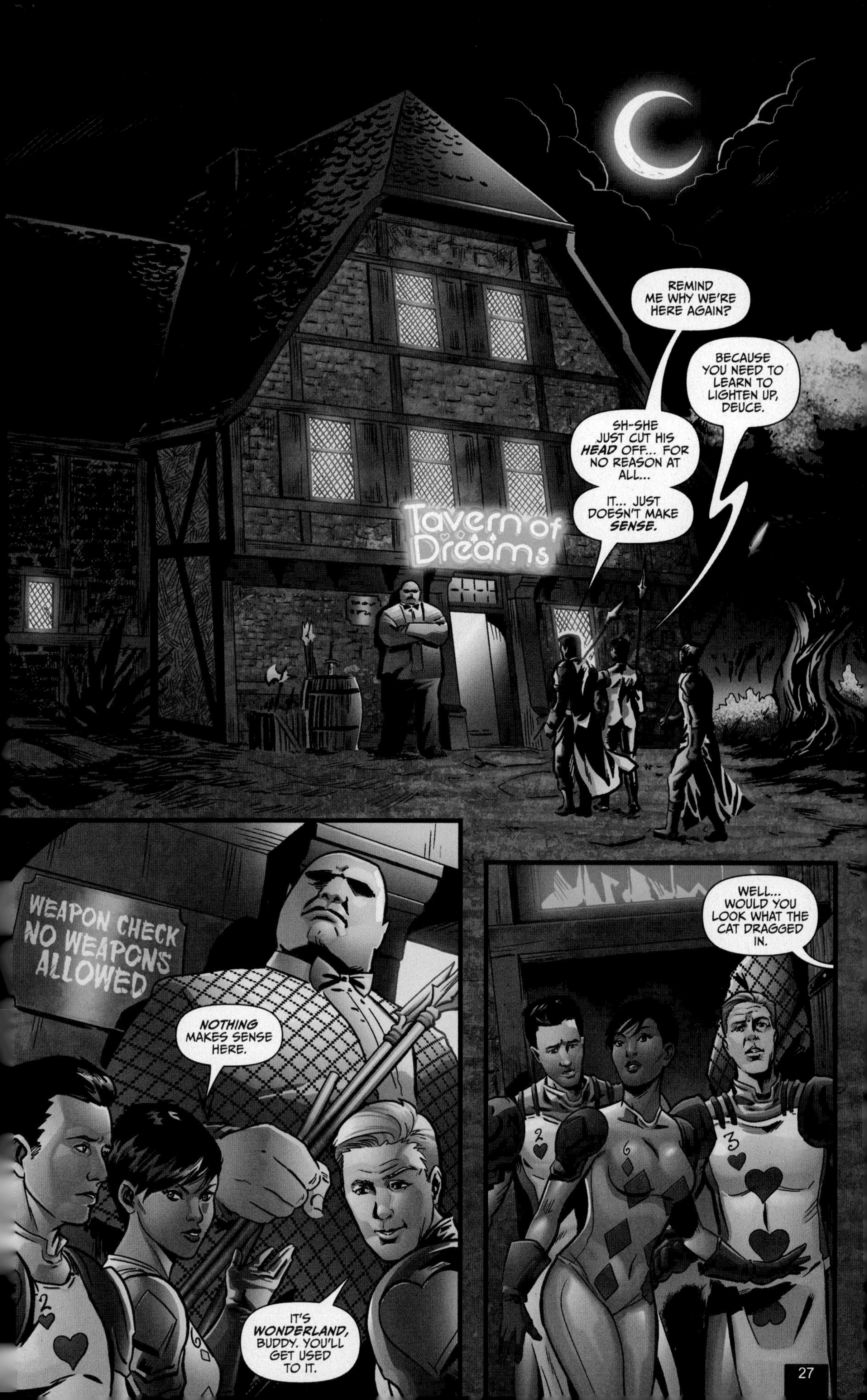
Tavern of Dreams
REMIND ME WHY WE'RE HERE AGAIN?
BECAUSE YOU NEED TO LEARN TO LIGHTEN UP, DEUCE.
SH-SHE JUST CUT HIS HEAD OFF... FOR NO REASON AT ALL...
IT... JUST DOESN'T MAKE SENSE.
WEAPON CHECK NO WEAPONS ALLOWED
NOTHING MAKES SENSE HERE.
IT'S WONDERLAND, BUDDY. YOU'LL GET USED TO IT.
WELL... WOULD YOU LOOK WHAT THE CAT DRAGGED IN.

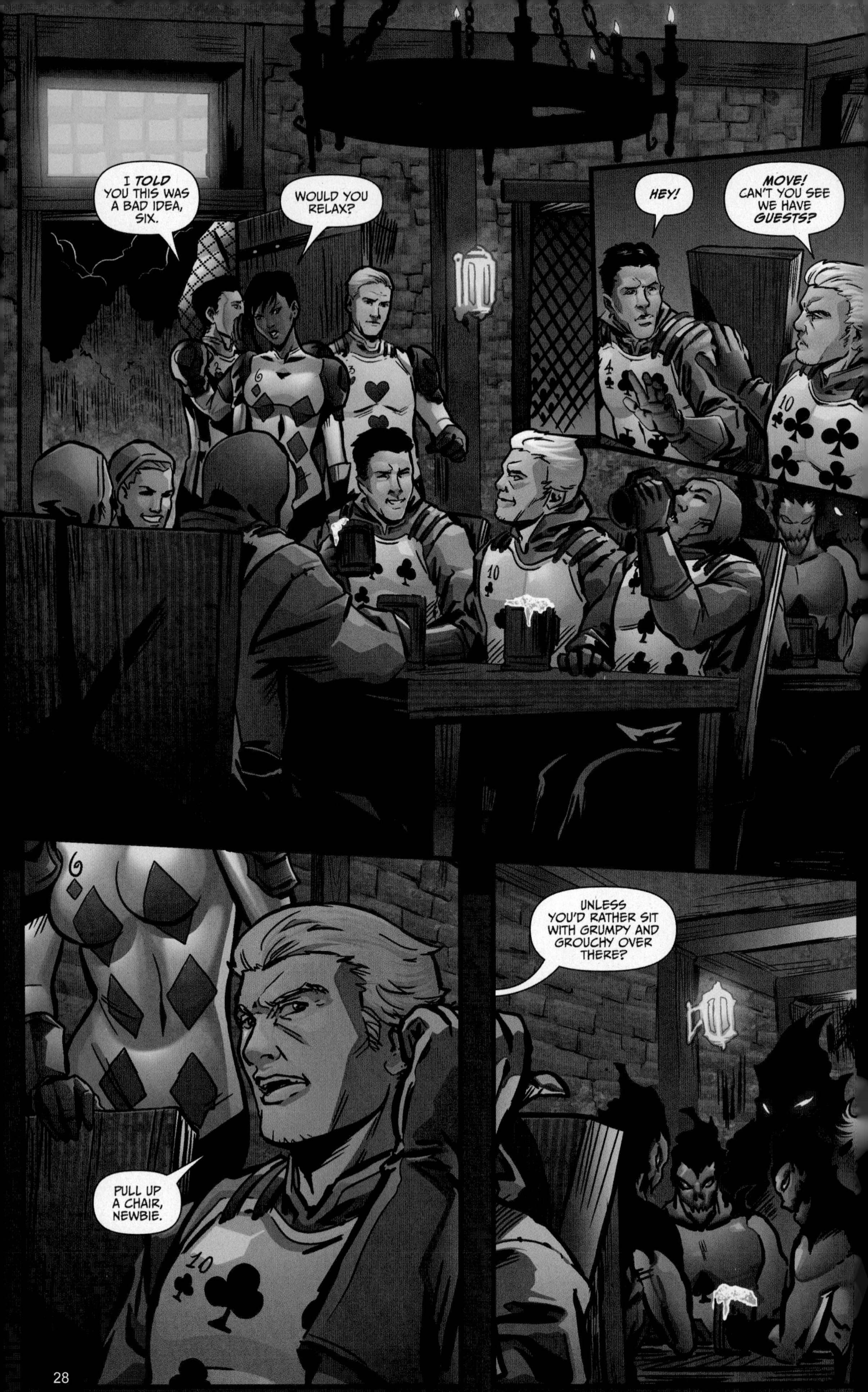
I TOLD YOU THIS WAS A BAD IDEA, SIX.
WOULD YOU RELAX?
HEY!
MOVE! CAN'T YOU SEE WE HAVE GUESTS?
PULL UP A CHAIR, NEWBIE.
UNLESS YOU'D RATHER SIT WITH GRUMPY AND GROUCHY OVER THERE?

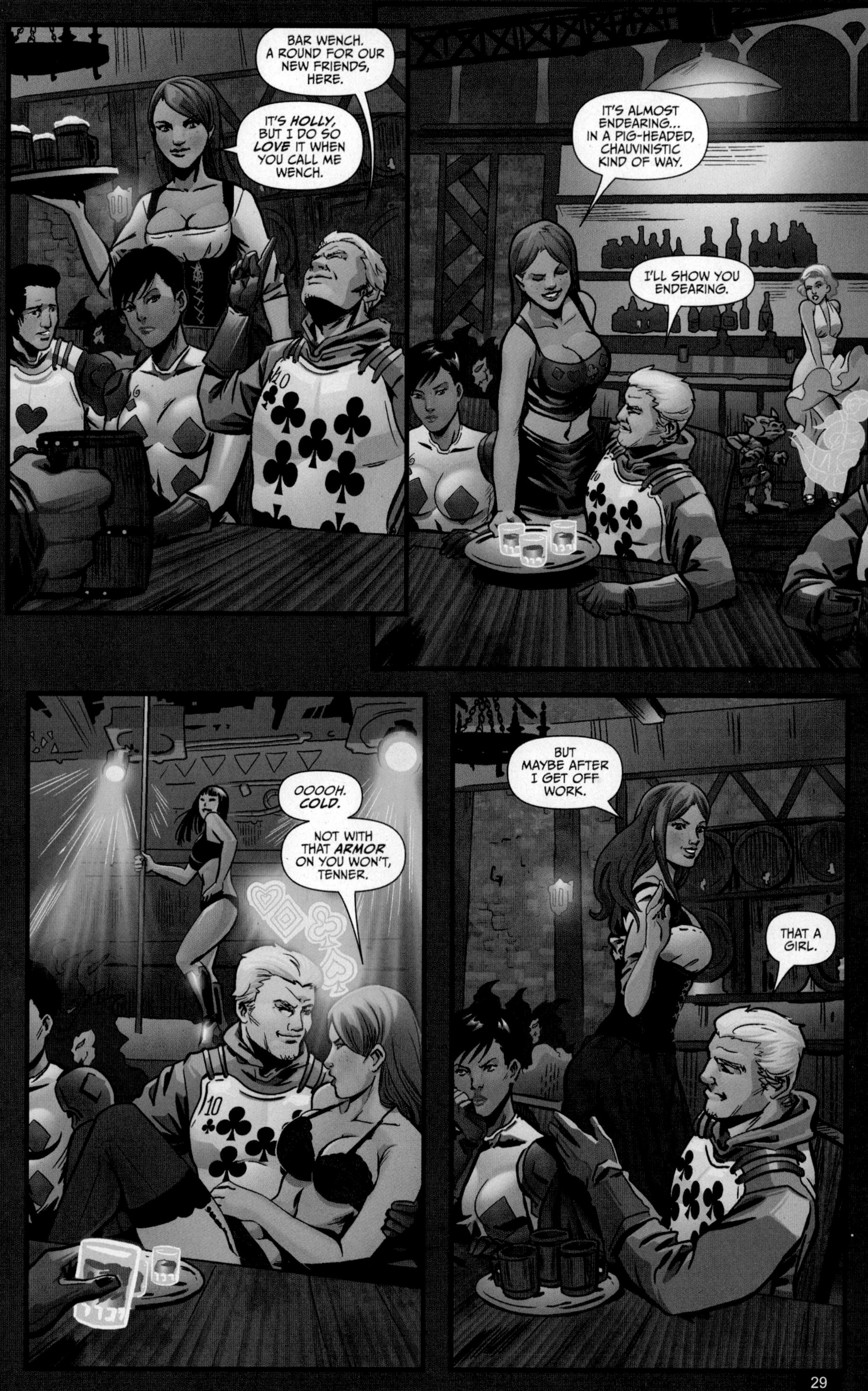

BAR WENCH. A ROUND FOR OUR NEW FRIENDS, HERE.
IT'S HOLLY, BUT I DO SO LOVE IT WHEN YOU CALL ME WENCH.
IT'S ALMOST ENDEARING... IN A PIG-HEADED, CHAUVINISTIC KIND OF WAY.
I'LL SHOW YOU ENDEARING.
OOOOH. COLD.
NOT WITH THAT ARMOR ON YOU WON'T, TENNER.
BUT MAYBE AFTER I GET OFF WORK.
THAT A GIRL.

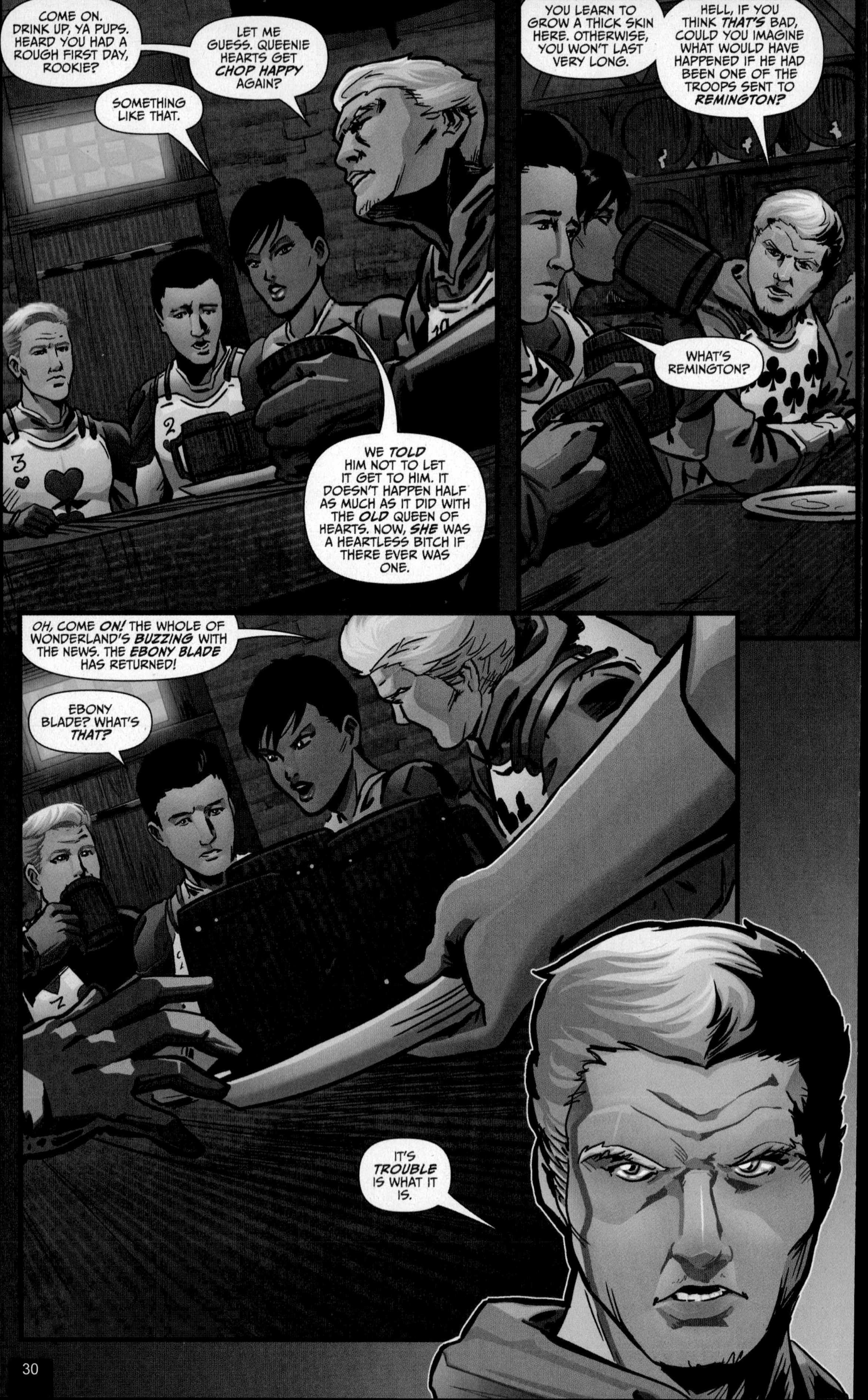
COME ON. DRINK UP, YA PUPS. HEARD YOU HAD A ROUGH FIRST DAY, ROOKIE?
LET ME GUESS. QUEENIE HEARTS GET CHOP HAPPY AGAIN?
SOMETHING LIKE THAT.
WE TOLD HIM NOT TO LET IT GET TO HIM. IT DOESN'T HAPPEN HALF AS MUCH AS IT DID WITH THE OLD QUEEN OF HEARTS. NOW, SHE WAS A HEARTLESS BITCH IF THERE EVER WAS ONE.
YOU LEARN TO GROW A THICK SKIN HERE. OTHERWISE, YOU WON'T LAST VERY LONG.
HELL, IF YOU THINK THAT'S BAD, COULD YOU IMAGINE WHAT WOULD HAVE HAPPENED IF HE HAD BEEN ONE OF THE TROOPS SENT TO REMINGTON?
WHAT'S REMINGTON?
OH, COME ON! THE WHOLE OF WONDERLAND'S BUZZING WITH THE NEWS. THE EBONY BLADE HAS RETURNED!
EBONY BLADE? WHAT'S THAT?
IT'S TROUBLE IS WHAT IT IS.

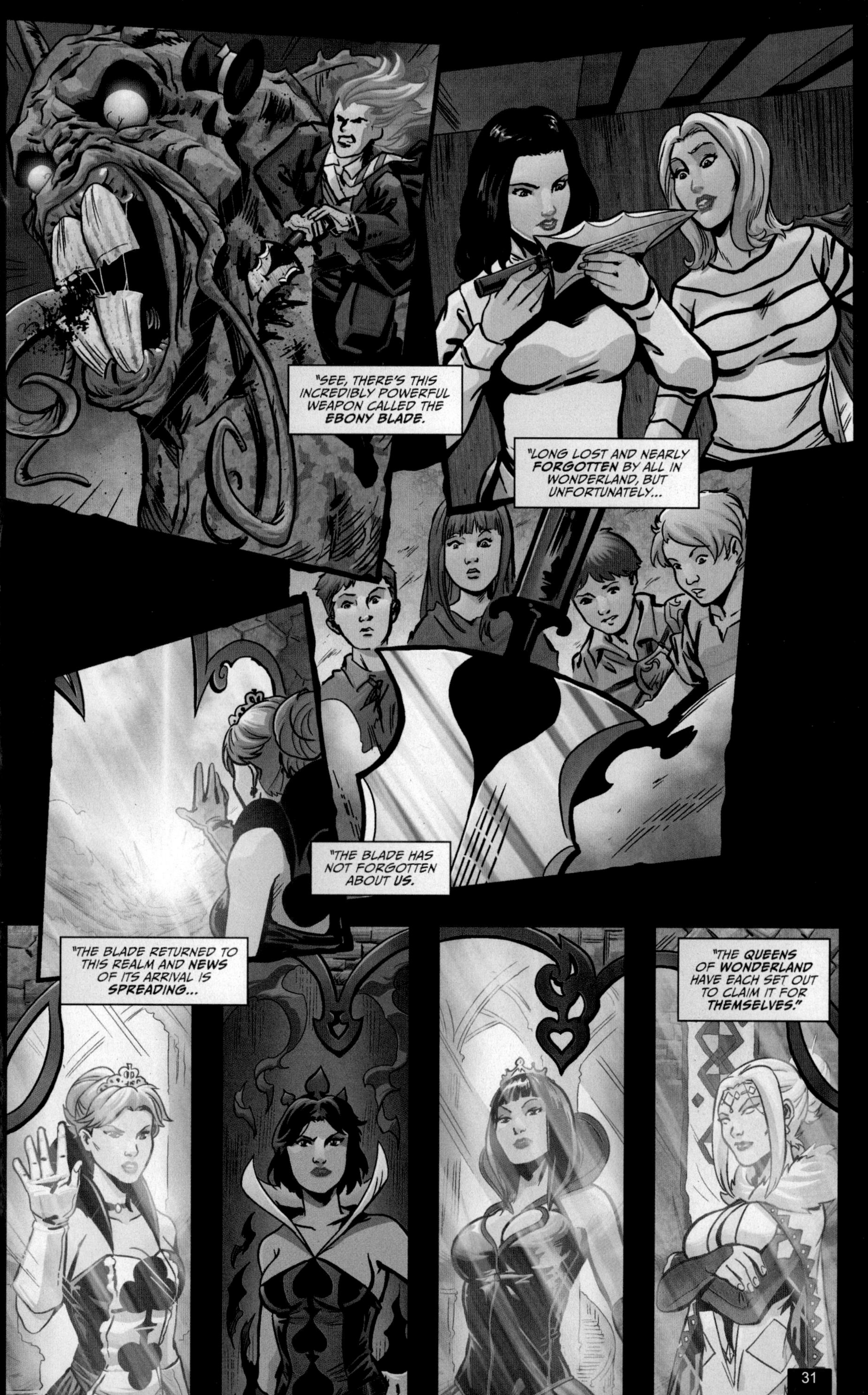
"SEE, THERE'S THIS INCREDIBLY POWERFUL WEAPON CALLED THE **EBONY BLADE.**
"LONG LOST AND NEARLY **FORGOTTEN** BY ALL IN WONDERLAND, BUT UNFORTUNATELY...
"THE BLADE HAS NOT FORGOTTEN ABOUT **US.**
"THE BLADE RETURNED TO THIS REALM AND **NEWS** OF ITS ARRIVAL IS **SPREADING...**
"THE **QUEENS** OF **WONDERLAND** HAVE EACH SET OUT TO CLAIM IT FOR **THEMSELVES.**"

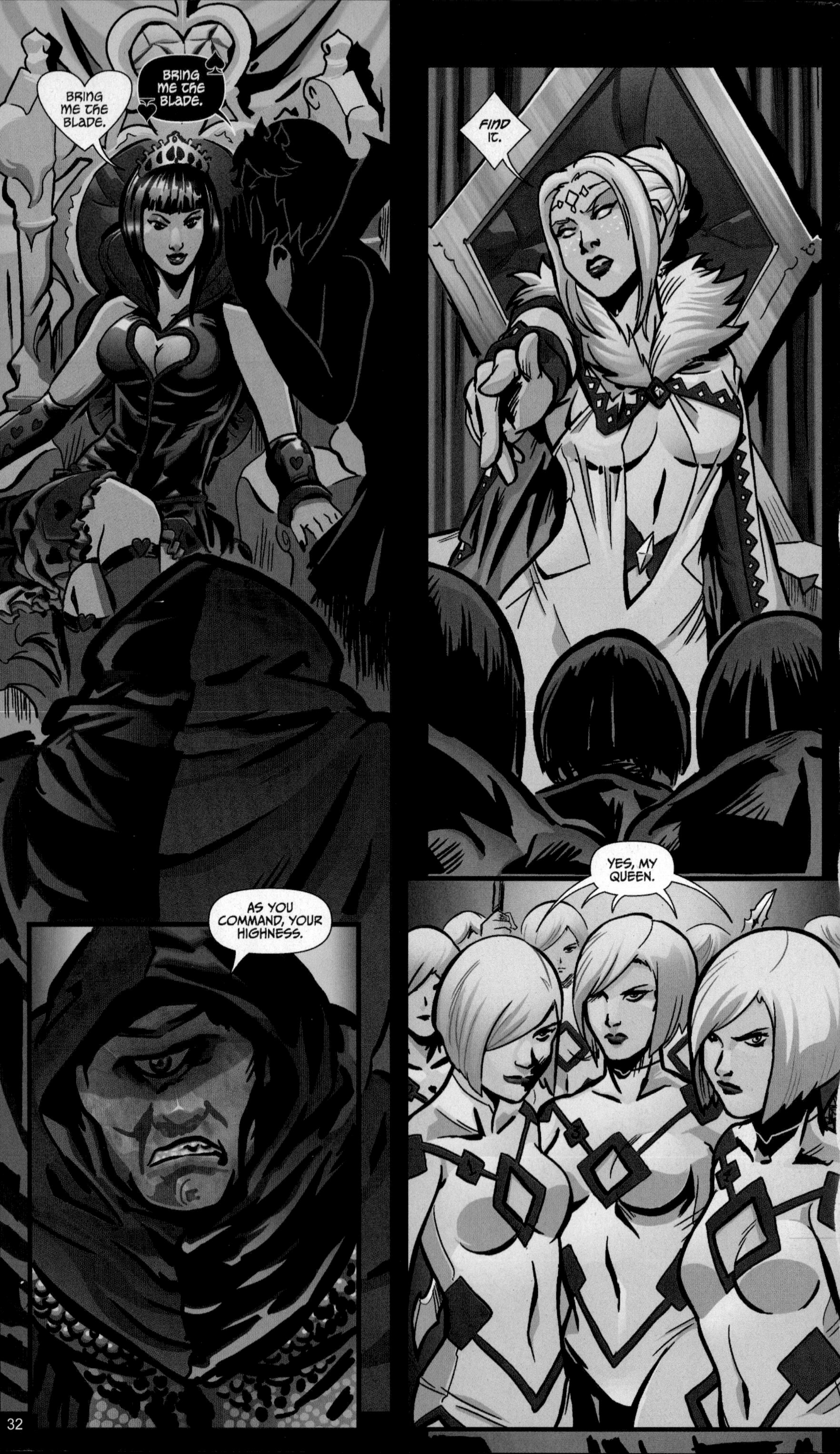
BRING ME THE BLADE.
BRING ME THE BLADE.
FIND IT.
AS YOU COMMAND, YOUR HIGHNESS.
YES, MY QUEEN.

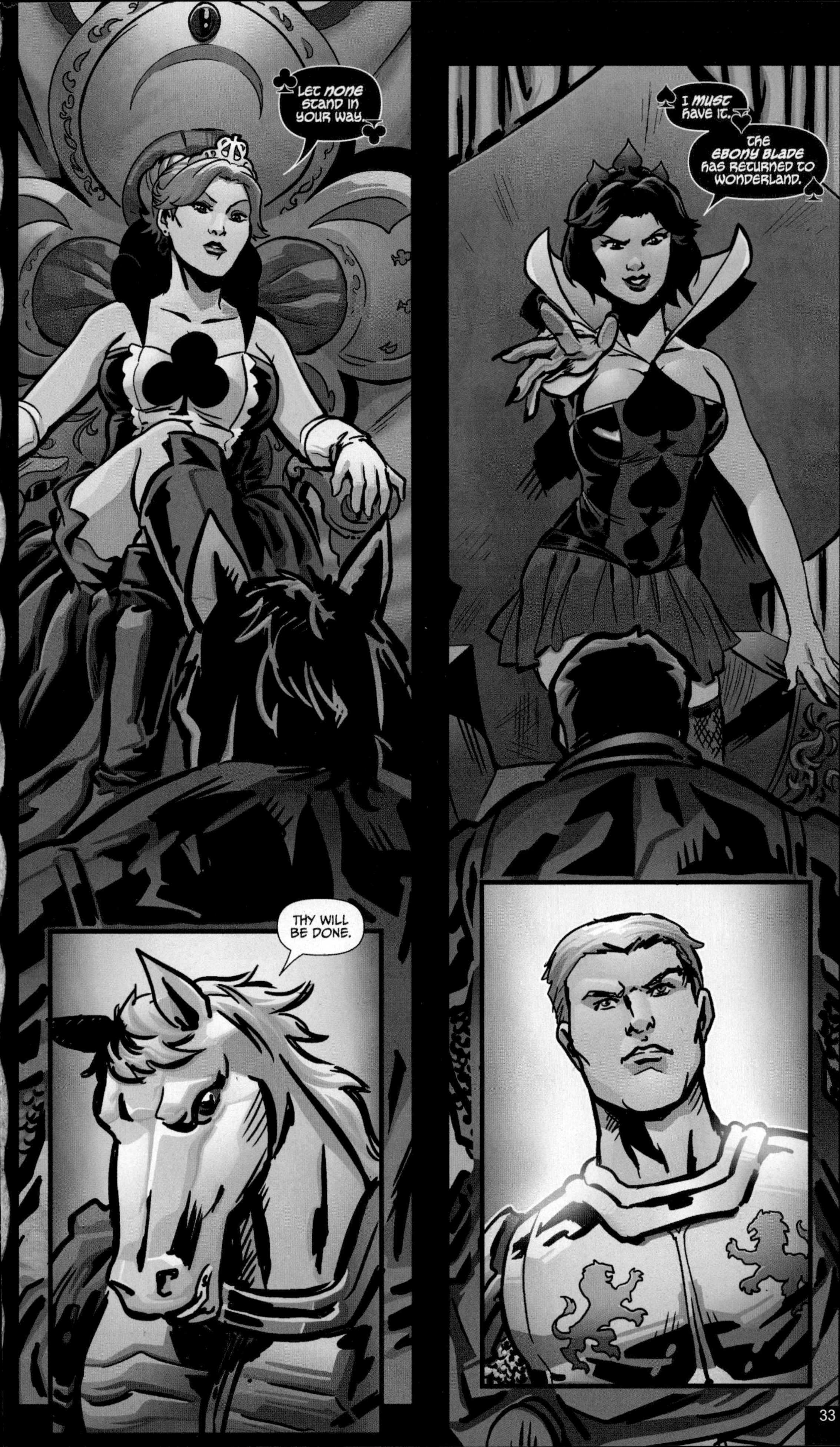
LET NONE STAND IN YOUR WAY.
THY WILL BE DONE.
I MUST HAVE IT.
THE EBONY BLADE HAS RETURNED TO WONDERLAND.

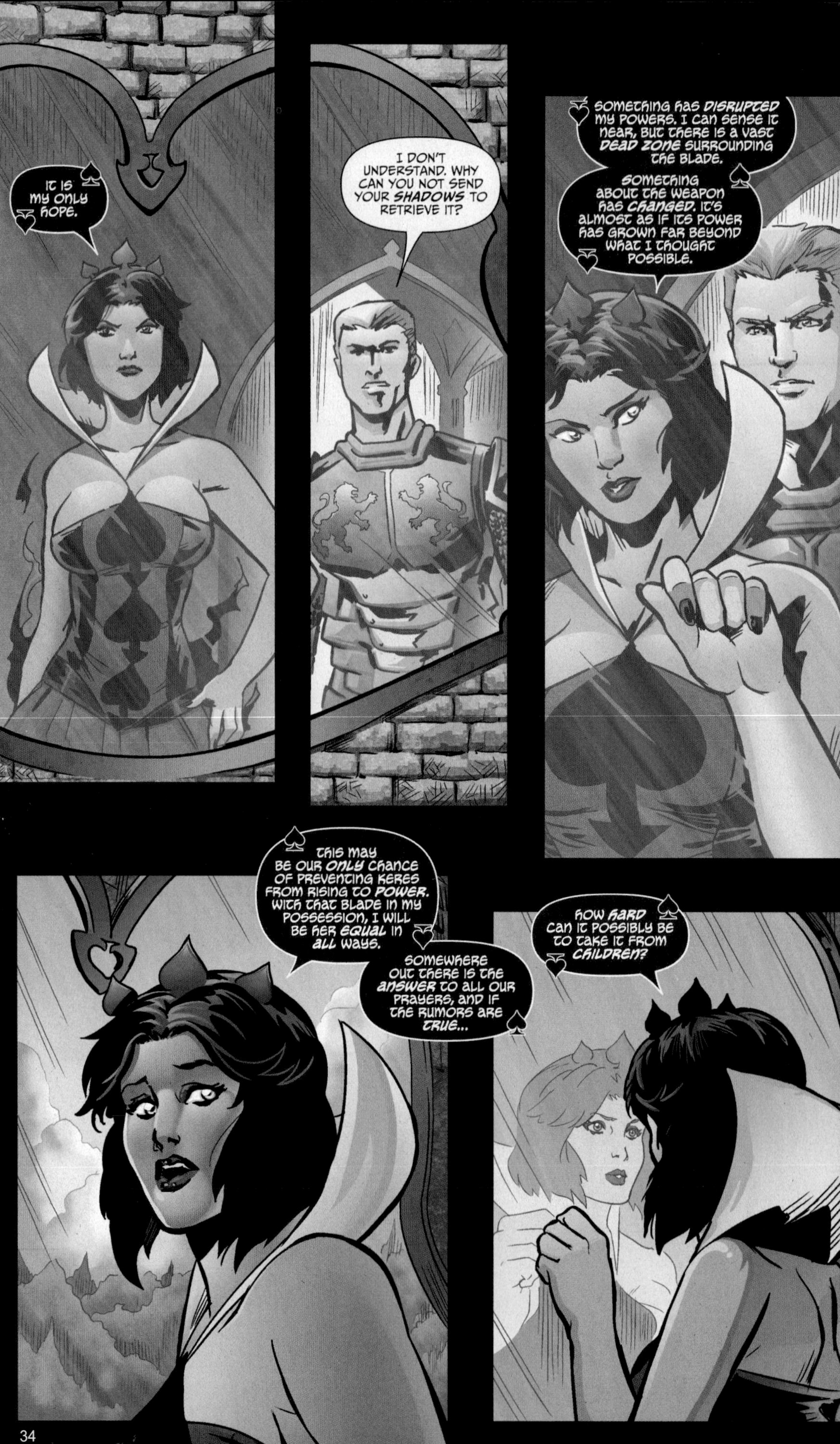

IT IS MY ONLY HOPE.
I DON'T UNDERSTAND. WHY CAN YOU NOT SEND YOUR SHADOWS TO RETRIEVE IT?
SOMETHING HAS DISRUPTED MY POWERS. I CAN SENSE IT NEAR, BUT THERE IS A VAST DEAD ZONE SURROUNDING THE BLADE.
SOMETHING ABOUT THE WEAPON HAS CHANGED. IT'S ALMOST AS IF ITS POWER HAS GROWN FAR BEYOND WHAT I THOUGHT POSSIBLE.
THIS MAY BE OUR ONLY CHANCE OF PREVENTING KERES FROM RISING TO POWER. WITH THAT BLADE IN MY POSSESSION, I WILL BE HER EQUAL IN ALL WAYS.
SOMEWHERE OUT THERE IS THE ANSWER TO ALL OUR PRAYERS, AND IF THE RUMORS ARE TRUE...
HOW HARD CAN IT POSSIBLY BE TO TAKE IT FROM CHILDREN?

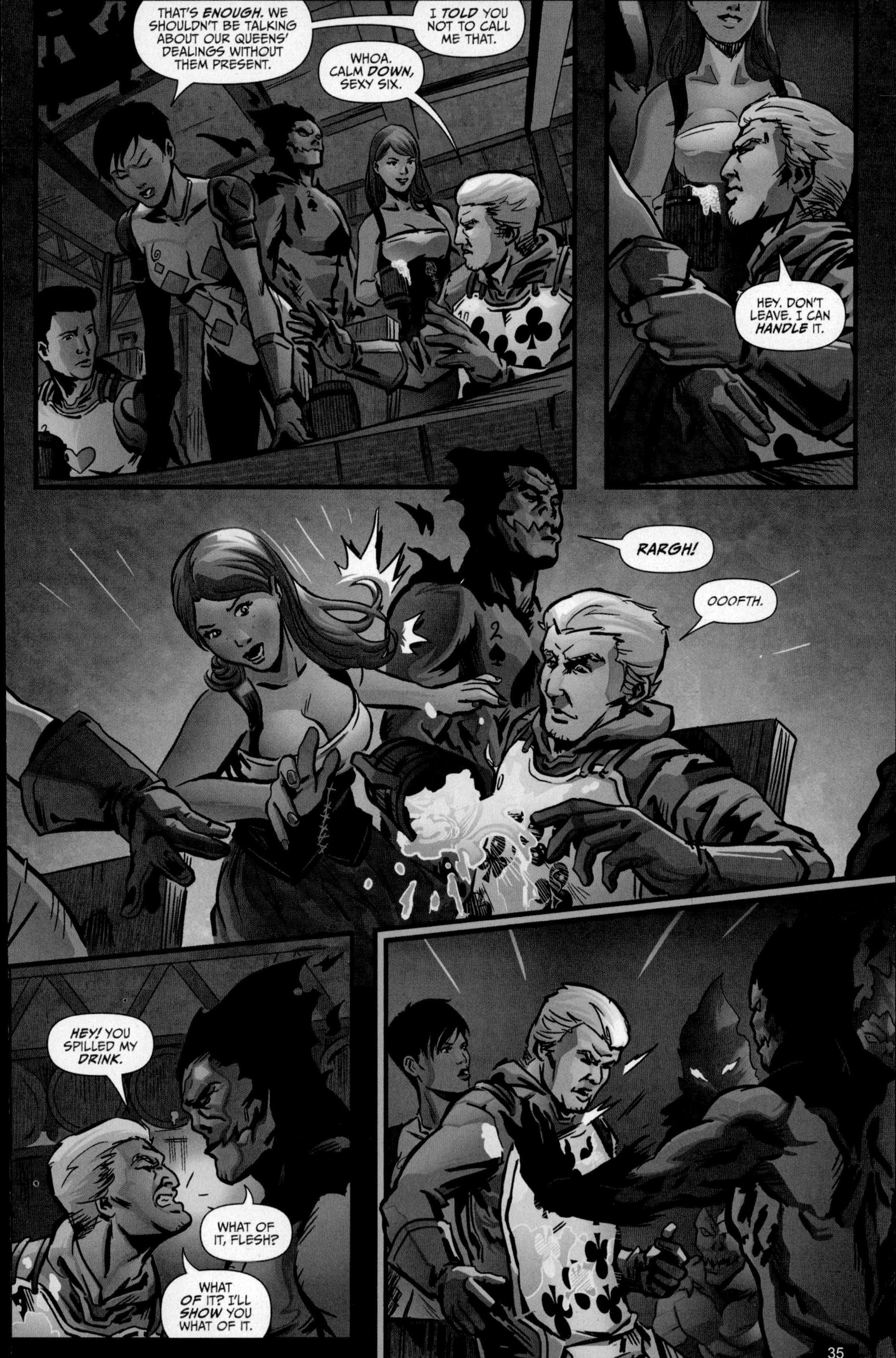
THAT'S ENOUGH. WE SHOULDN'T BE TALKING ABOUT OUR QUEENS' DEALINGS WITHOUT THEM PRESENT.
I TOLD YOU NOT TO CALL ME THAT.
WHOA. CALM DOWN, SEXY SIX.
HEY. DON'T LEAVE. I CAN HANDLE IT.
RARGH!
OOOFTH.
HEY! YOU SPILLED MY DRINK.
WHAT OF IT, FLESH?
WHAT OF IT? I'LL SHOW YOU WHAT OF IT.

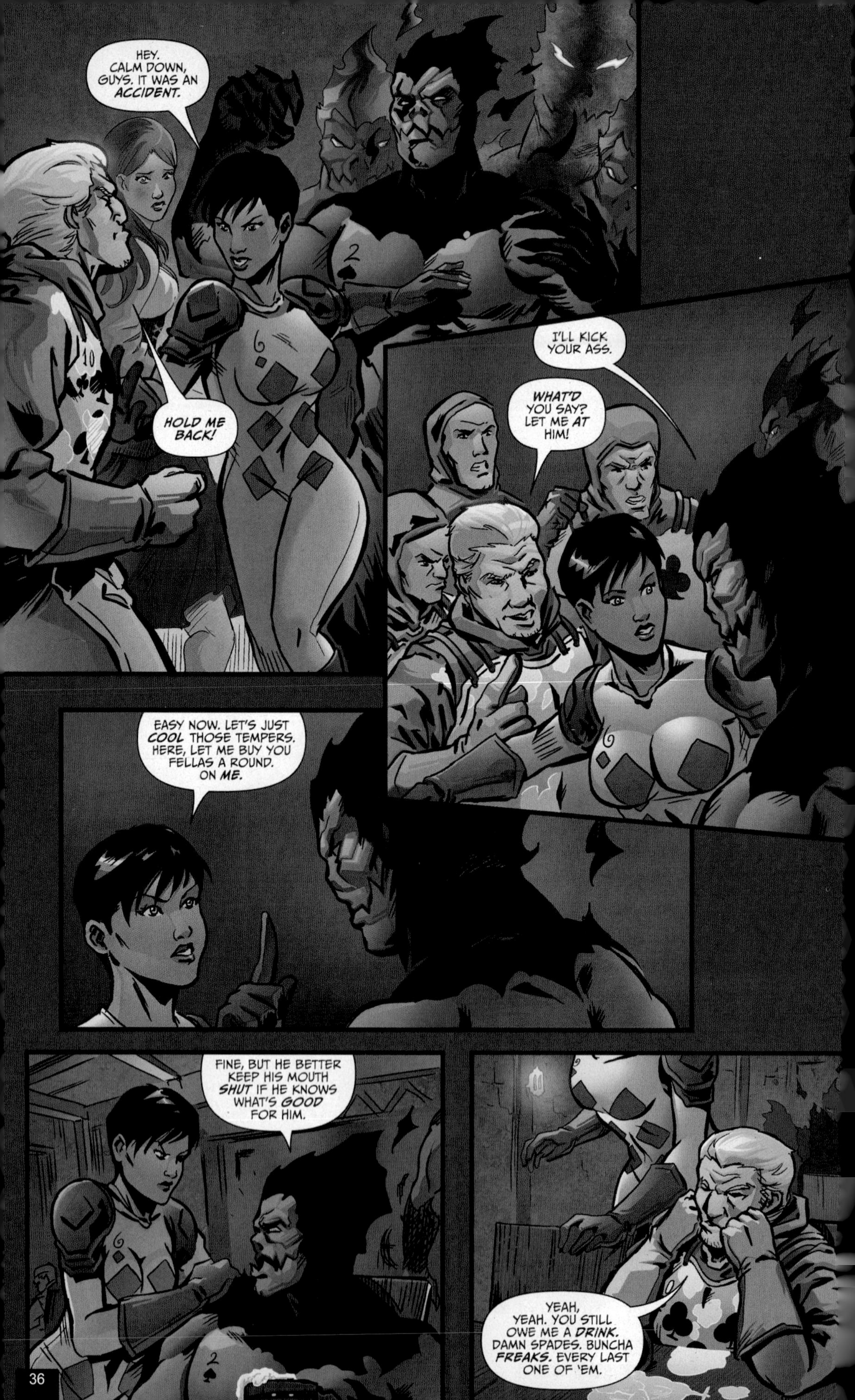
HEY. CALM DOWN, GUYS. IT WAS AN ACCIDENT.
HOLD ME BACK!
I'LL KICK YOUR ASS.
WHAT'D YOU SAY? LET ME AT HIM!
EASY NOW. LET'S JUST COOL THOSE TEMPERS. HERE, LET ME BUY YOU FELLAS A ROUND. ON ME.
FINE, BUT HE BETTER KEEP HIS MOUTH SHUT IF HE KNOWS WHAT'S GOOD FOR HIM.
YEAH, YEAH. YOU STILL OWE ME A DRINK. DAMN SPADES. BUNCHA FREAKS. EVERY LAST ONE OF 'EM.

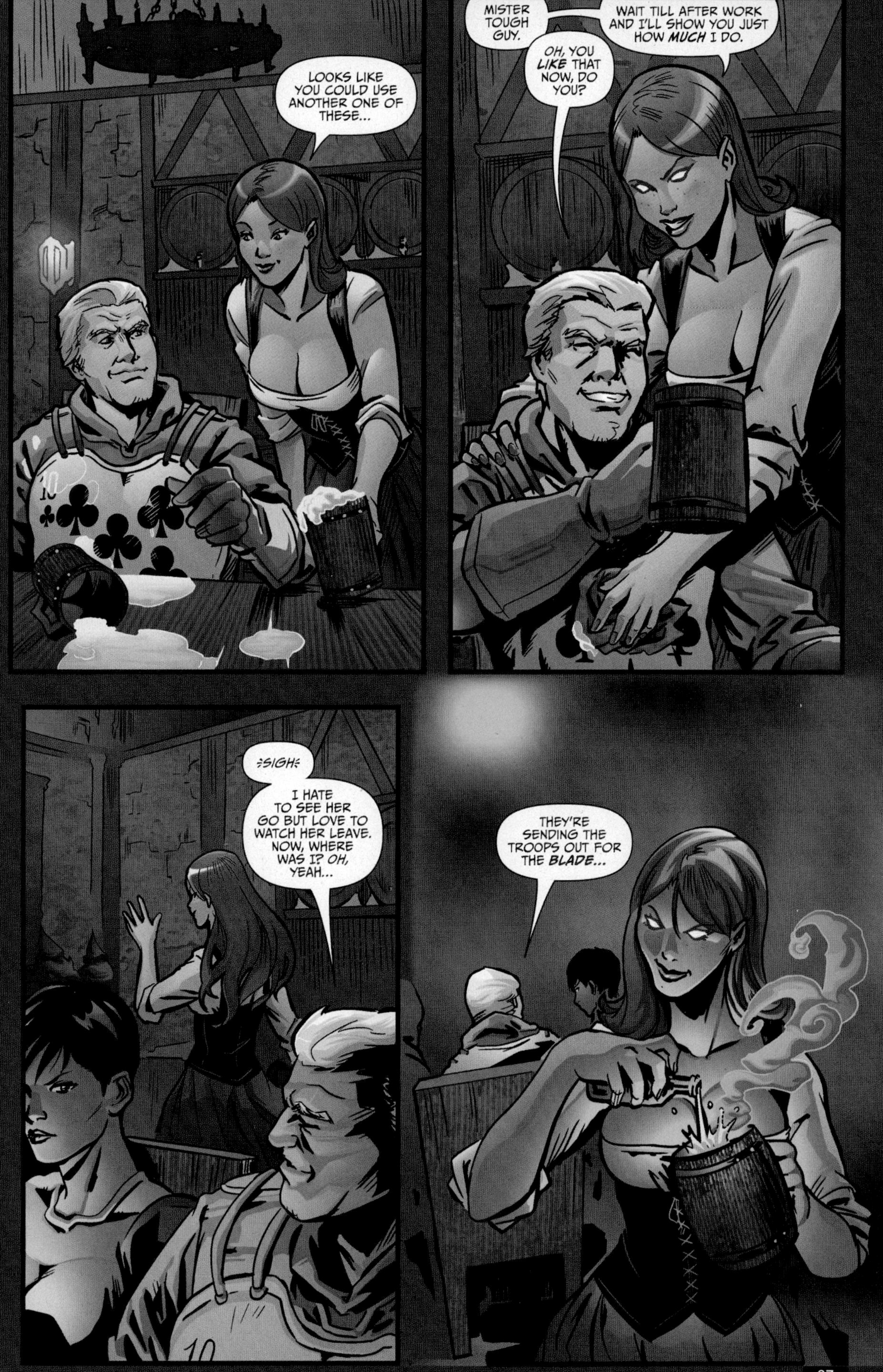
LOOKS LIKE YOU COULD USE ANOTHER ONE OF THESE...
MISTER TOUGH GUY.
OH, YOU LIKE THAT NOW, DO YOU?
WAIT TILL AFTER WORK AND I'LL SHOW YOU JUST HOW MUCH I DO.
SIGH
I HATE TO SEE HER GO BUT LOVE TO WATCH HER LEAVE. NOW, WHERE WAS I? OH, YEAH...
THEY'RE SENDING THE TROOPS OUT FOR THE BLADE...

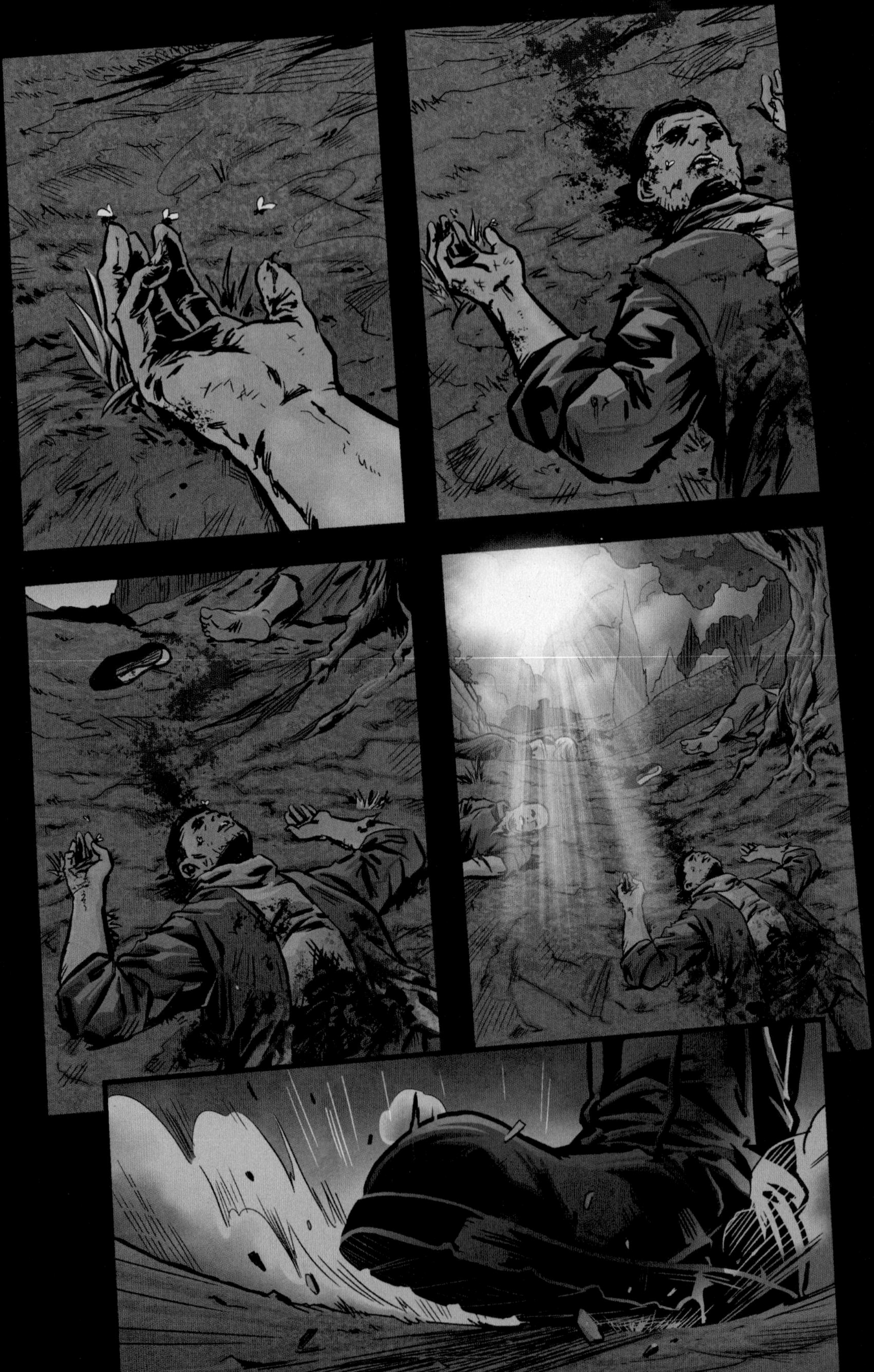

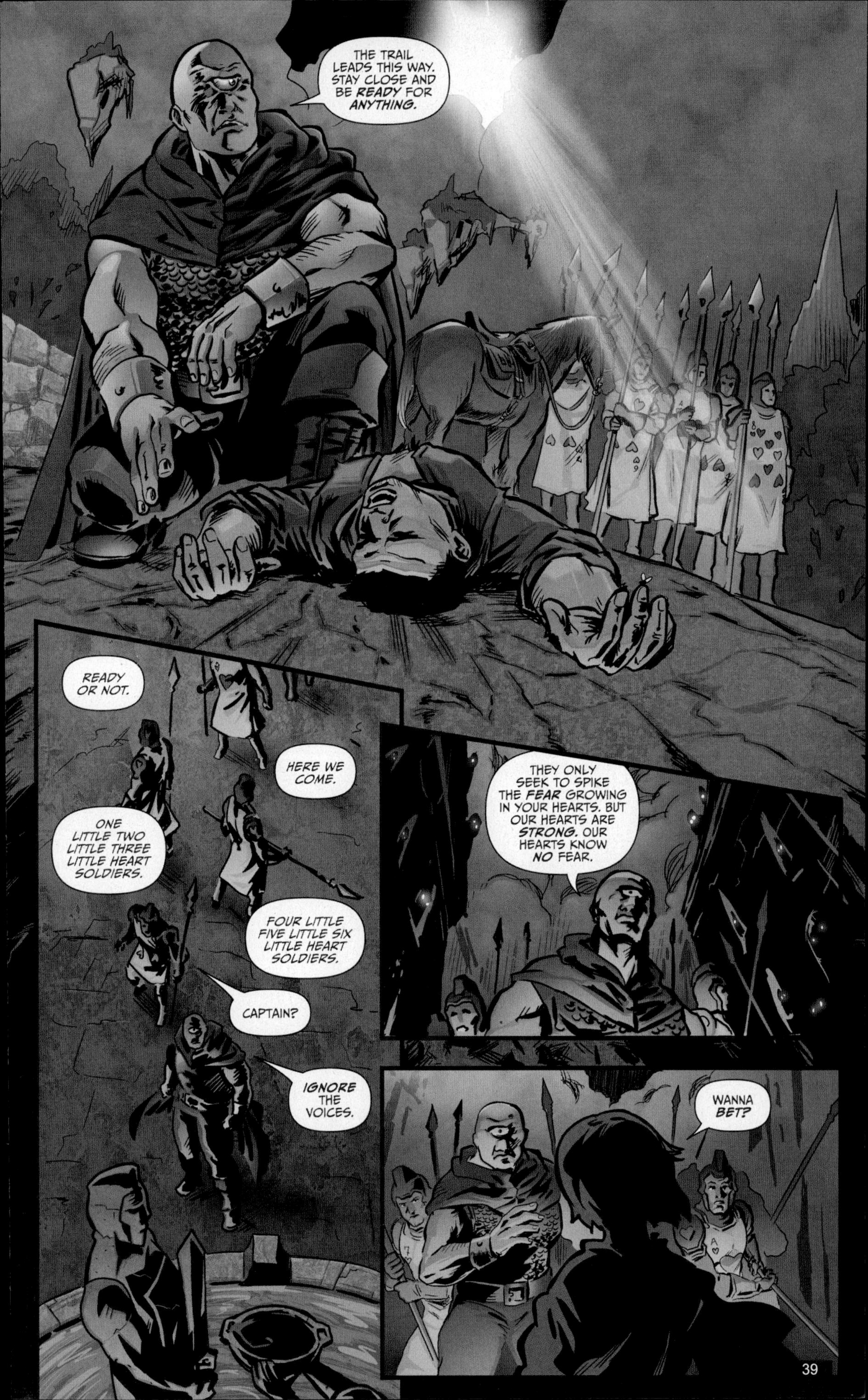
THE TRAIL LEADS THIS WAY. STAY CLOSE AND BE READY FOR ANYTHING.
READY OR NOT.
HERE WE COME.
ONE LITTLE TWO LITTLE THREE LITTLE HEART SOLDIERS.
FOUR LITTLE FIVE LITTLE SIX LITTLE HEART SOLDIERS.
CAPTAIN?
IGNORE THE VOICES.
THEY ONLY SEEK TO SPIKE THE FEAR GROWING IN YOUR HEARTS. BUT OUR HEARTS ARE STRONG. OUR HEARTS KNOW NO FEAR.
WANNA BET?

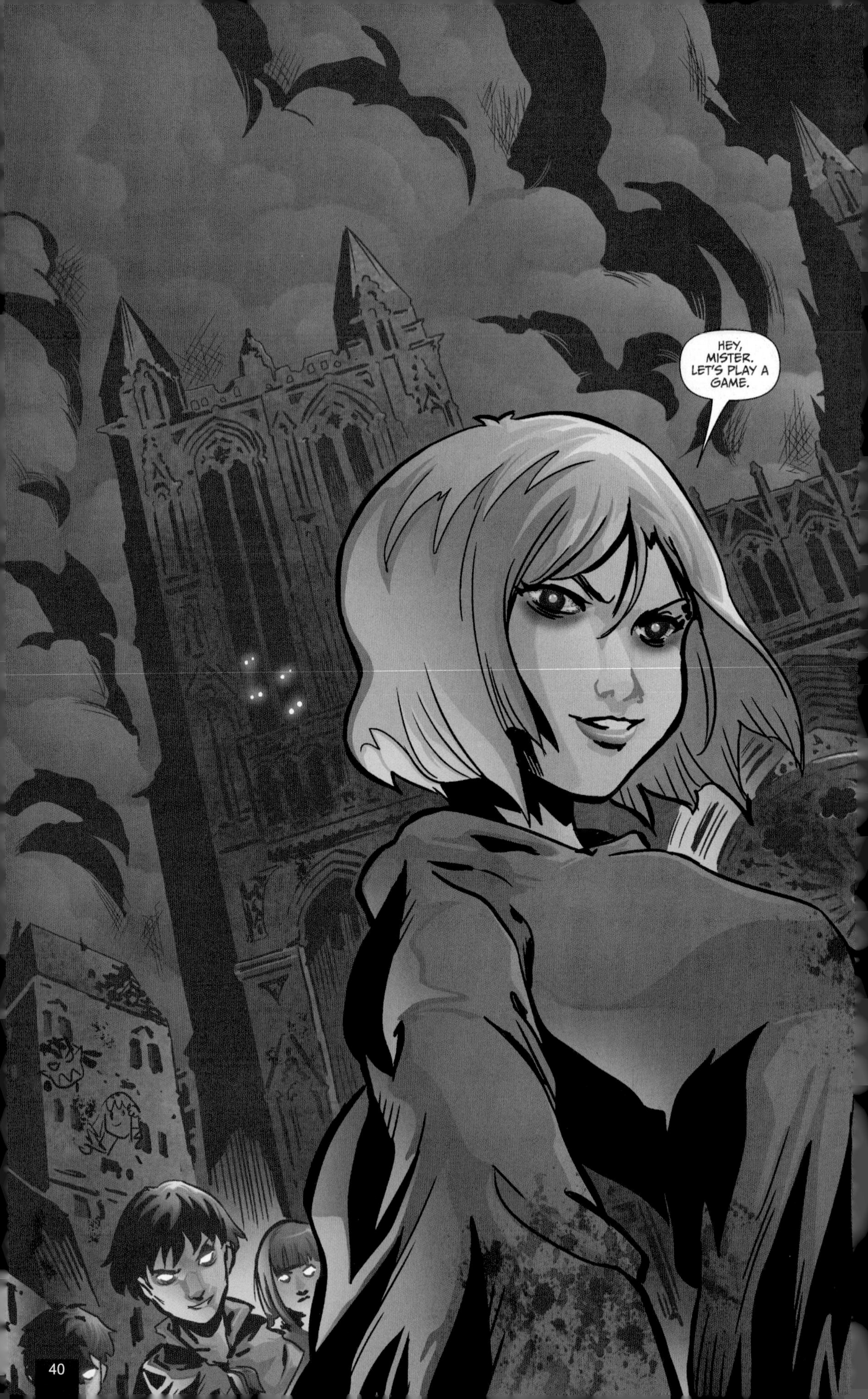
HEY, MISTER. LET'S PLAY A GAME.

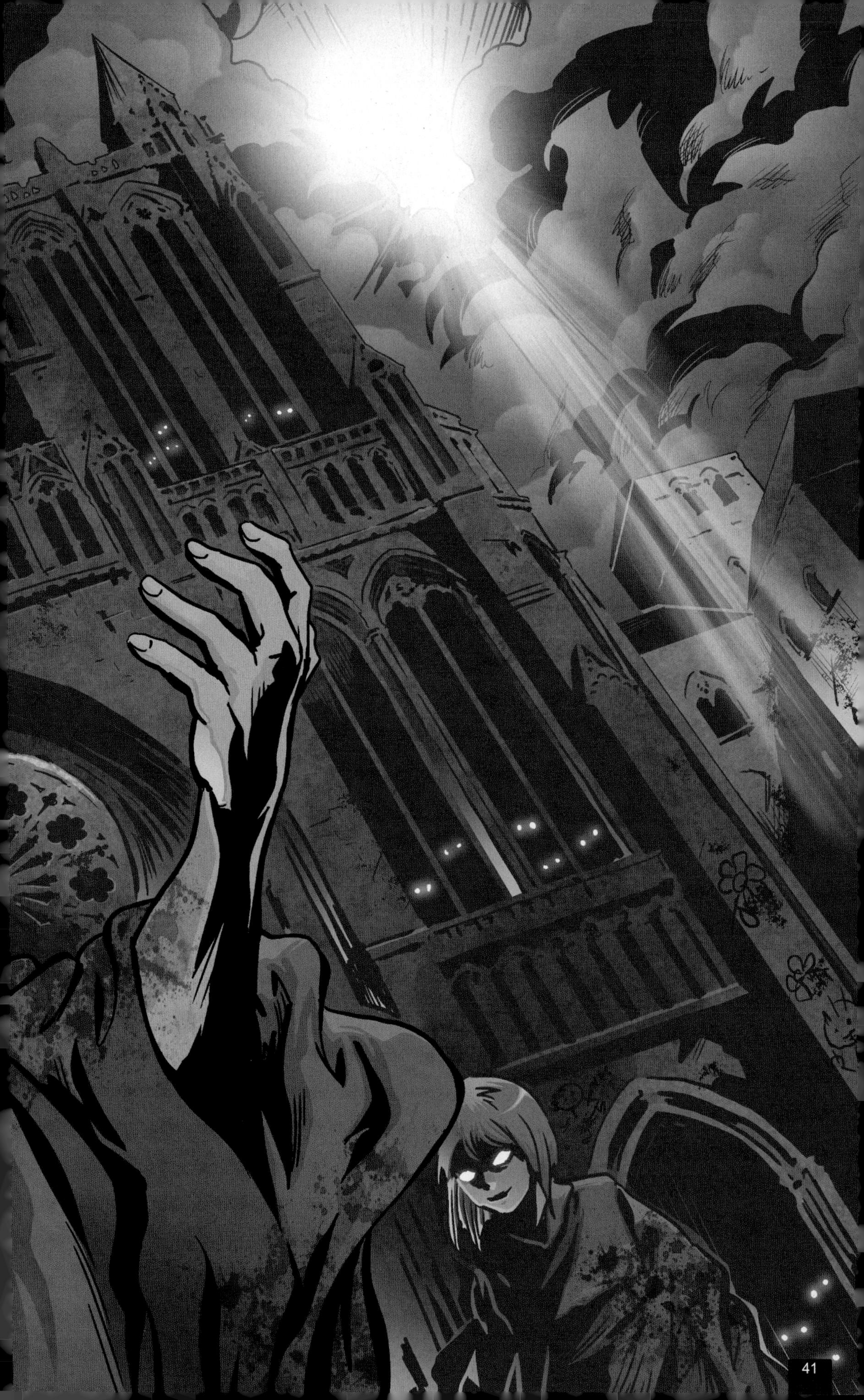

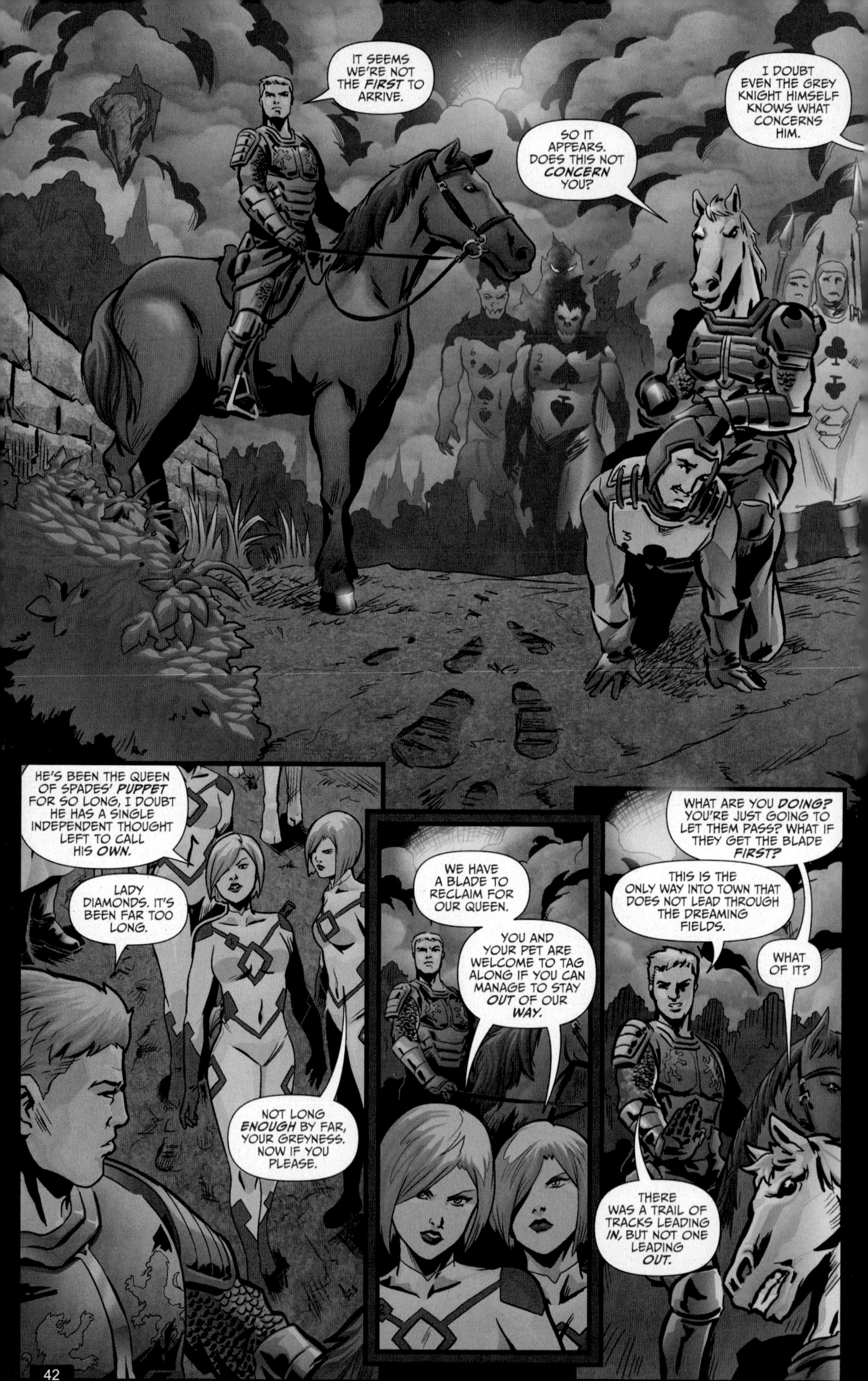
IT SEEMS WE'RE NOT THE FIRST TO ARRIVE.
SO IT APPEARS. DOES THIS NOT CONCERN YOU?
I DOUBT EVEN THE GREY KNIGHT HIMSELF KNOWS WHAT CONCERNS HIM.
HE'S BEEN THE QUEEN OF SPADES' PUPPET FOR SO LONG, I DOUBT HE HAS A SINGLE INDEPENDENT THOUGHT LEFT TO CALL HIS OWN.
LADY DIAMONDS. IT'S BEEN FAR TOO LONG.
NOT LONG ENOUGH BY FAR, YOUR GREYNESS. NOW IF YOU PLEASE.
WE HAVE A BLADE TO RECLAIM FOR OUR QUEEN.
YOU AND YOUR PET ARE WELCOME TO TAG ALONG IF YOU CAN MANAGE TO STAY OUT OF OUR WAY.
WHAT ARE YOU DOING? YOU'RE JUST GOING TO LET THEM PASS? WHAT IF THEY GET THE BLADE FIRST?
THIS IS THE ONLY WAY INTO TOWN THAT DOES NOT LEAD THROUGH THE DREAMING FIELDS.
WHAT OF IT?
THERE WAS A TRAIL OF TRACKS LEADING IN, BUT NOT ONE LEADING OUT.

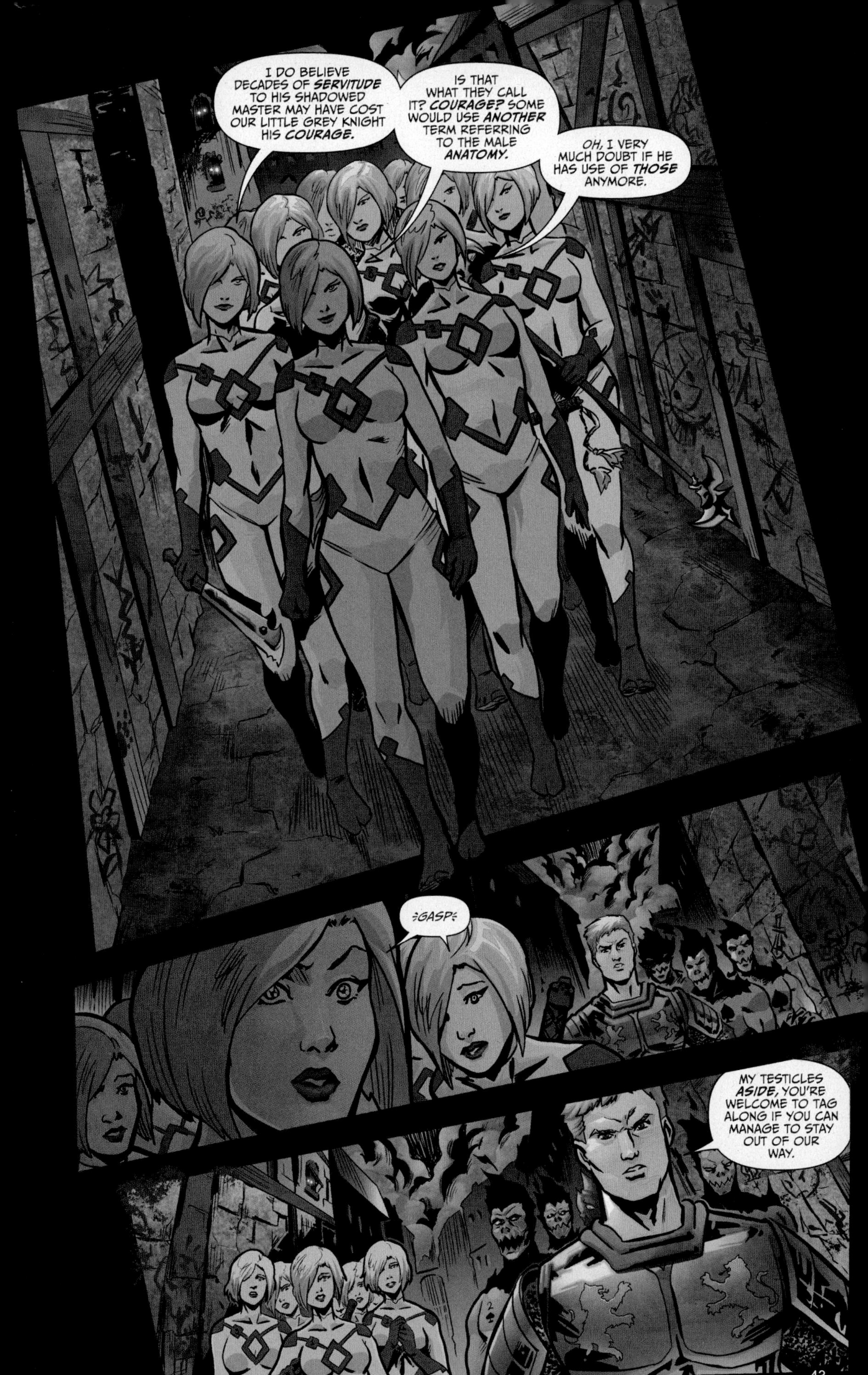
I DO BELIEVE DECADES OF SERVITUDE TO HIS SHADOWED MASTER MAY HAVE COST OUR LITTLE GREY KNIGHT HIS COURAGE.
IS THAT WHAT THEY CALL IT? COURAGE? SOME WOULD USE ANOTHER TERM REFERRING TO THE MALE ANATOMY.
OH, I VERY MUCH DOUBT IF HE HAS USE OF THOSE ANYMORE.
GASP
MY TESTICLES ASIDE, YOU'RE WELCOME TO TAG ALONG IF YOU CAN MANAGE TO STAY OUT OF OUR WAY.

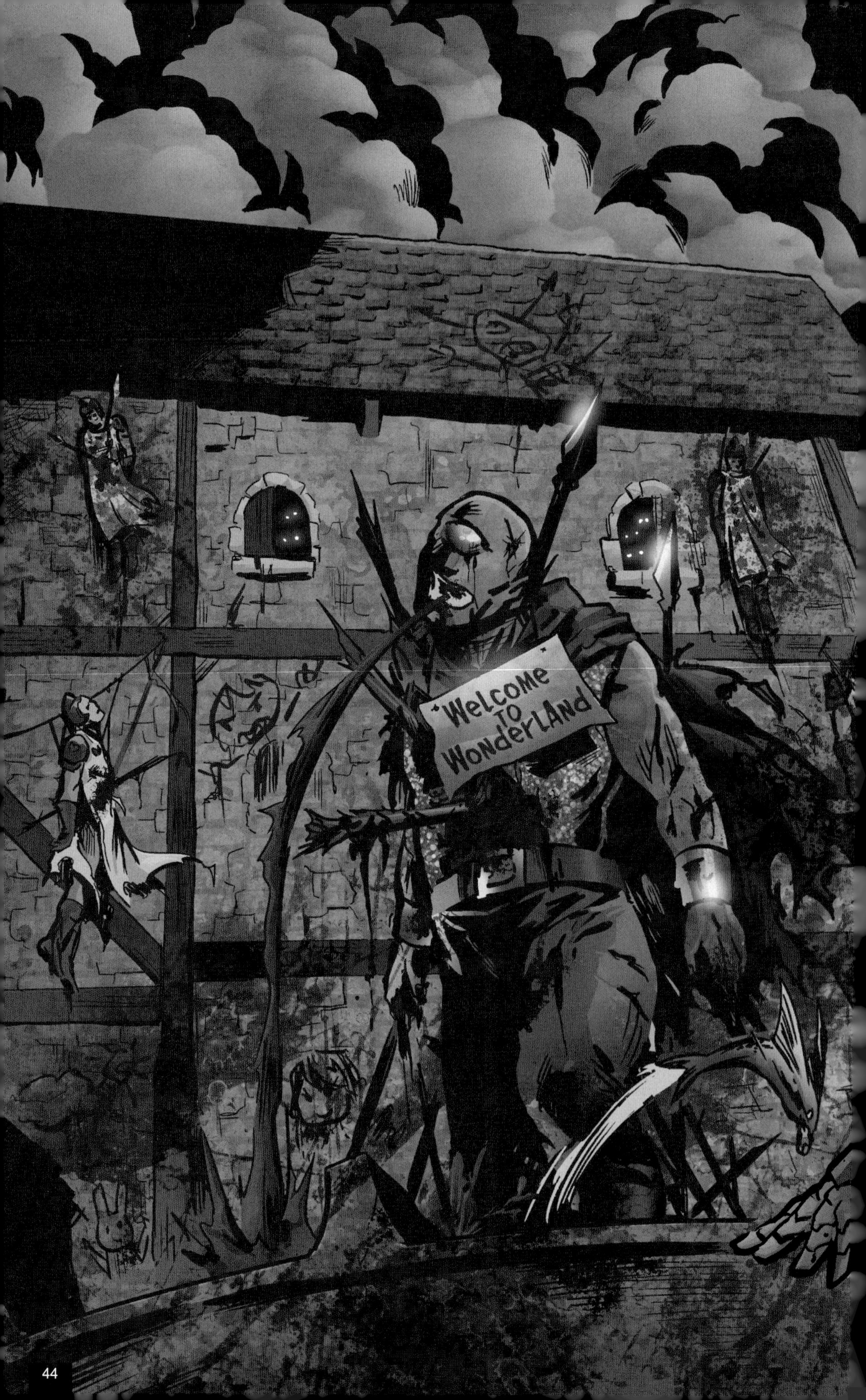
Welcome
TO
WonderLANd

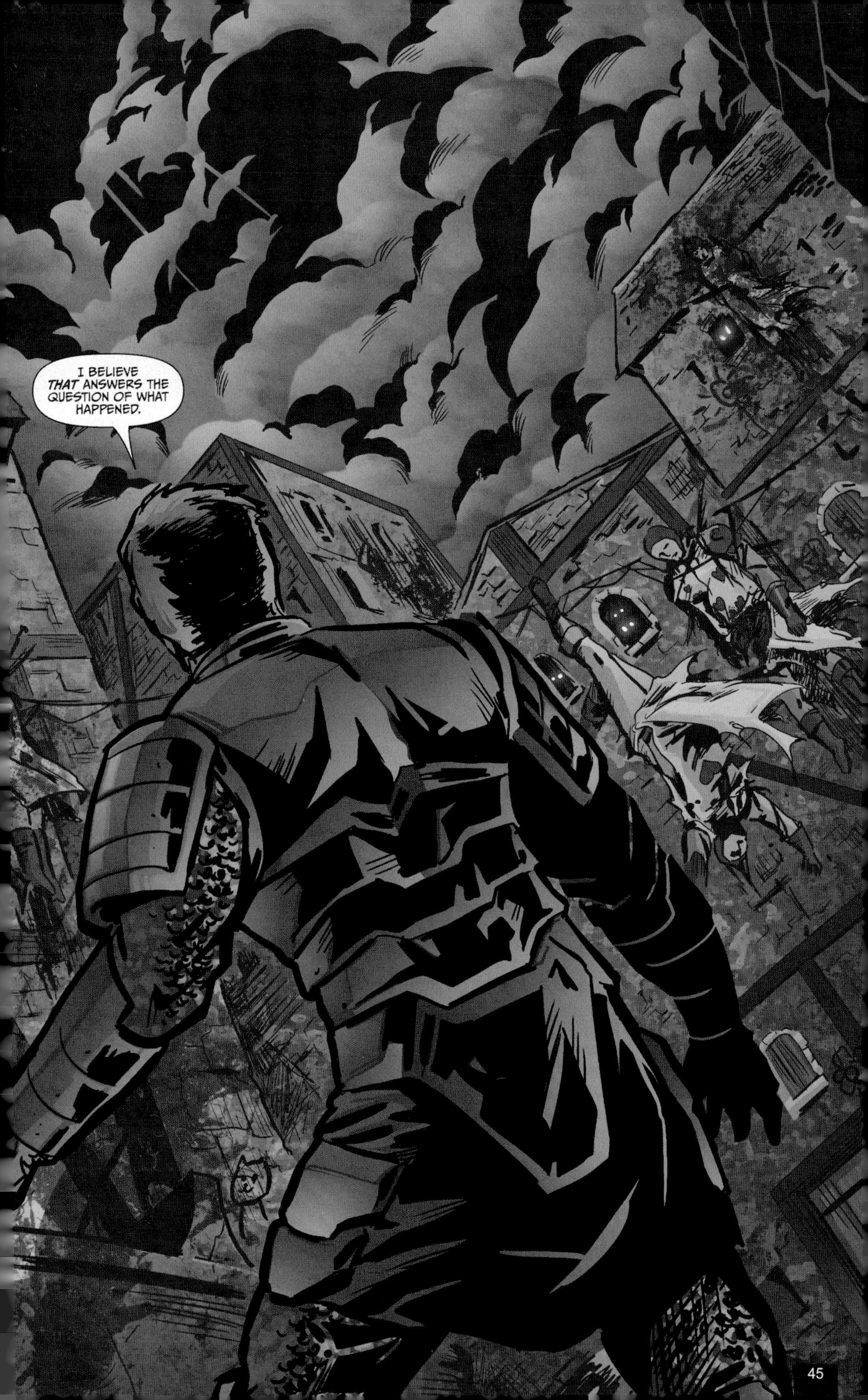
I BELIEVE *THAT* ANSWERS THE QUESTION OF WHAT HAPPENED.

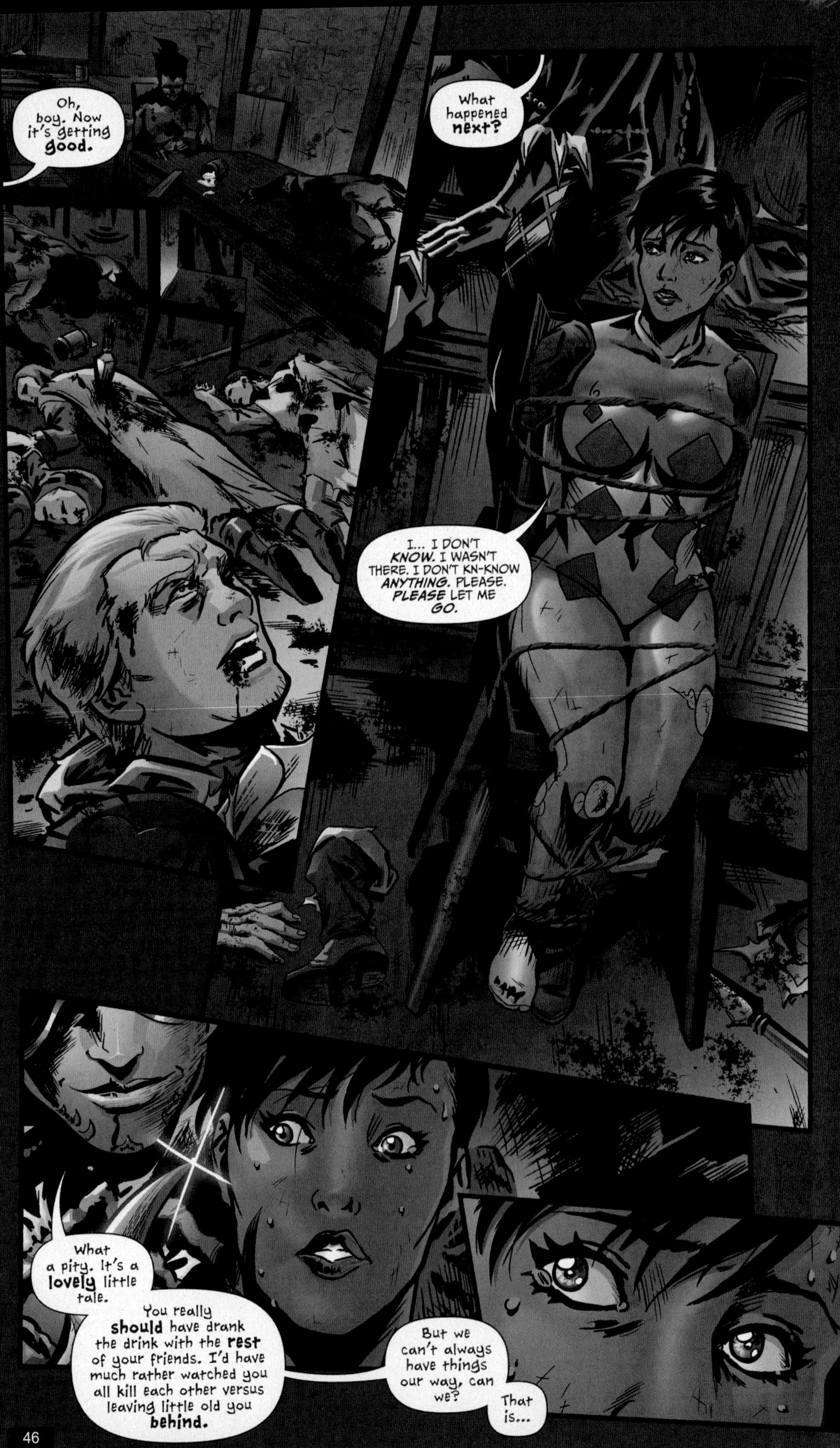
Oh, boy. Now it's getting good.
What happened next?
I... I DON'T KNOW. I WASN'T THERE. I DON'T KN-KNOW ANYTHING. PLEASE. PLEASE LET ME GO.
What a pity. It's a lovely little tale.
You really should have drank the drink with the rest of your friends. I'd have much rather watched you all kill each other versus leaving little old you behind.
But we can't always have things our way, can we?
That is...

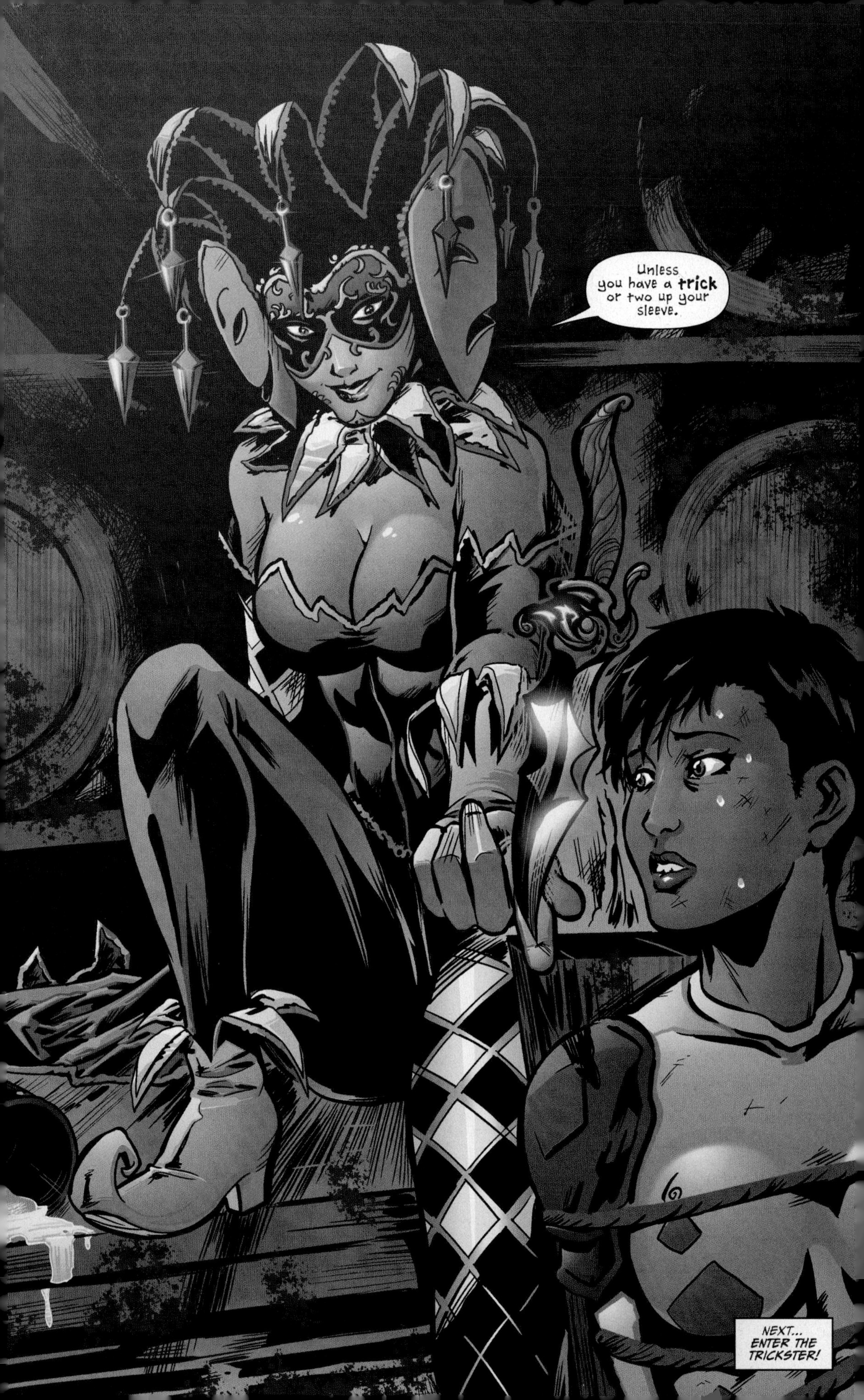
Unless you have a trick or two up your sleeve.
NEXT... ENTER THE TRICKSTER!

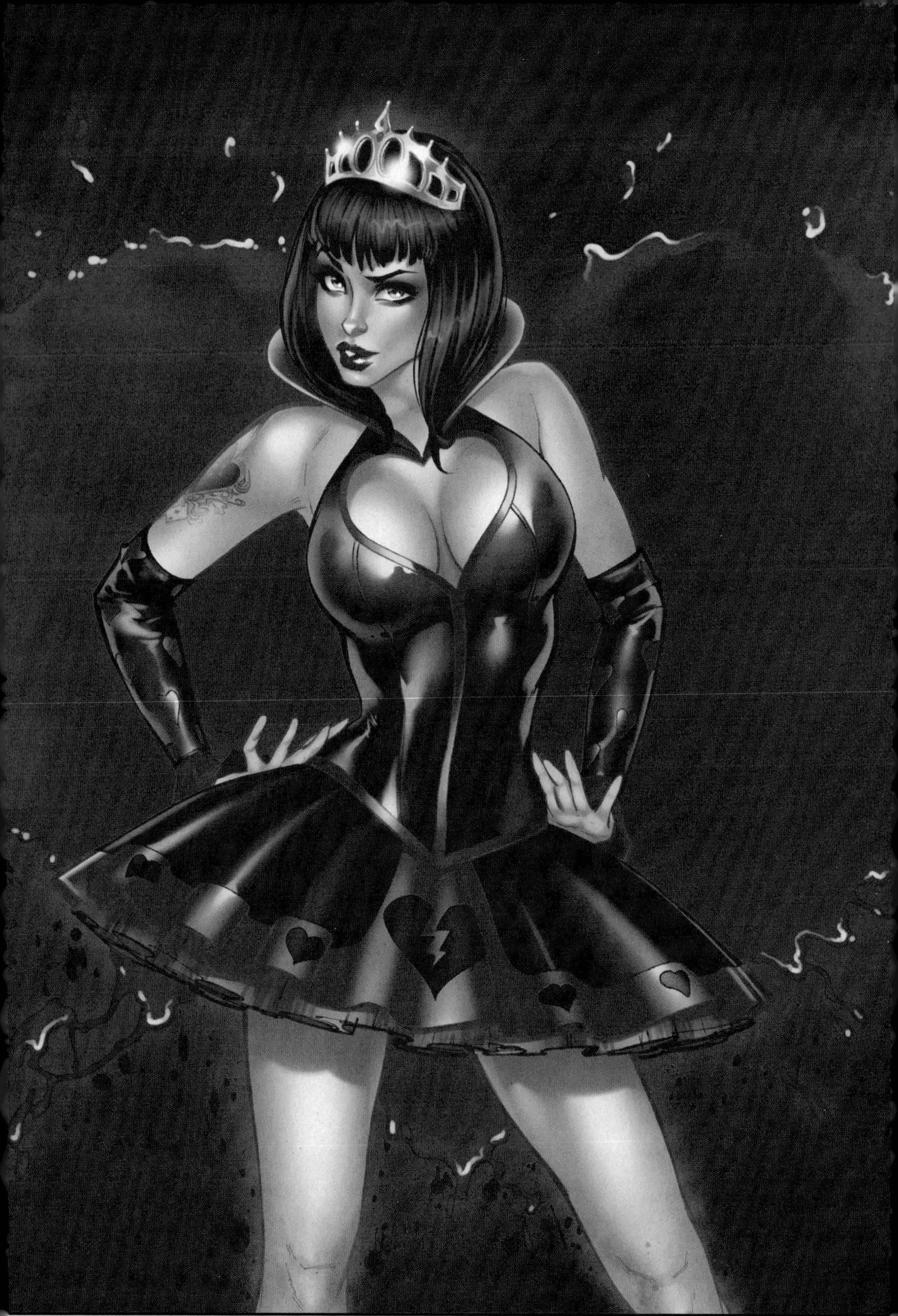

CHAPTER THREE

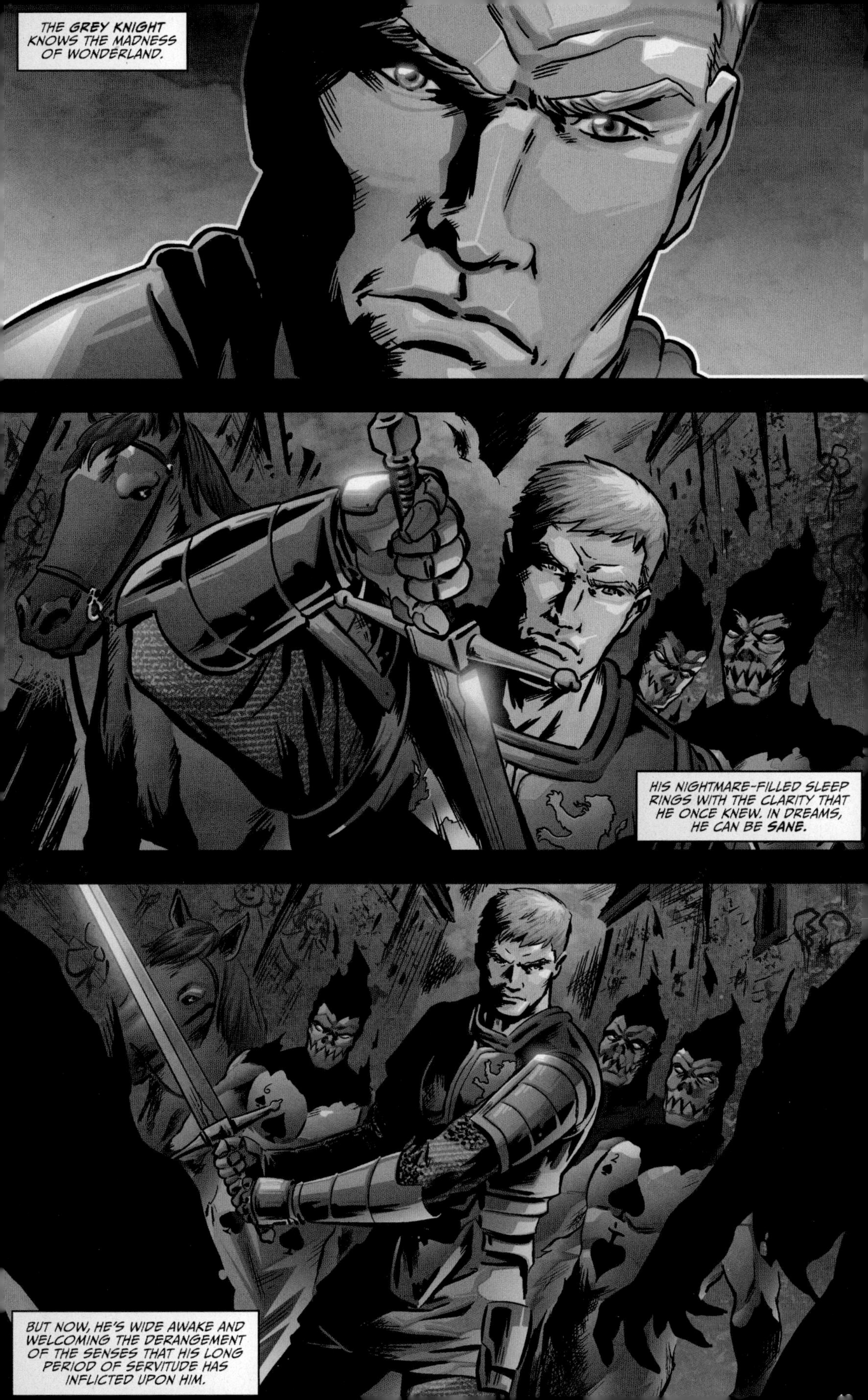
THE GREY KNIGHT KNOWS THE MADNESS OF WONDERLAND.
HIS NIGHTMARE-FILLED SLEEP RINGS WITH THE CLARITY THAT HE ONCE KNEW. IN DREAMS, HE CAN BE SANE.
BUT NOW, HE'S WIDE AWAKE AND WELCOMING THE DERANGEMENT OF THE SENSES THAT HIS LONG PERIOD OF SERVITUDE HAS INFLICTED UPON HIM.

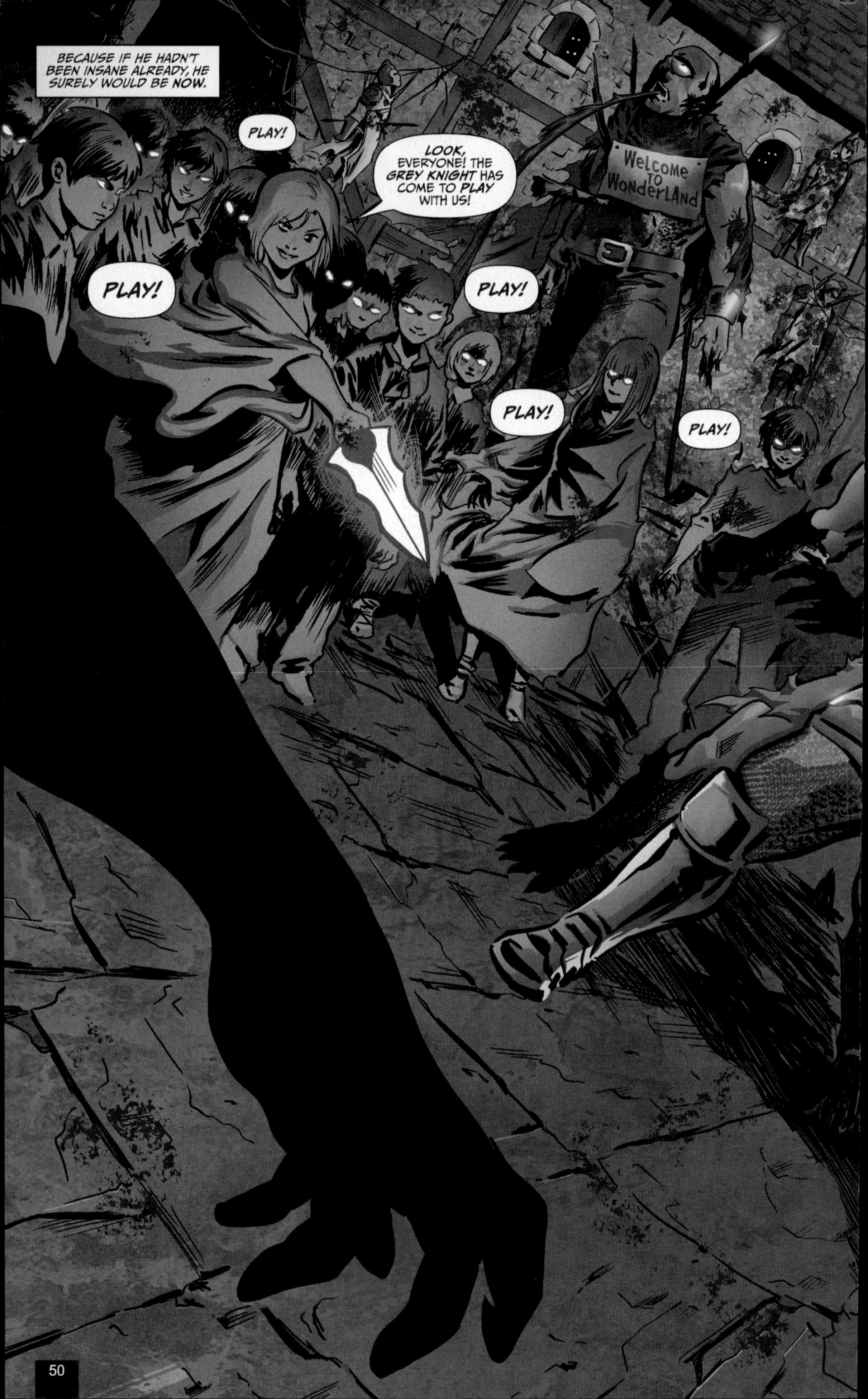
BECAUSE IF HE HADN'T BEEN INSANE ALREADY, HE SURELY WOULD BE NOW.
PLAY!
LOOK, EVERYONE! THE GREY KNIGHT HAS COME TO PLAY WITH US!
Welcome TO WonderLAnd
PLAY!
PLAY!
PLAY!
PLAY!

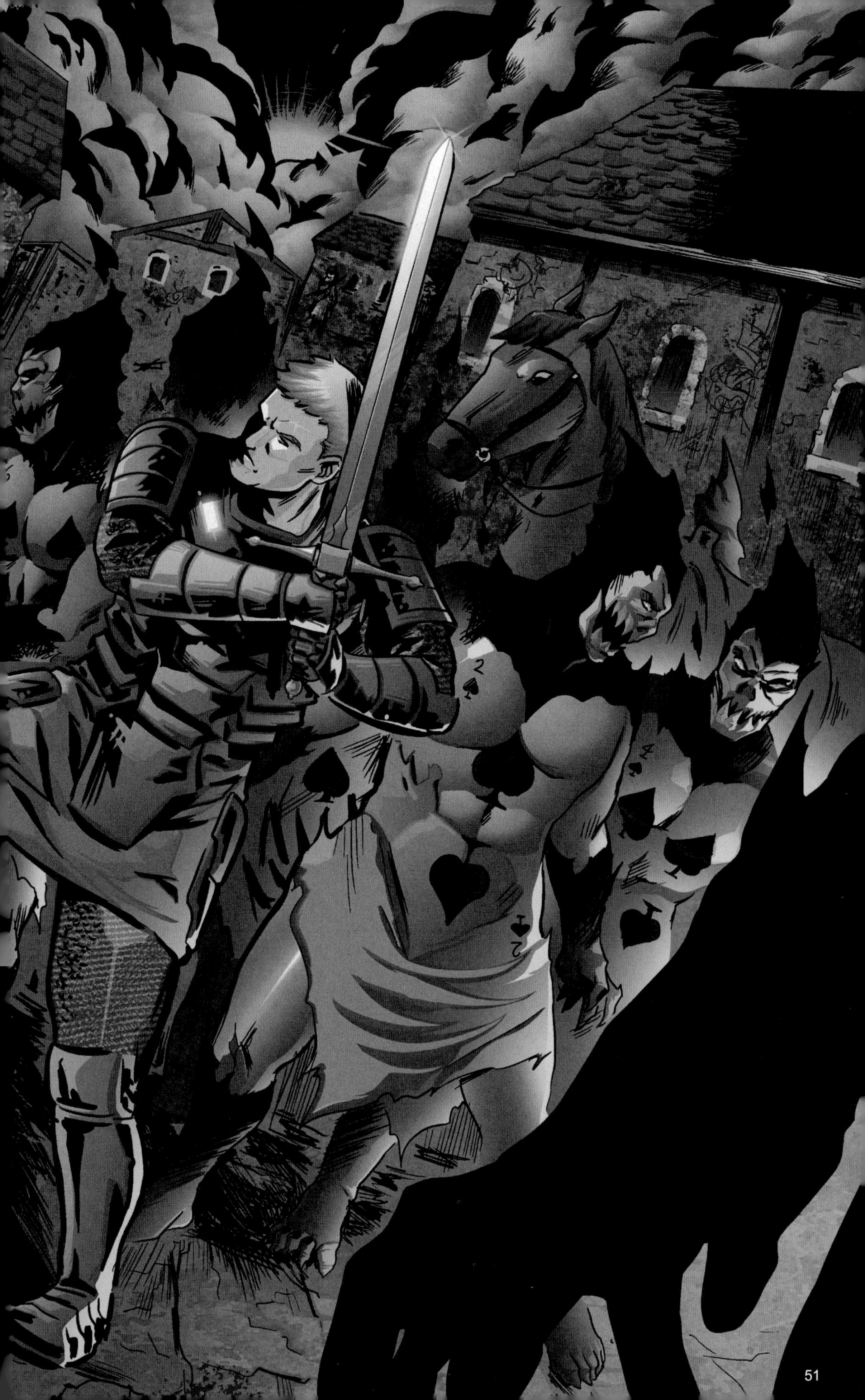

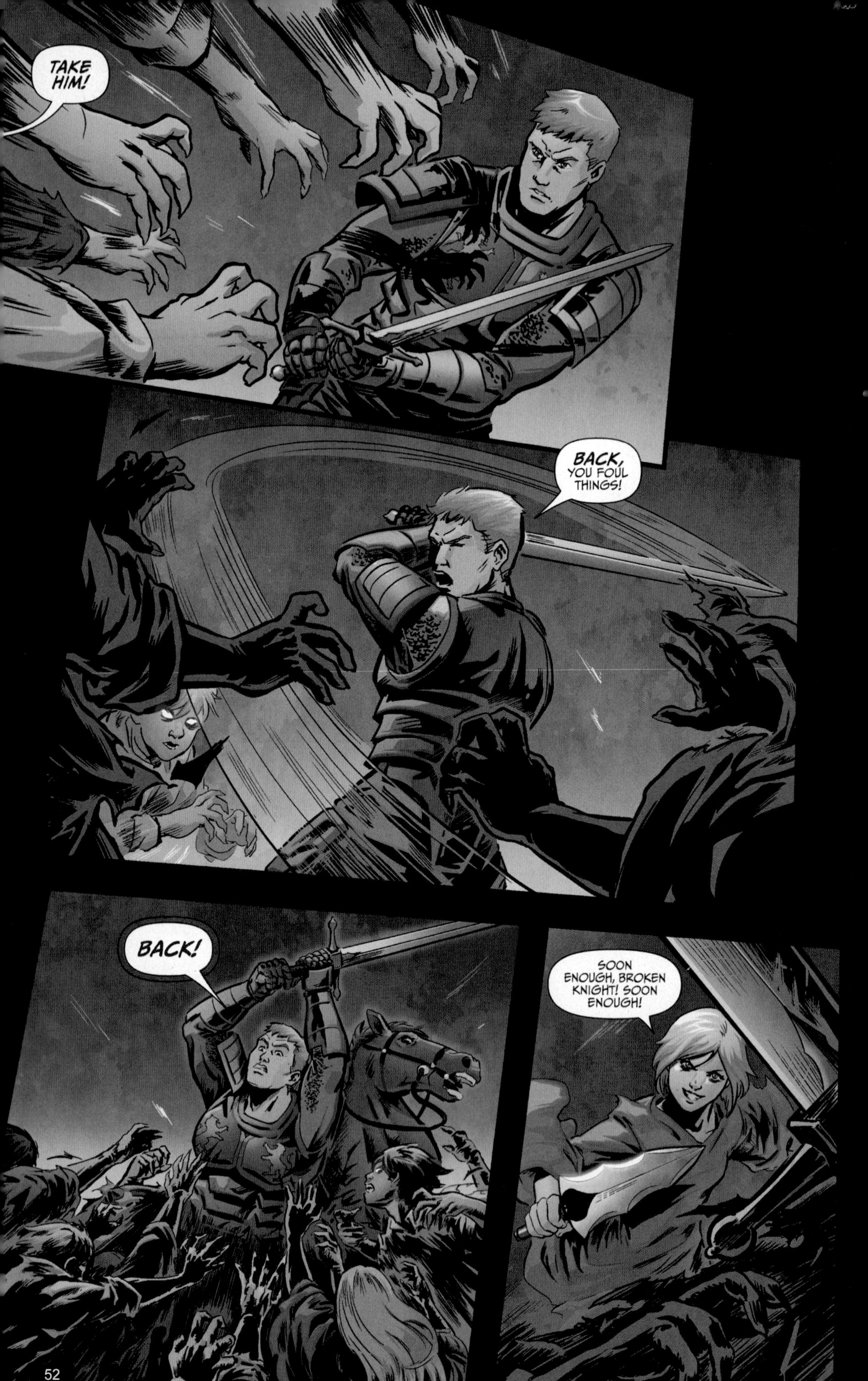
TAKE HIM!
BACK, YOU FOUL THINGS!
BACK!
SOON ENOUGH, BROKEN KNIGHT! SOON ENOUGH!

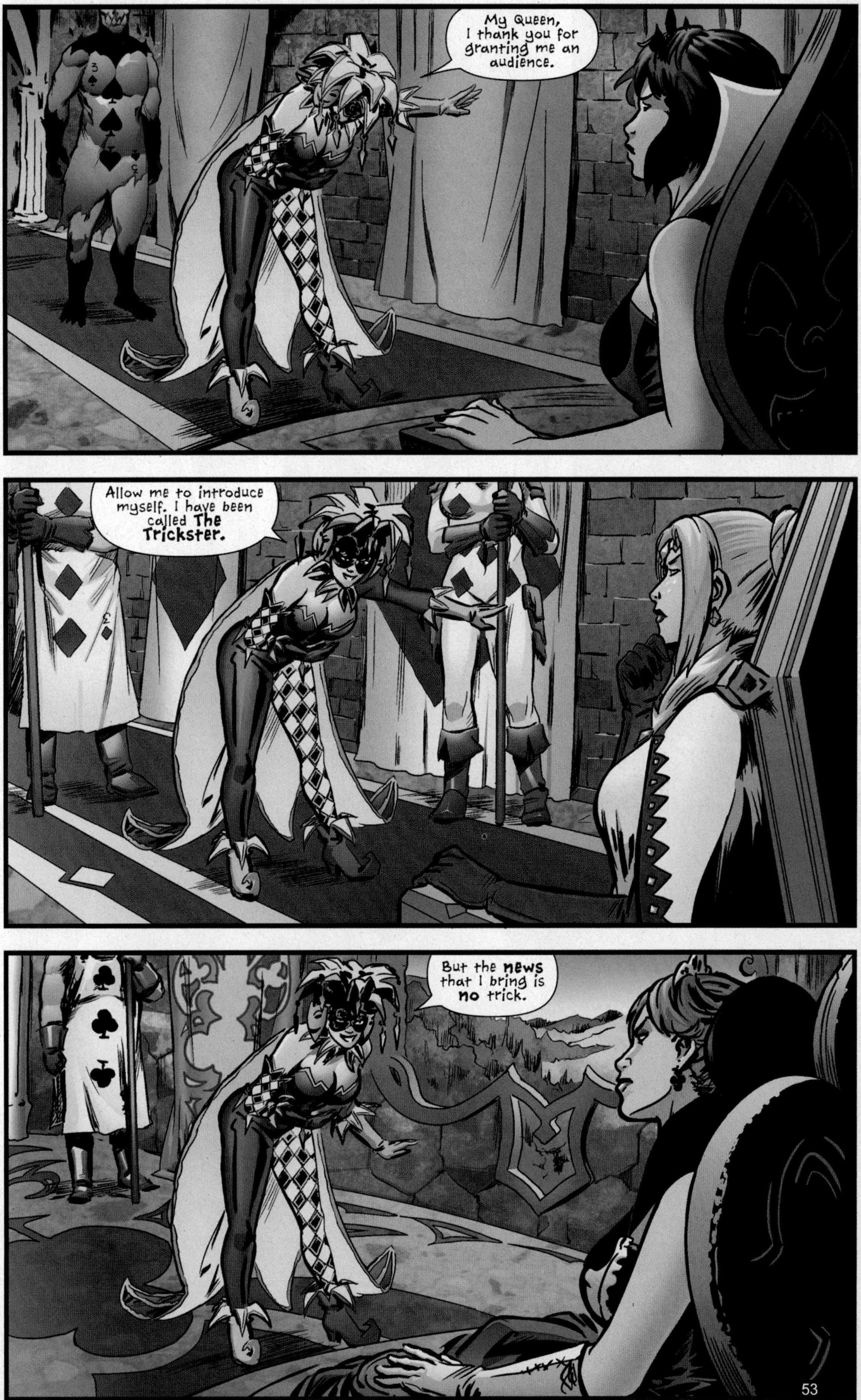
My Queen, I thank you for granting me an audience.
Allow me to introduce myself. I have been called **The Trickster.**
But the **news** that I bring is **no** trick.

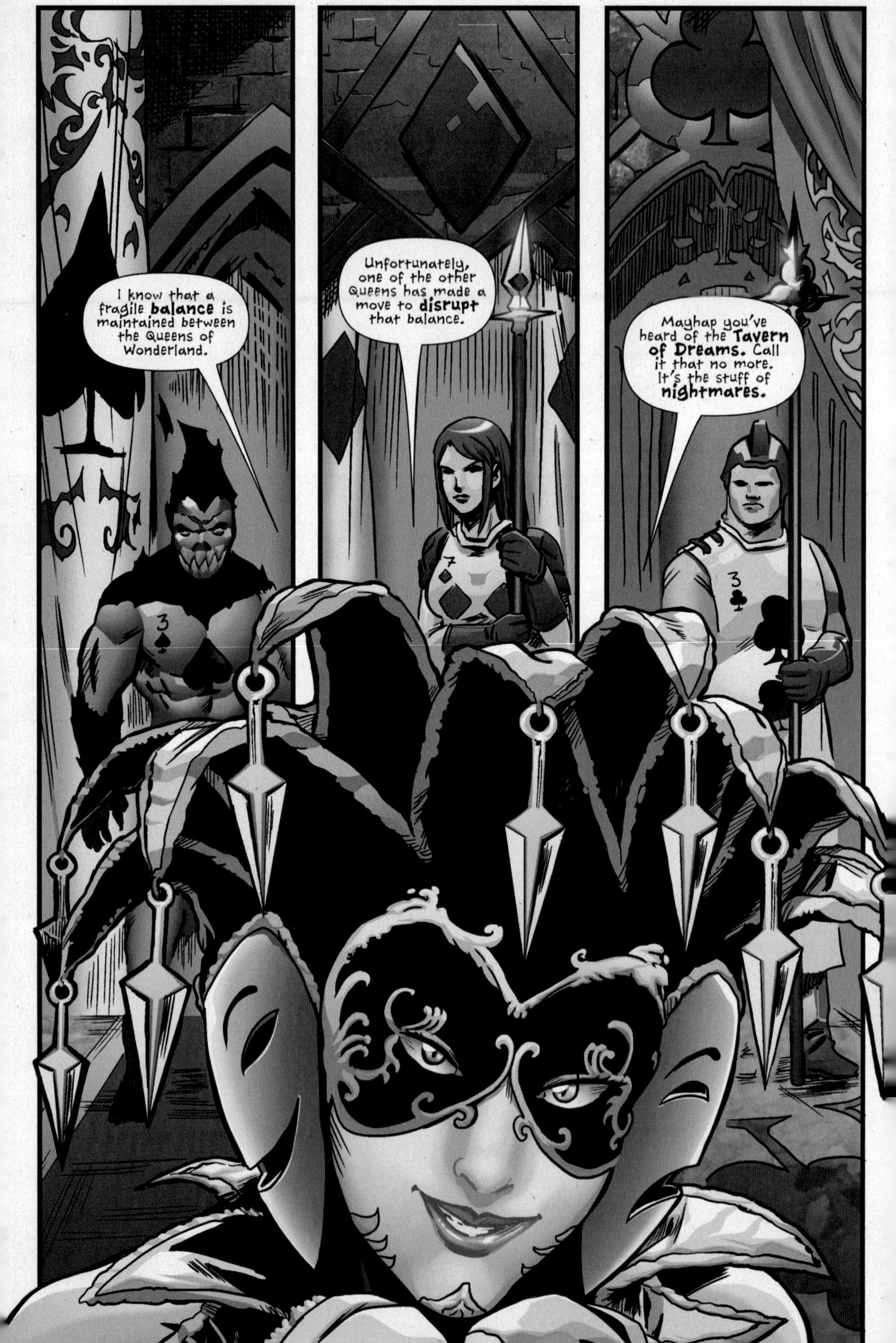
I know that a fragile **balance** is maintained between the Queens of Wonderland.
Unfortunately, one of the other Queens has made a move to **disrupt** that balance.
Mayhap you've heard of the **Tavern of Dreams.** Call it that no more. It's the stuff of **nightmares.**

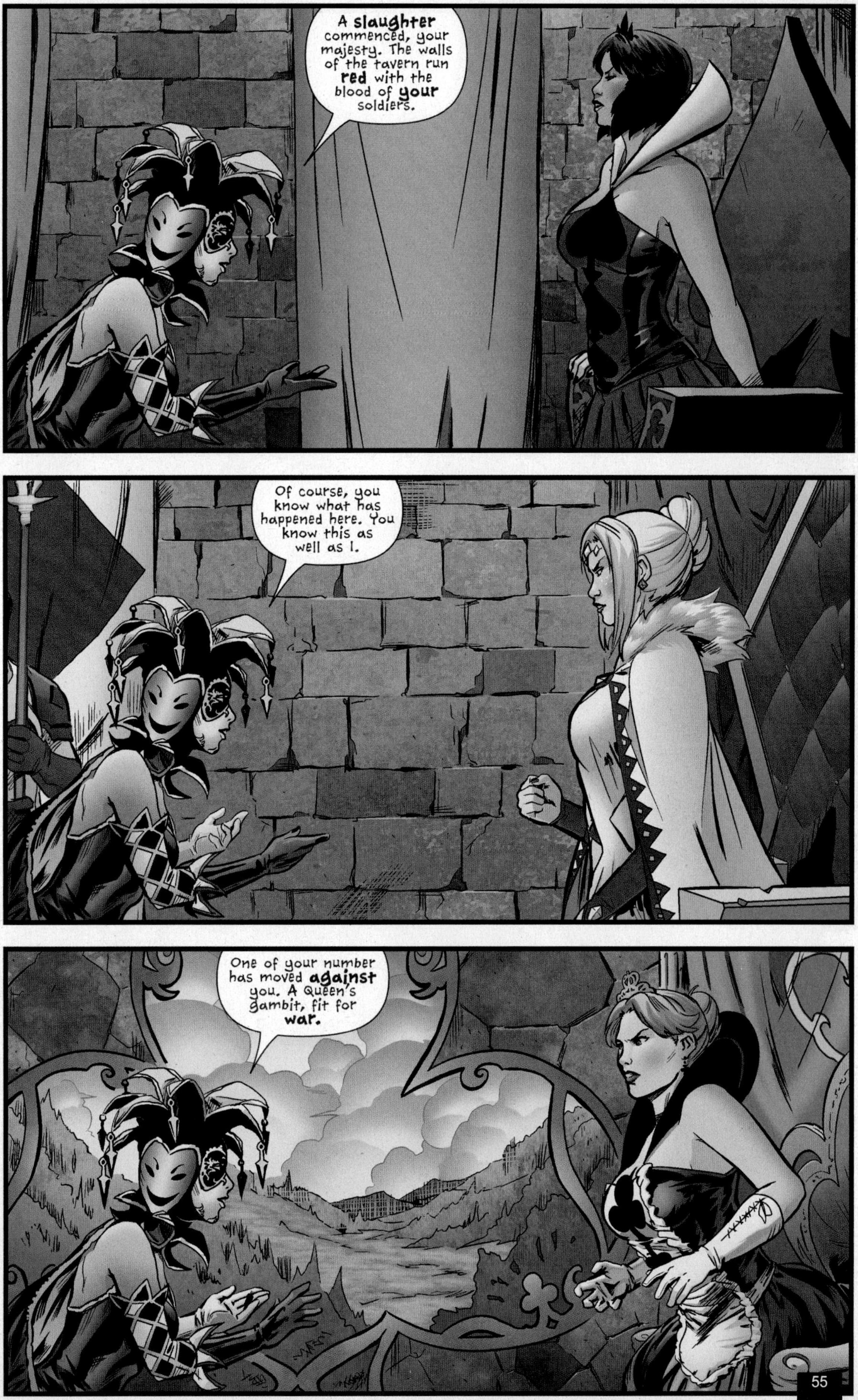
A slaughter commenced, your majesty. The walls of the tavern run red with the blood of your soldiers.
Of course, you know what has happened here. You know this as well as I.
One of your number has moved against you. A Queen's gambit, fit for war.

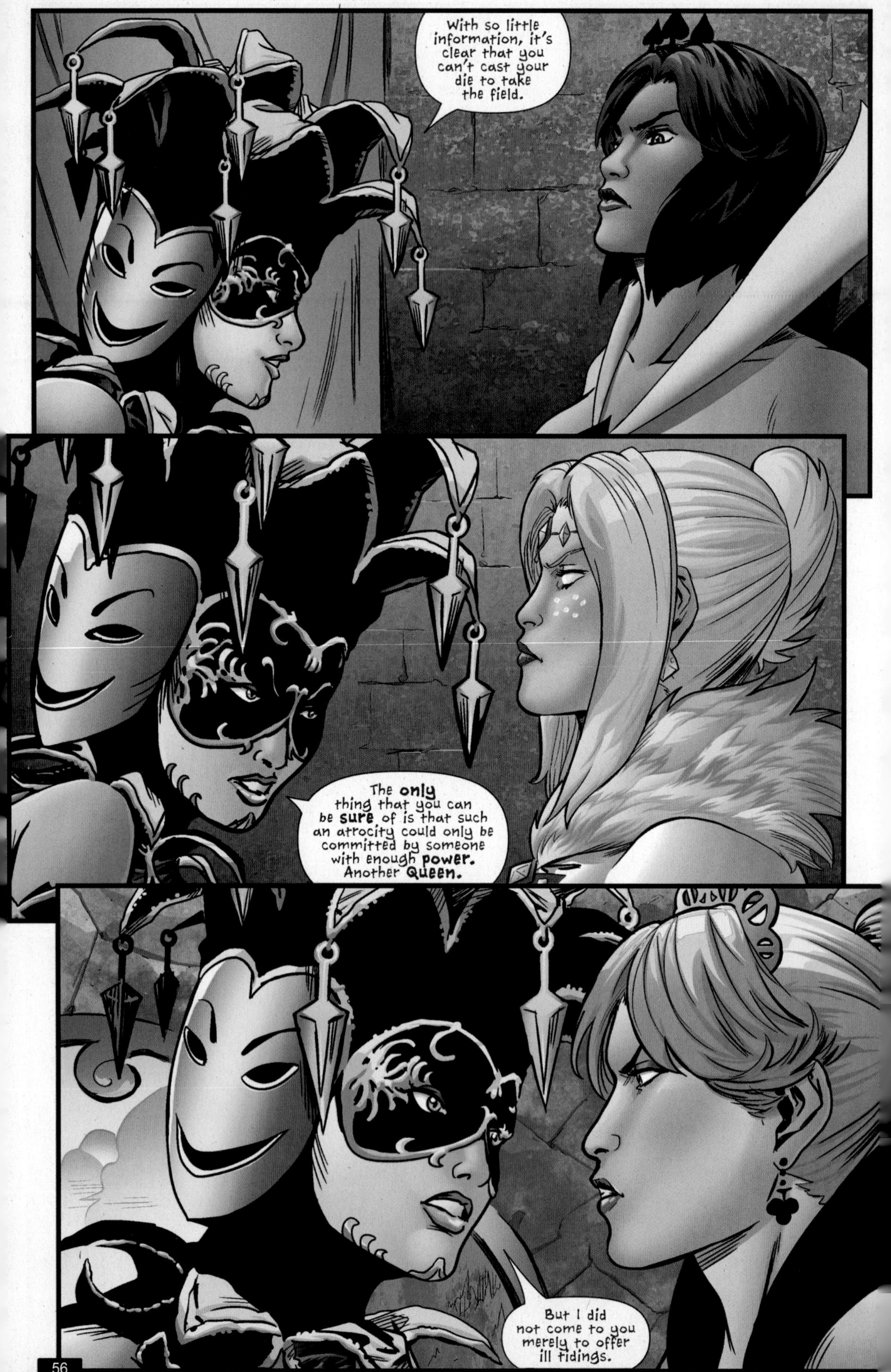

With so little information, it's clear that you can't cast your die to take the field.
The only thing that you can be sure of is that such an atrocity could only be committed by someone with enough power. Another Queen.
But I did not come to you merely to offer ill tidings.

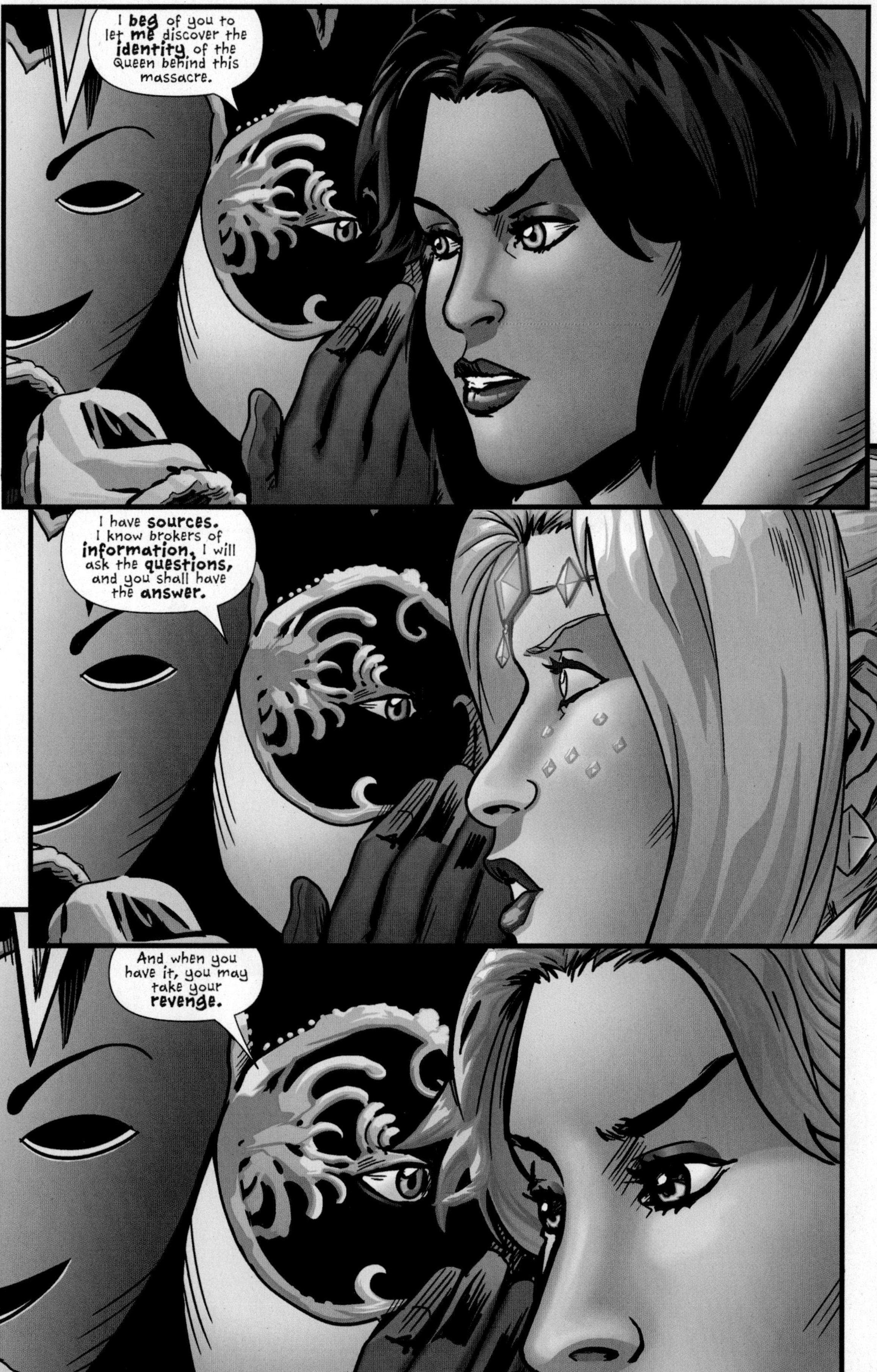
I beg of you to let me discover the identity of the Queen behind this massacre.
I have sources. I know brokers of information. I will ask the questions, and you shall have the answer.
And when you have it, you may take your revenge.

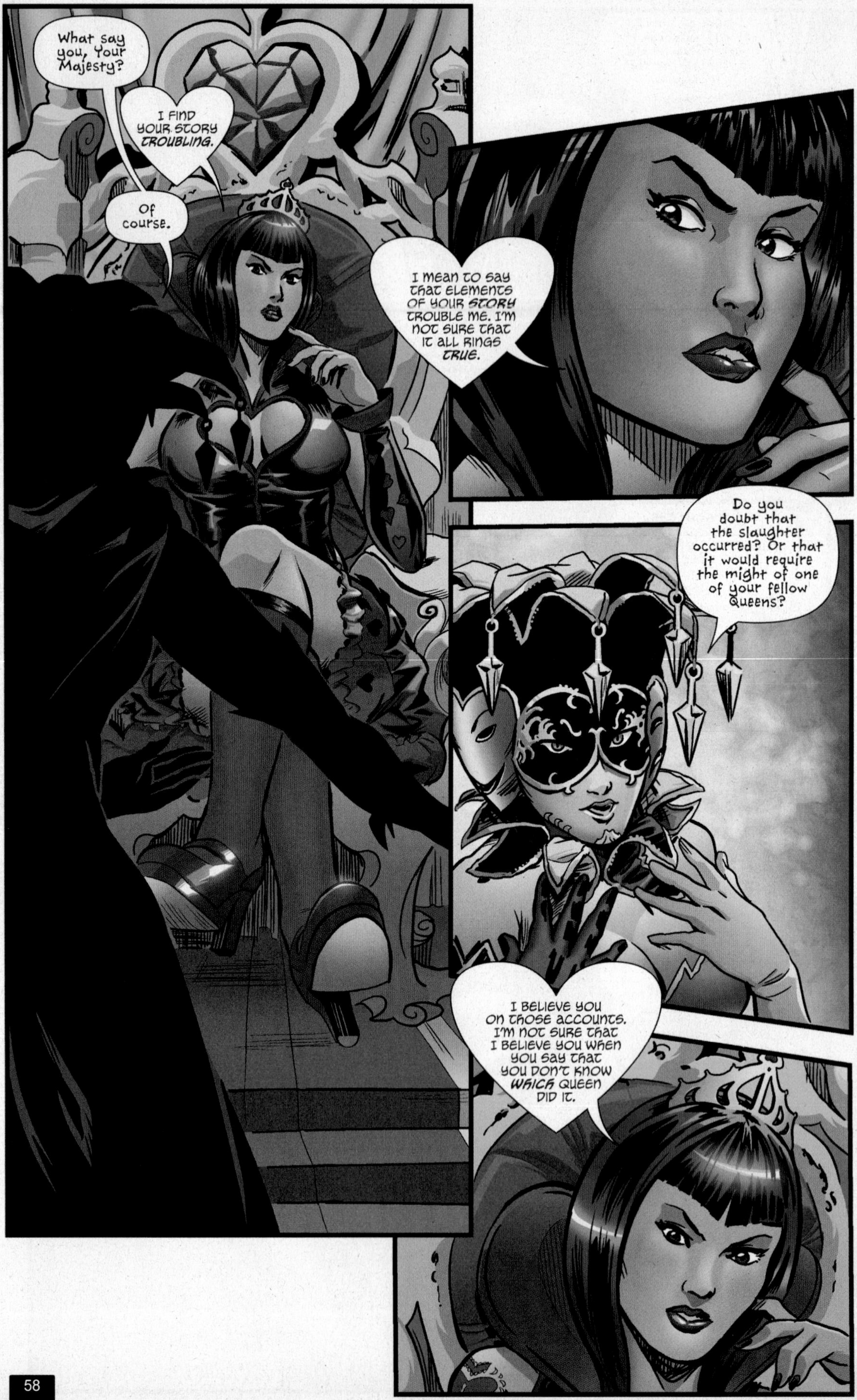
What say you, Your Majesty?
I FIND YOUR STORY TROUBLING.
Of course.
I MEAN TO SAY THAT ELEMENTS OF YOUR STORY TROUBLE ME. I'M NOT SURE THAT IT ALL RINGS TRUE.
Do you doubt that the slaughter occurred? Or that it would require the might of one of your fellow Queens?
I BELIEVE YOU ON THOSE ACCOUNTS. I'M NOT SURE THAT I BELIEVE YOU WHEN YOU SAY THAT YOU DON'T KNOW WHICH QUEEN DID IT.

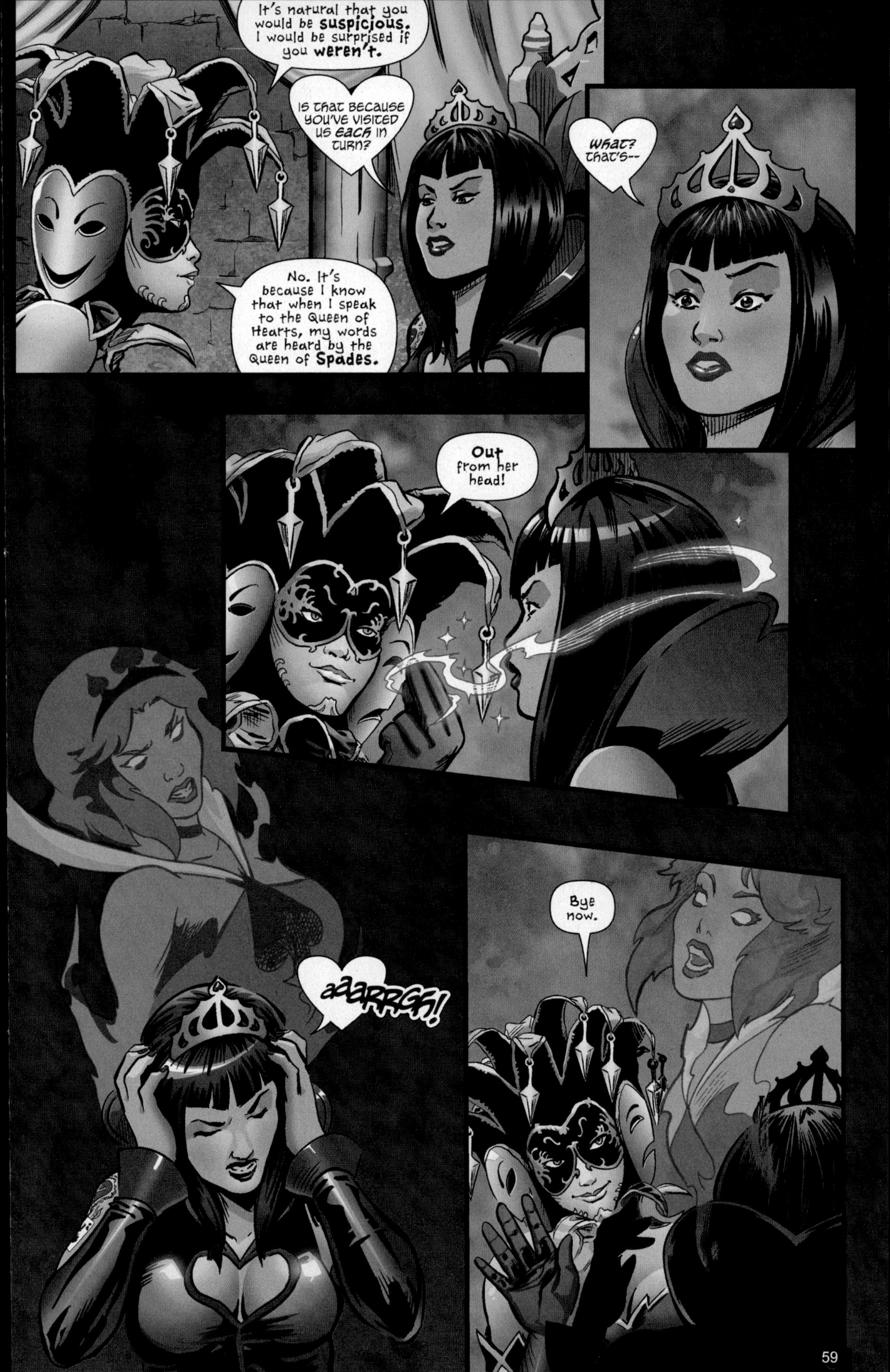
It's natural that you would be suspicious. I would be surprised if you weren't.
Is that because you've visited us each in turn?
No. It's because I know that when I speak to the Queen of Hearts, my words are heard by the Queen of Spades.
What? That's--
Out from her head!
aaarrgh!
Bye now.

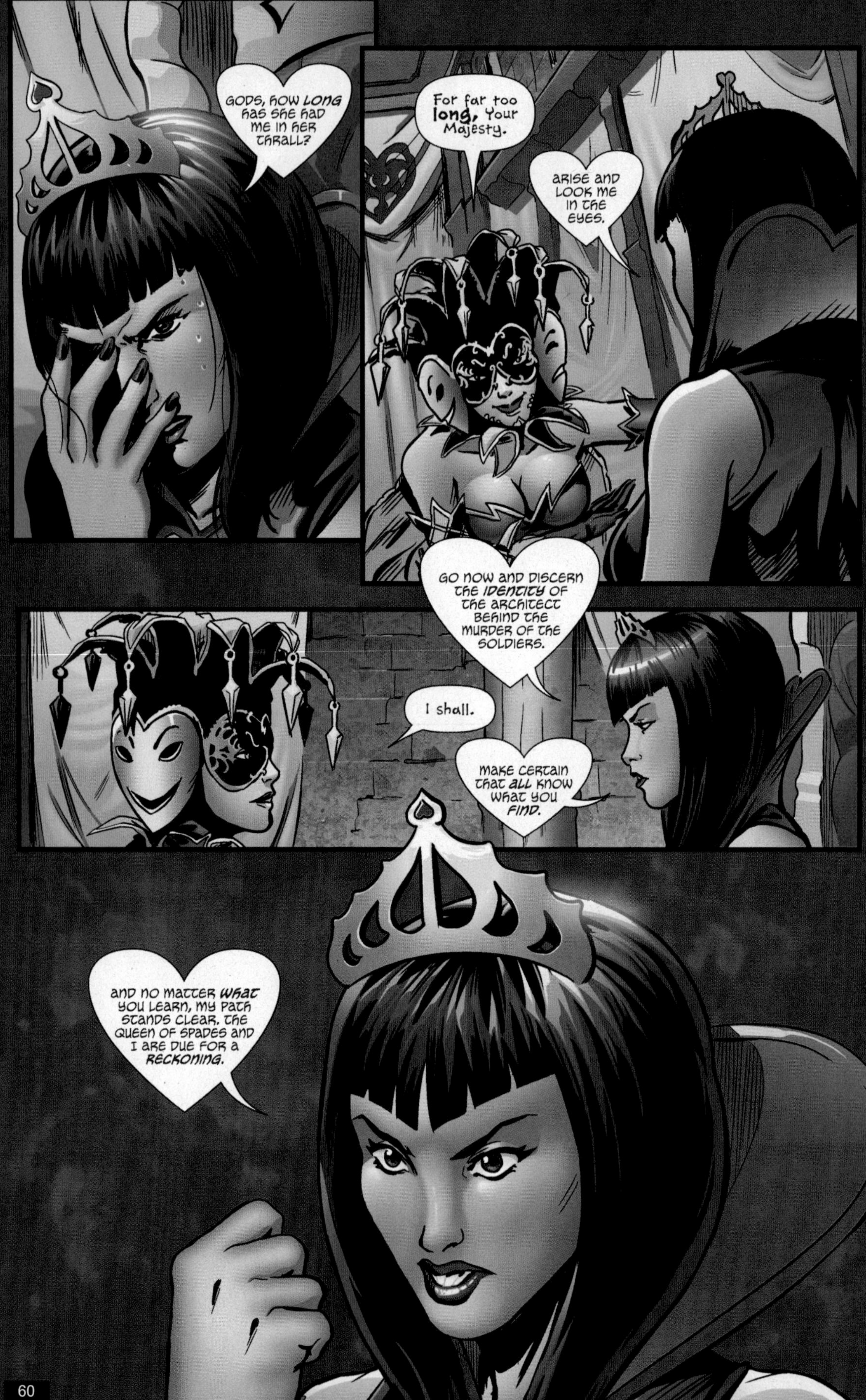
GODS, HOW *LONG* HAS SHE HAD ME IN HER THRALL?
For far too **long,** Your Majesty.
ARISE AND LOOK ME IN THE EYES.
GO NOW AND DISCERN THE *IDENTITY* OF THE ARCHITECT BEHIND THE MURDER OF THE SOLDIERS.
I shall.
MAKE CERTAIN THAT *ALL* KNOW WHAT YOU *FIND.*
AND NO MATTER *WHAT* YOU LEARN, MY PATH STANDS CLEAR. THE QUEEN OF SPADES AND I ARE DUE FOR A *RECKONING.*

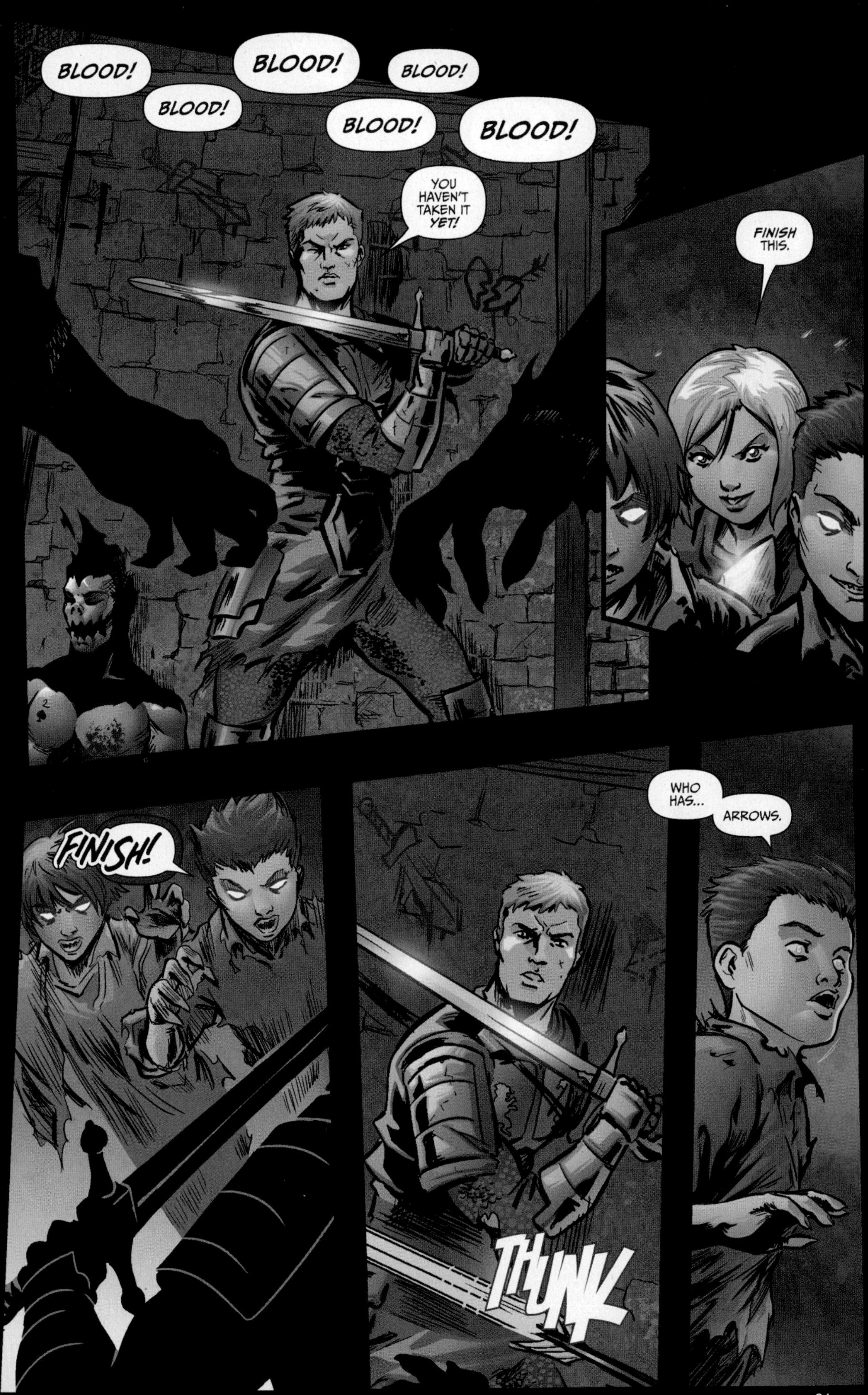
BLOOD!
BLOOD!
BLOOD!
BLOOD!
BLOOD!
BLOOD!
YOU HAVEN'T TAKEN IT YET!
FINISH THIS.
FINISH!
WHO HAS...
ARROWS.
THUNK

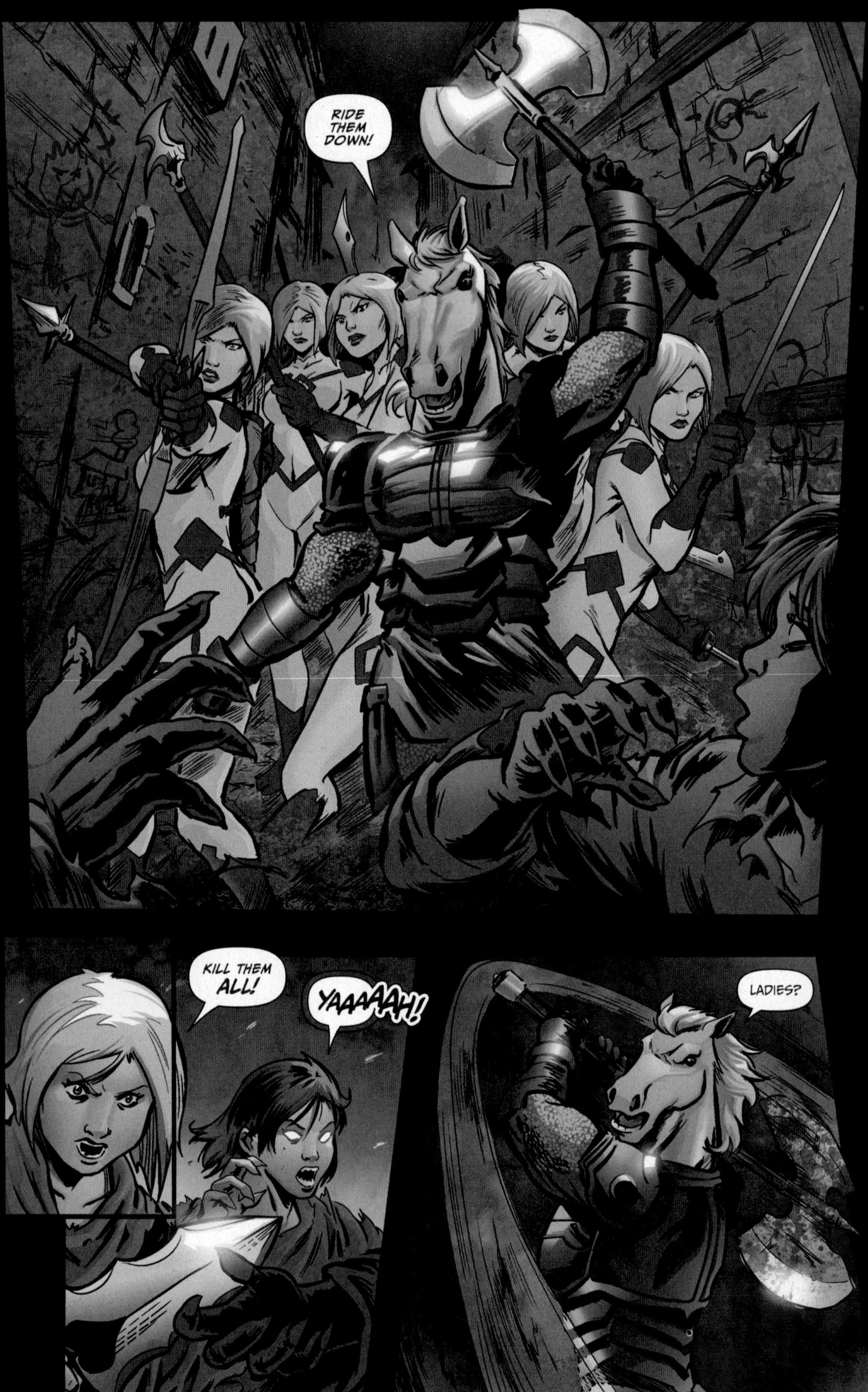
RIDE THEM DOWN!
KILL THEM ALL!
YAAAAAH!
LADIES?

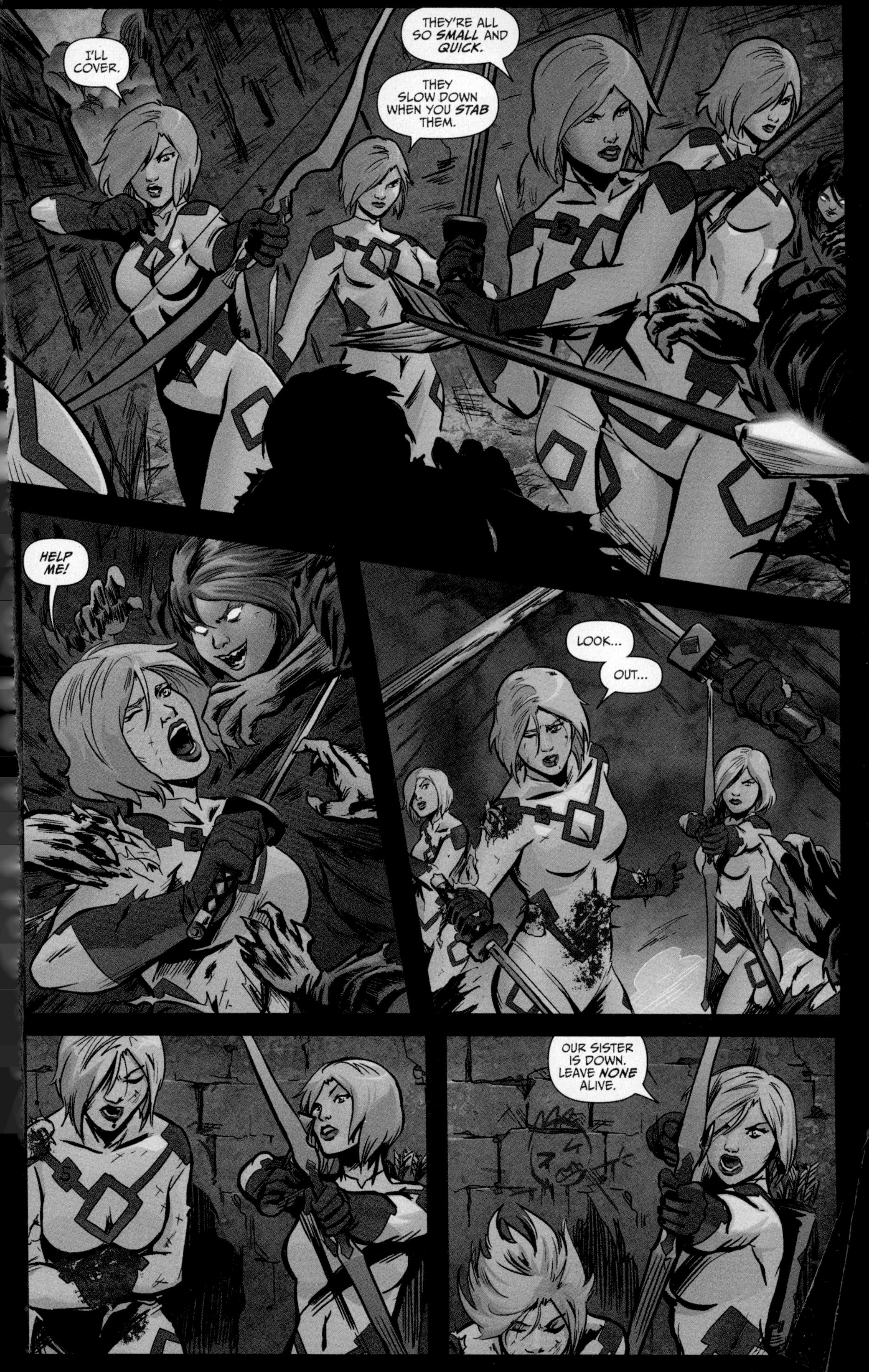
I'LL COVER.
THEY'RE ALL SO SMALL AND QUICK.
THEY SLOW DOWN WHEN YOU STAB THEM.
HELP ME!
LOOK...
OUT...
OUR SISTER IS DOWN. LEAVE NONE ALIVE.

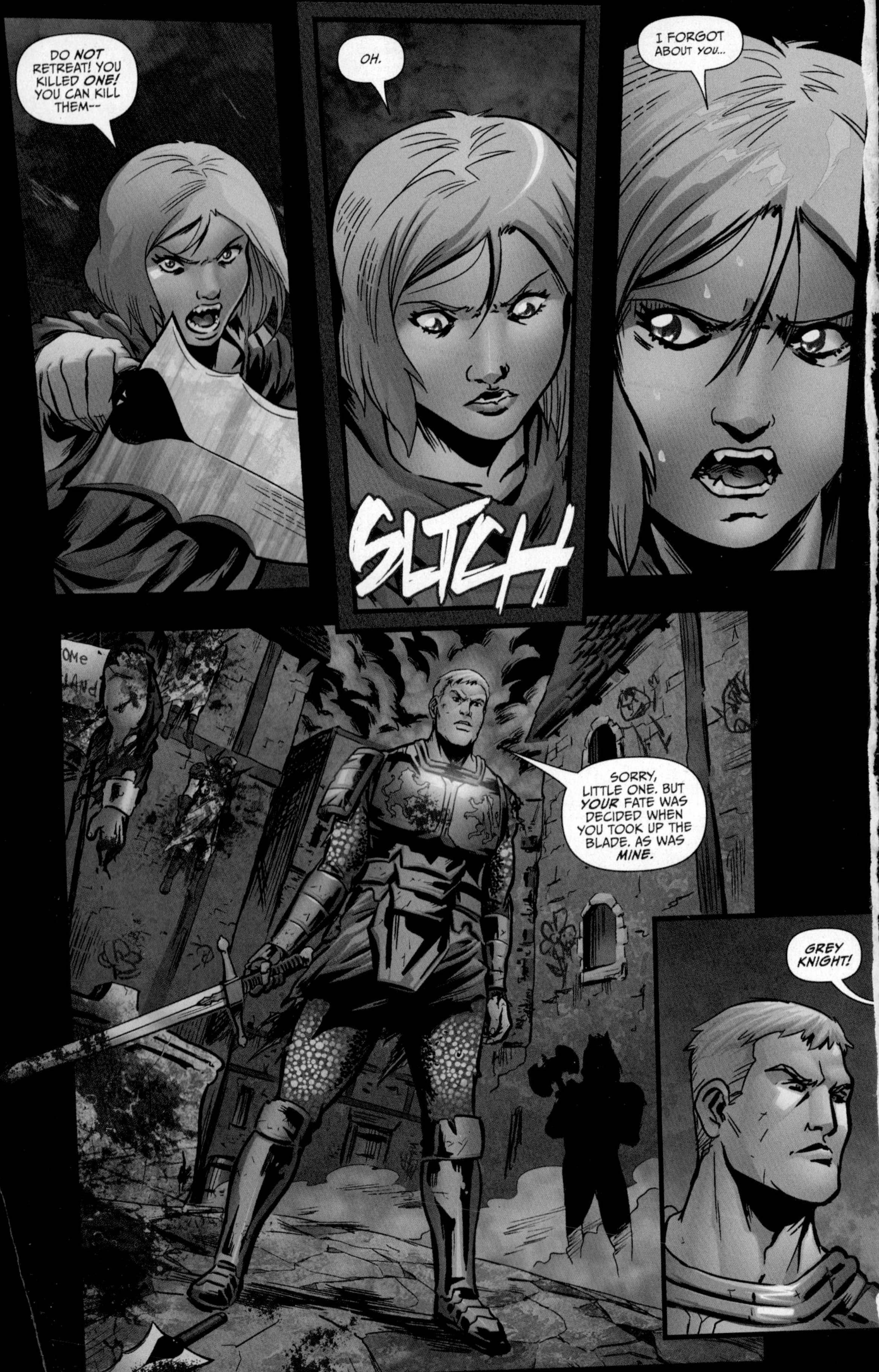
DO NOT RETREAT! YOU KILLED ONE! YOU CAN KILL THEM--
OH.
SLTCH
I FORGOT ABOUT YOU...
SORRY, LITTLE ONE. BUT YOUR FATE WAS DECIDED WHEN YOU TOOK UP THE BLADE. AS WAS MINE.
GREY KNIGHT!

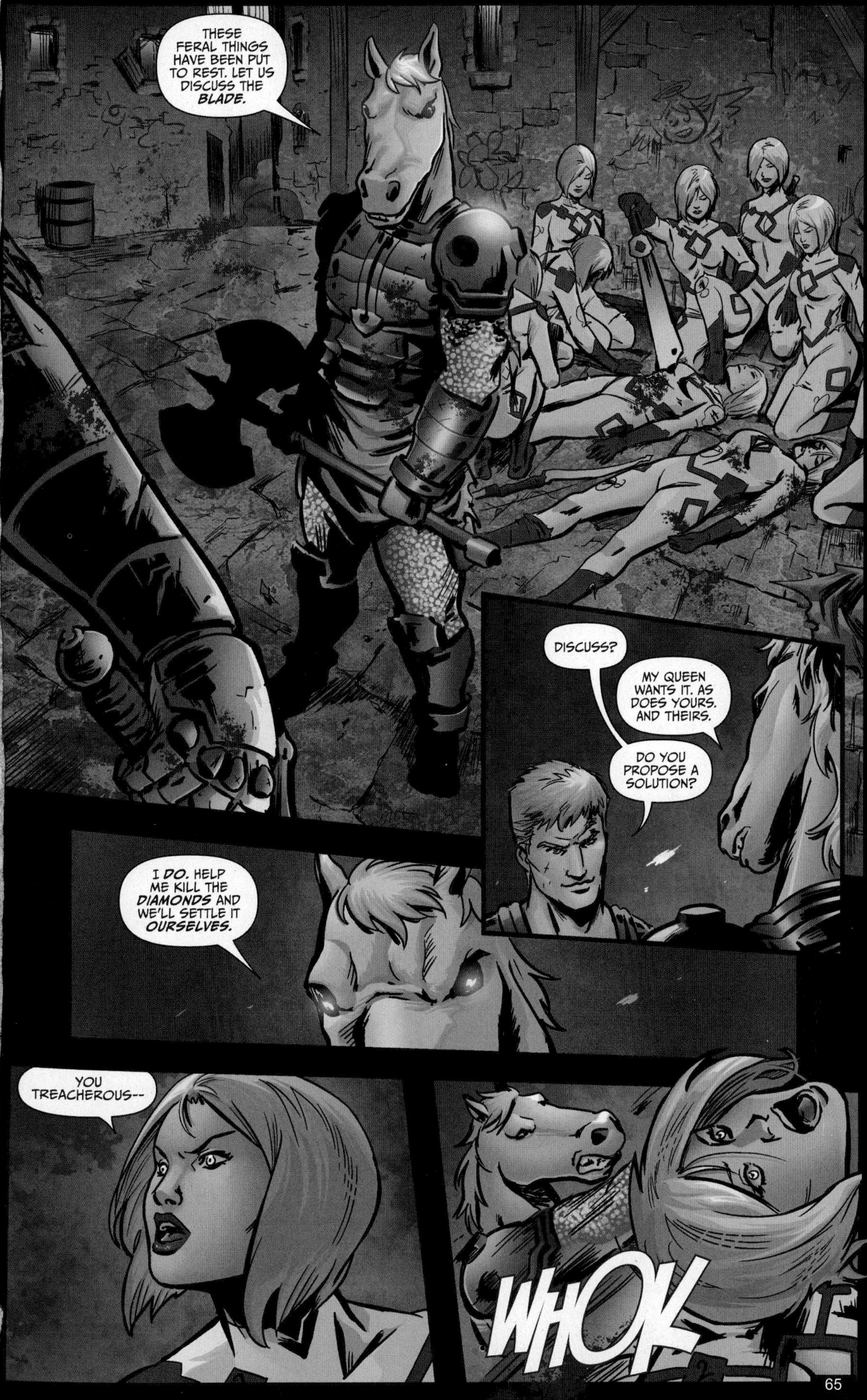
THESE FERAL THINGS HAVE BEEN PUT TO REST. LET US DISCUSS THE *BLADE.*
DISCUSS?
MY QUEEN WANTS IT. AS DOES YOURS. AND THEIRS.
DO YOU PROPOSE A SOLUTION?
I *DO.* HELP ME KILL THE *DIAMONDS* AND WE'LL SETTLE IT *OURSELVES.*
YOU TREACHEROUS--
WHOK

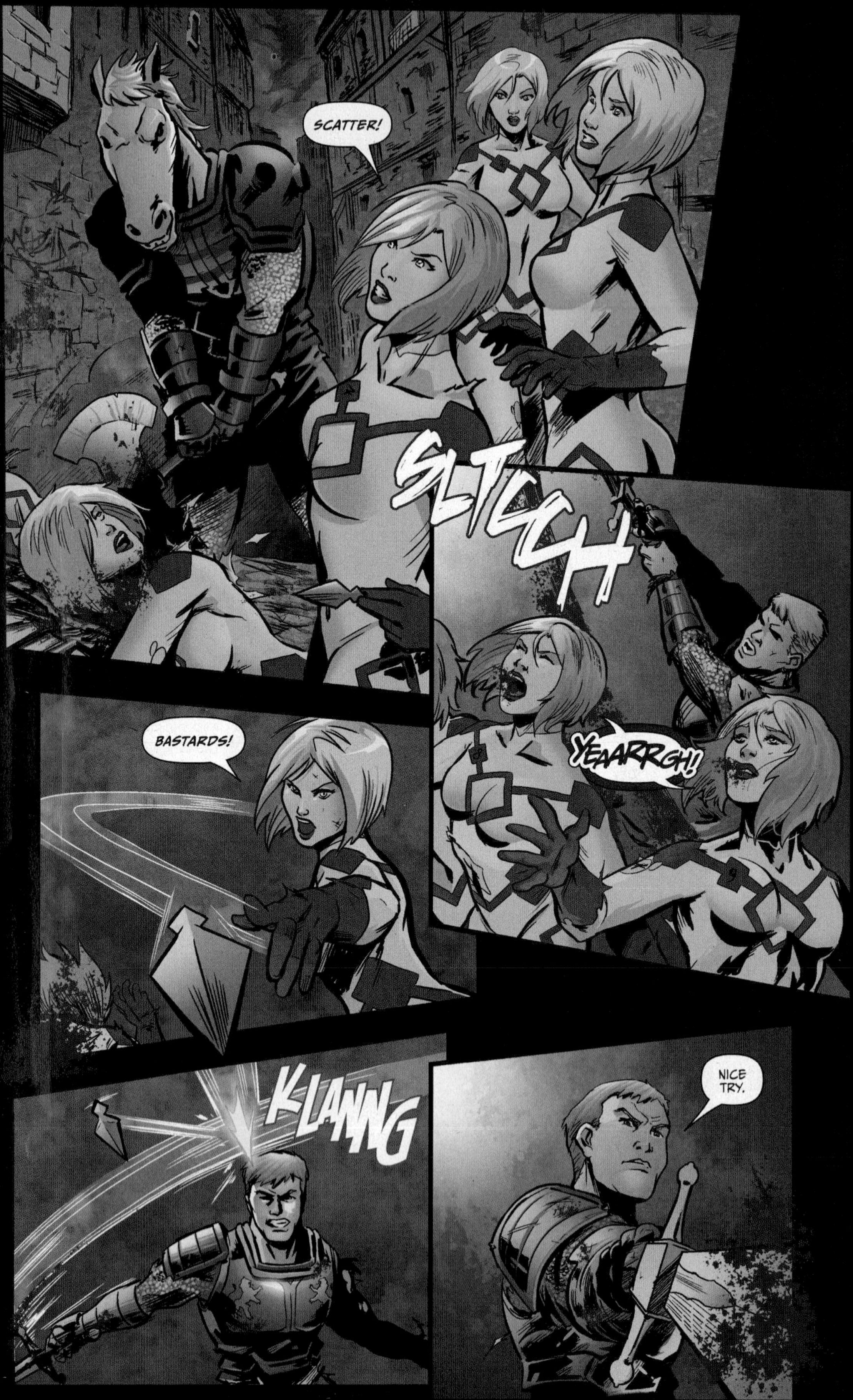
SCATTER!
SLTCCH
YEAARRGH!
BASTARDS!
KLANNG
NICE TRY.

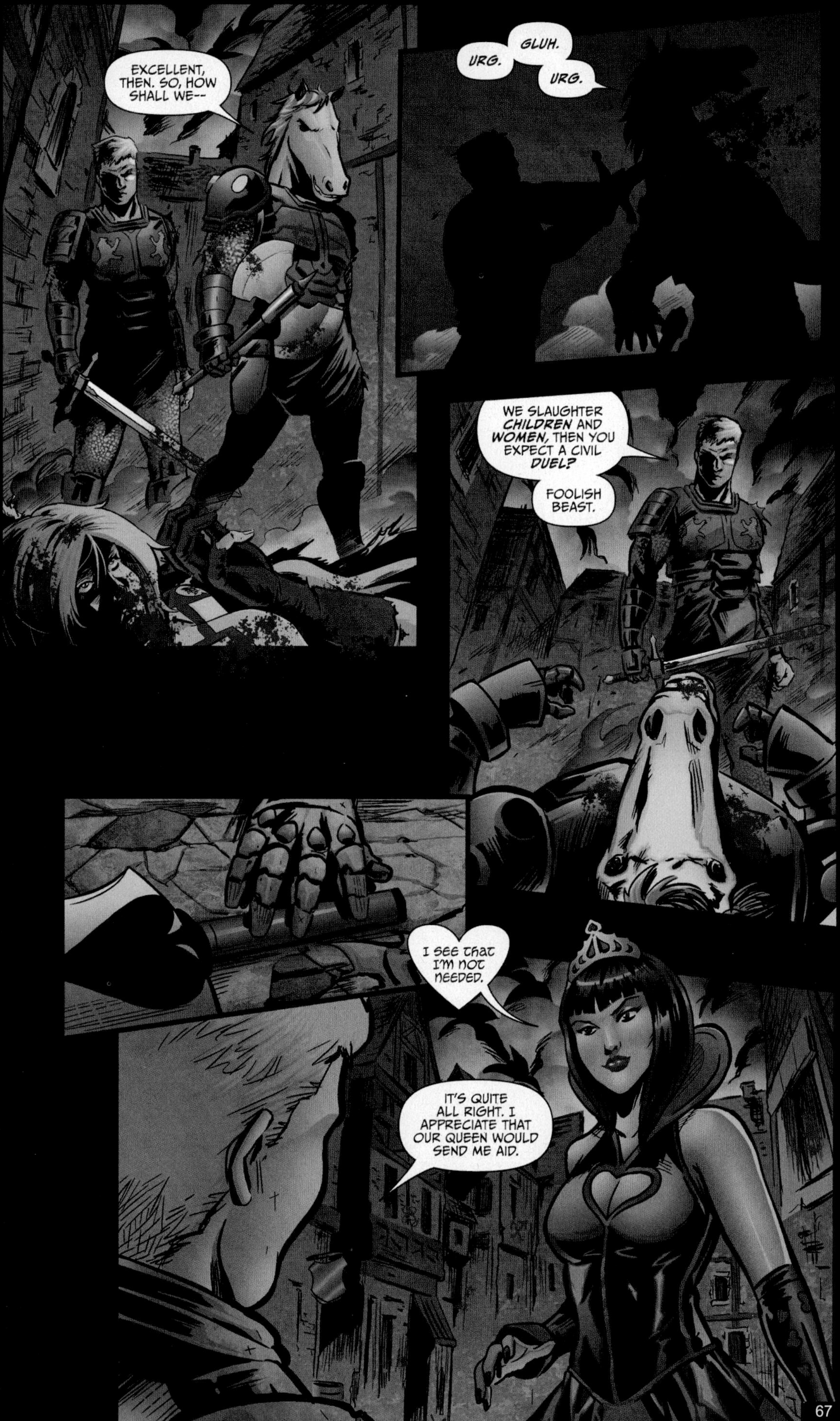
EXCELLENT, THEN. SO, HOW SHALL WE--
URG.
GLUH.
URG.
WE SLAUGHTER CHILDREN AND WOMEN, THEN YOU EXPECT A CIVIL DUEL?
FOOLISH BEAST.
I SEE THAT I'M NOT NEEDED.
IT'S QUITE ALL RIGHT. I APPRECIATE THAT OUR QUEEN WOULD SEND ME AID.

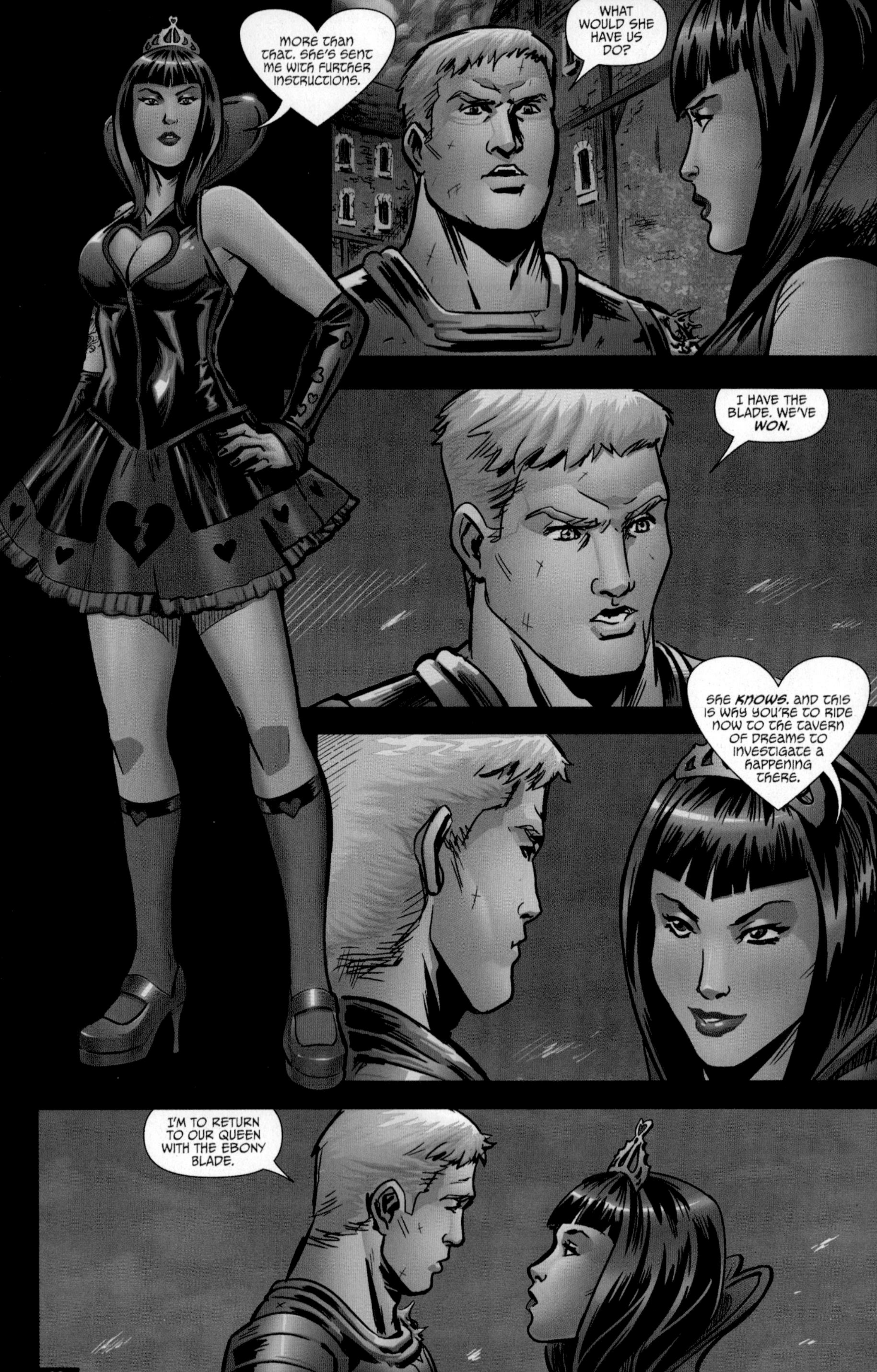
MORE THAN THAT. SHE'S SENT ME WITH FURTHER INSTRUCTIONS.
WHAT WOULD SHE HAVE US DO?
I HAVE THE BLADE. WE'VE WON.
SHE KNOWS. AND THIS IS WHY YOU'RE TO RIDE NOW TO THE TAVERN OF DREAMS TO INVESTIGATE A HAPPENING THERE.
I'M TO RETURN TO OUR QUEEN WITH THE EBONY BLADE.

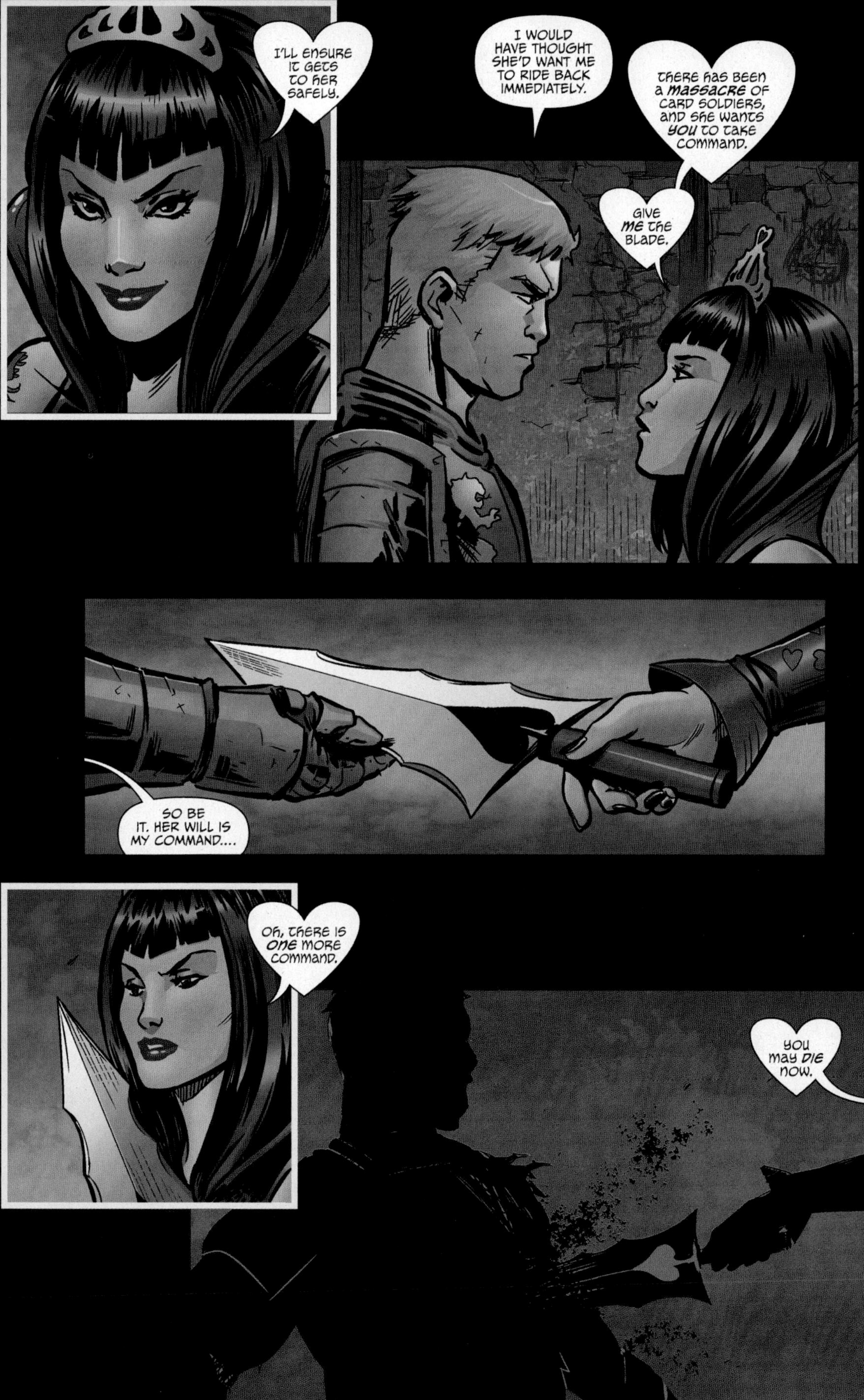
I'LL ENSURE IT GETS TO HER SAFELY.
I WOULD HAVE THOUGHT SHE'D WANT ME TO RIDE BACK IMMEDIATELY.
THERE HAS BEEN A MASSACRE OF CARD SOLDIERS, AND SHE WANTS YOU TO TAKE COMMAND.
GIVE ME THE BLADE.
SO BE IT. HER WILL IS MY COMMAND....
OH, THERE IS ONE MORE COMMAND.
YOU MAY DIE NOW.

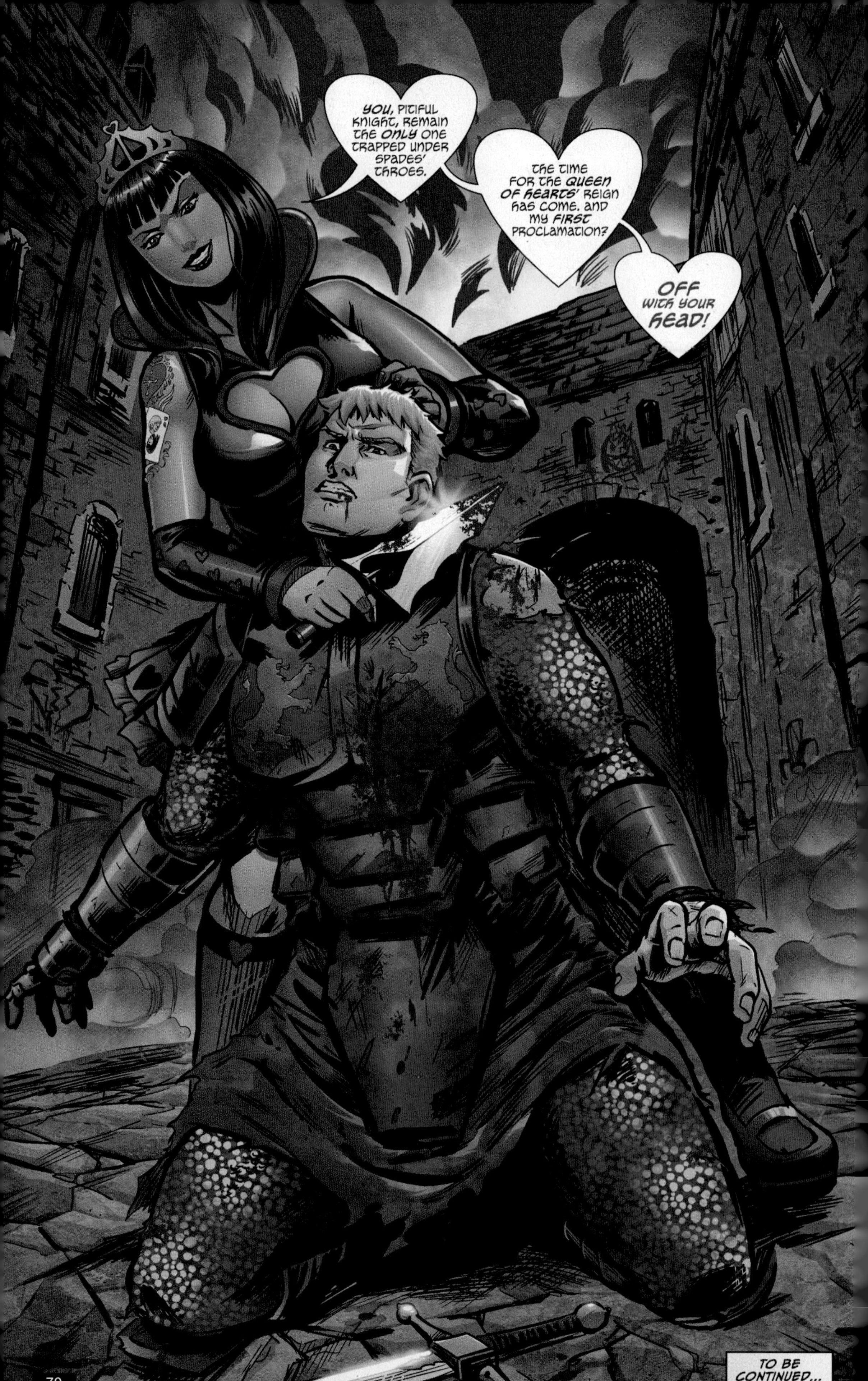
YOU, PITIFUL KNIGHT, REMAIN THE ONLY ONE TRAPPED UNDER SPADES' THROES.
THE TIME FOR THE QUEEN OF HEARTS' REIGN HAS COME. AND MY FIRST PROCLAMATION?
OFF WITH YOUR HEAD!
TO BE CONTINUED...

Grimm Fairy Tales presents

Wonderland

Clash of Queens

Age of Darkness

CHAPTER FOUR

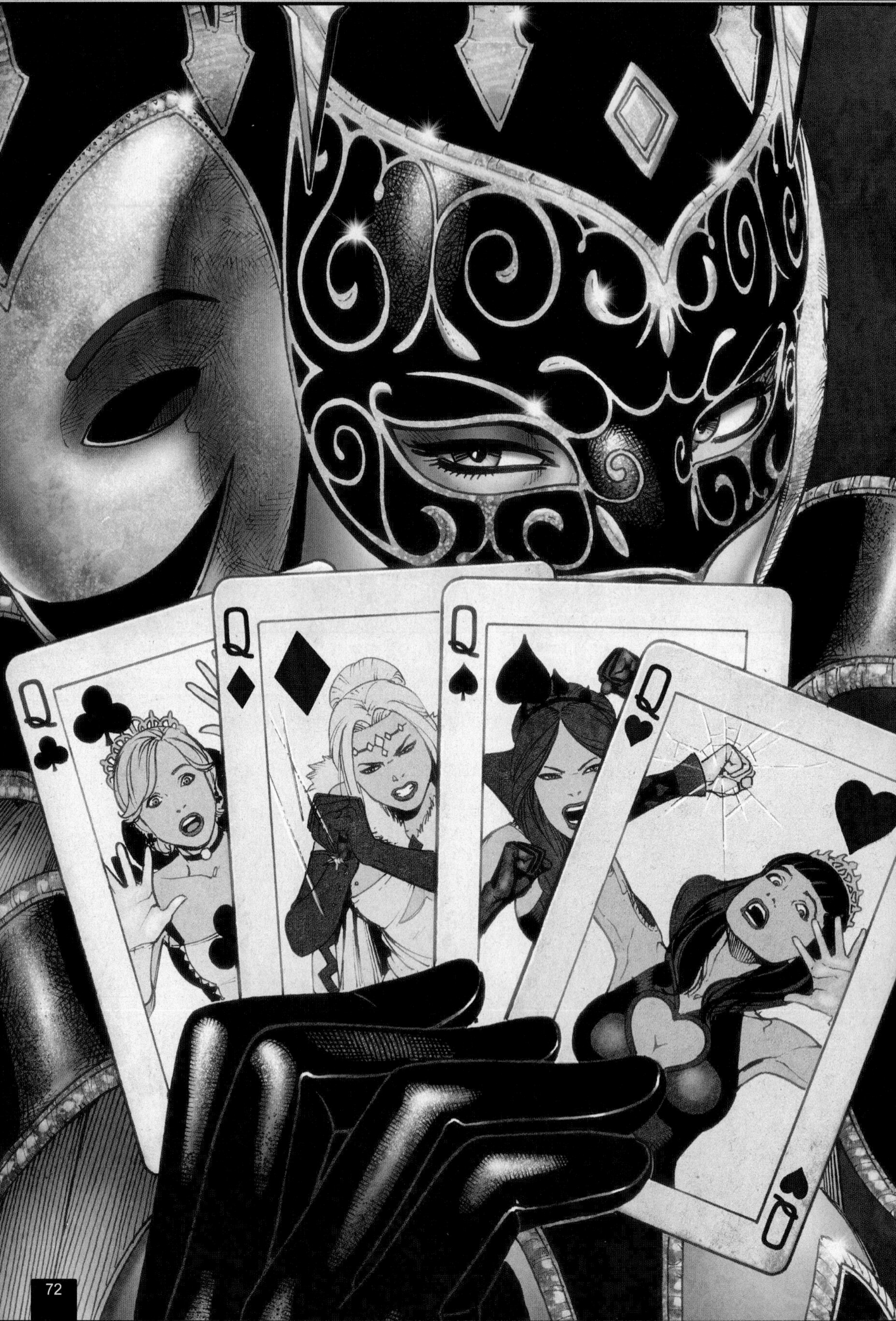

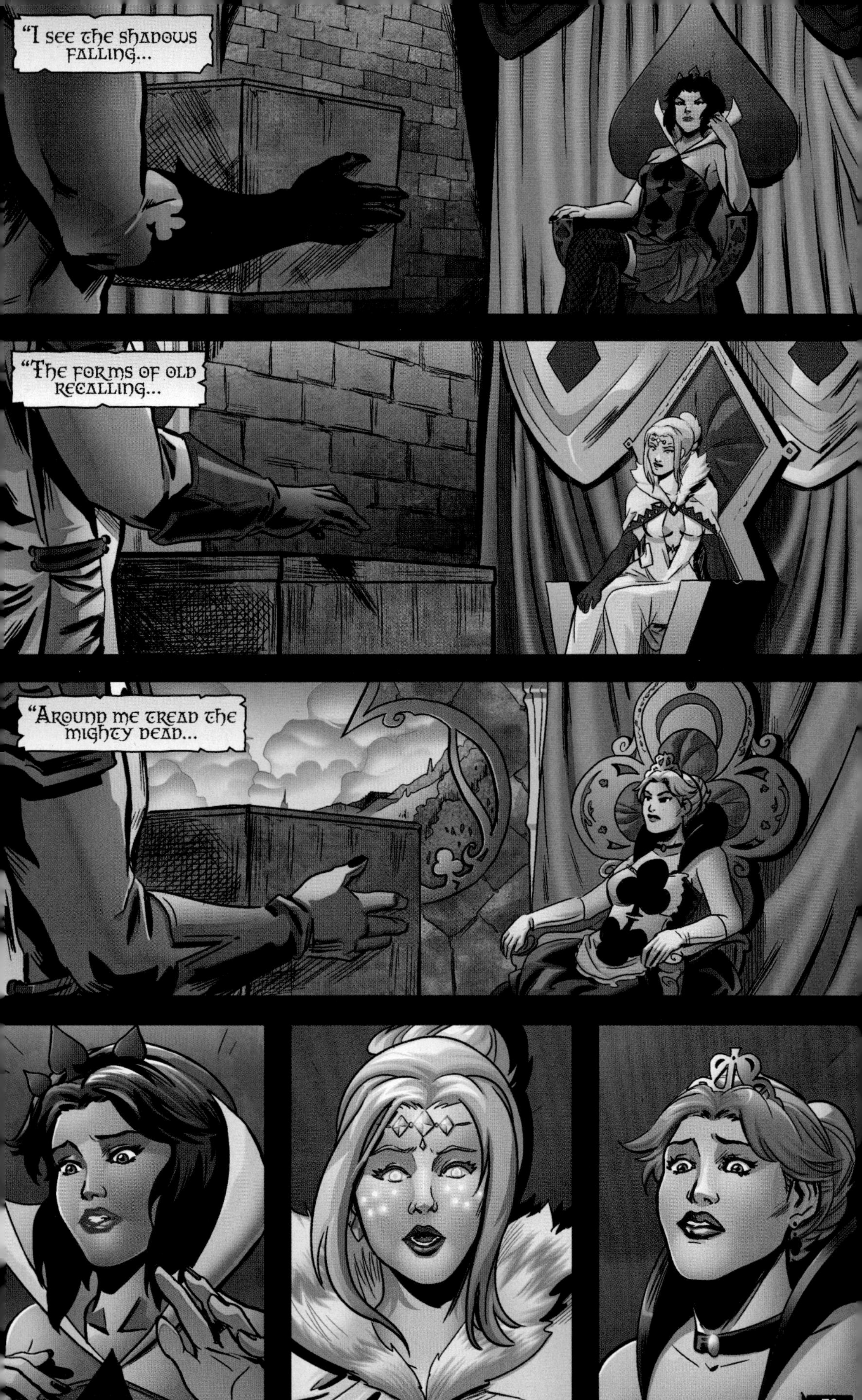

"I see the shadows falling...
"The forms of old recalling...
"Around me tread the mighty dead...

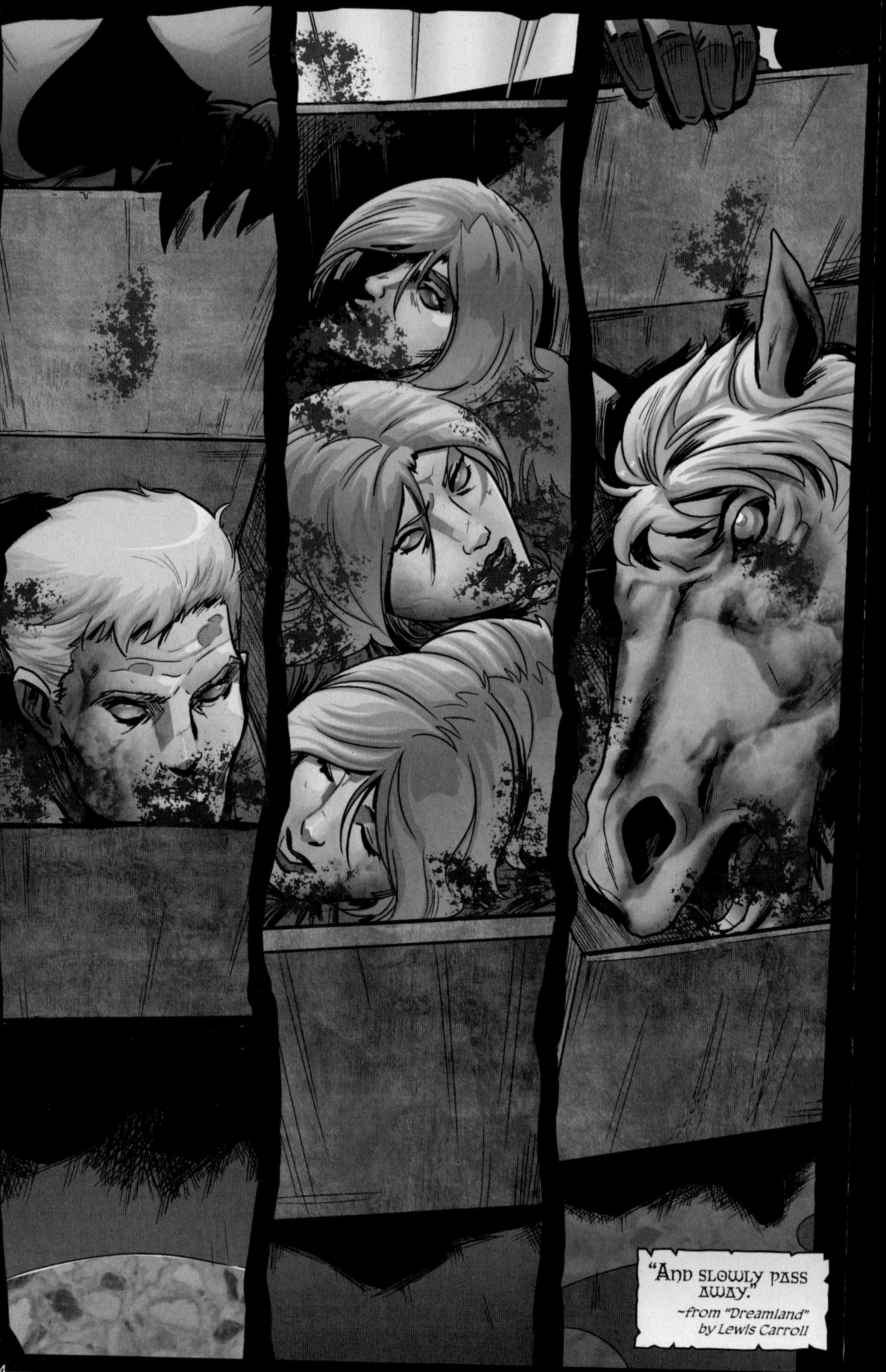
"And slowly pass away."
~from "Dreamland" by Lewis Carroll

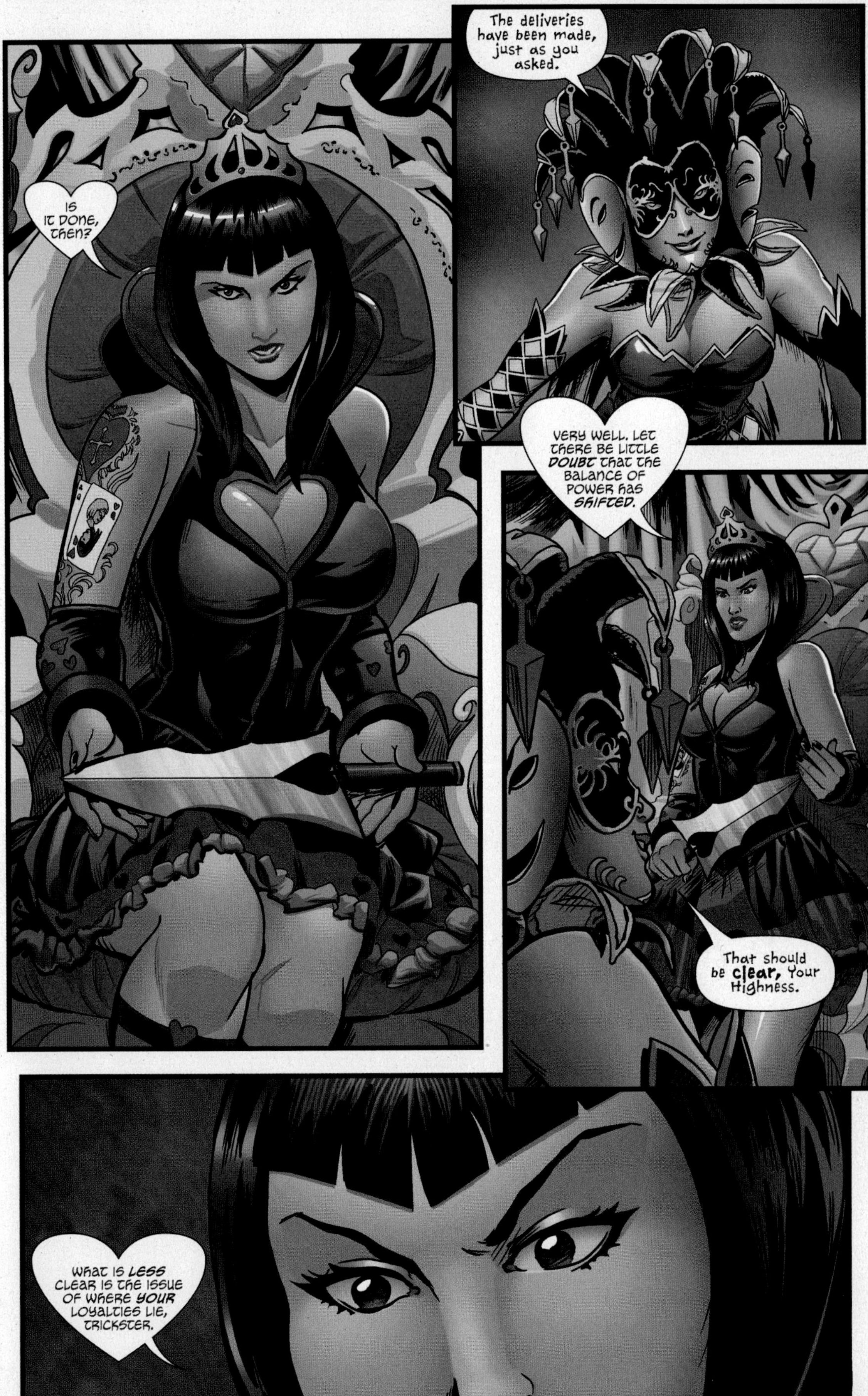
IS IT DONE, THEN?
The deliveries have been made, just as you asked.
VERY WELL. LET THERE BE LITTLE *DOUBT* THAT THE BALANCE OF POWER HAS *SHIFTED*.
That should be **clear,** Your Highness.
WHAT IS *LESS* CLEAR IS THE ISSUE OF WHERE ***YOUR*** LOYALTIES LIE, TRICKSTER.

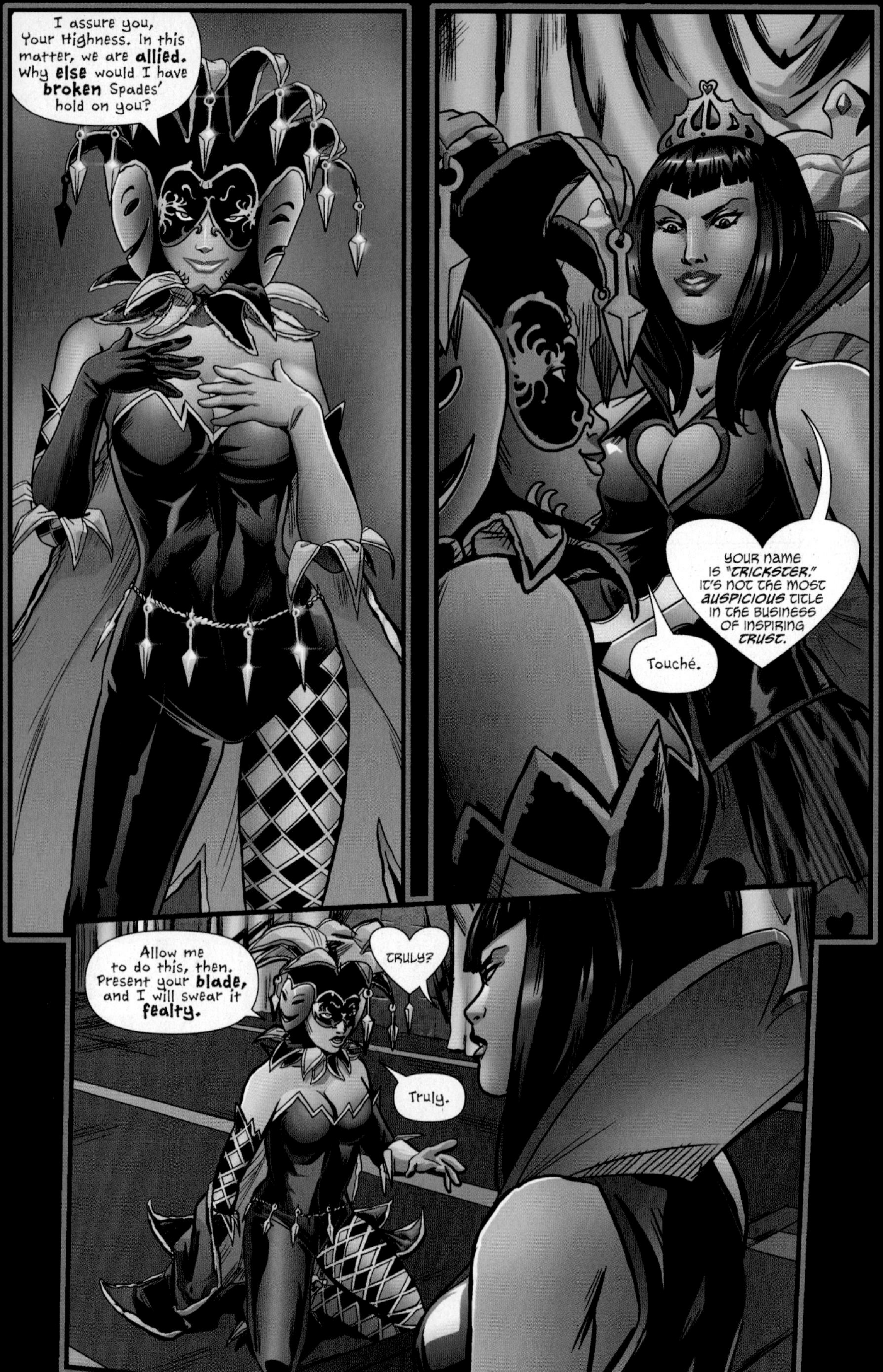
I assure you, Your Highness. In this matter, we are allied. Why else would I have broken Spades' hold on you?
YOUR NAME IS "TRICKSTER." IT'S NOT THE MOST AUSPICIOUS TITLE IN THE BUSINESS OF INSPIRING TRUST.
Touché.
Allow me to do this, then. Present your blade, and I will swear it fealty.
TRULY?
Truly.

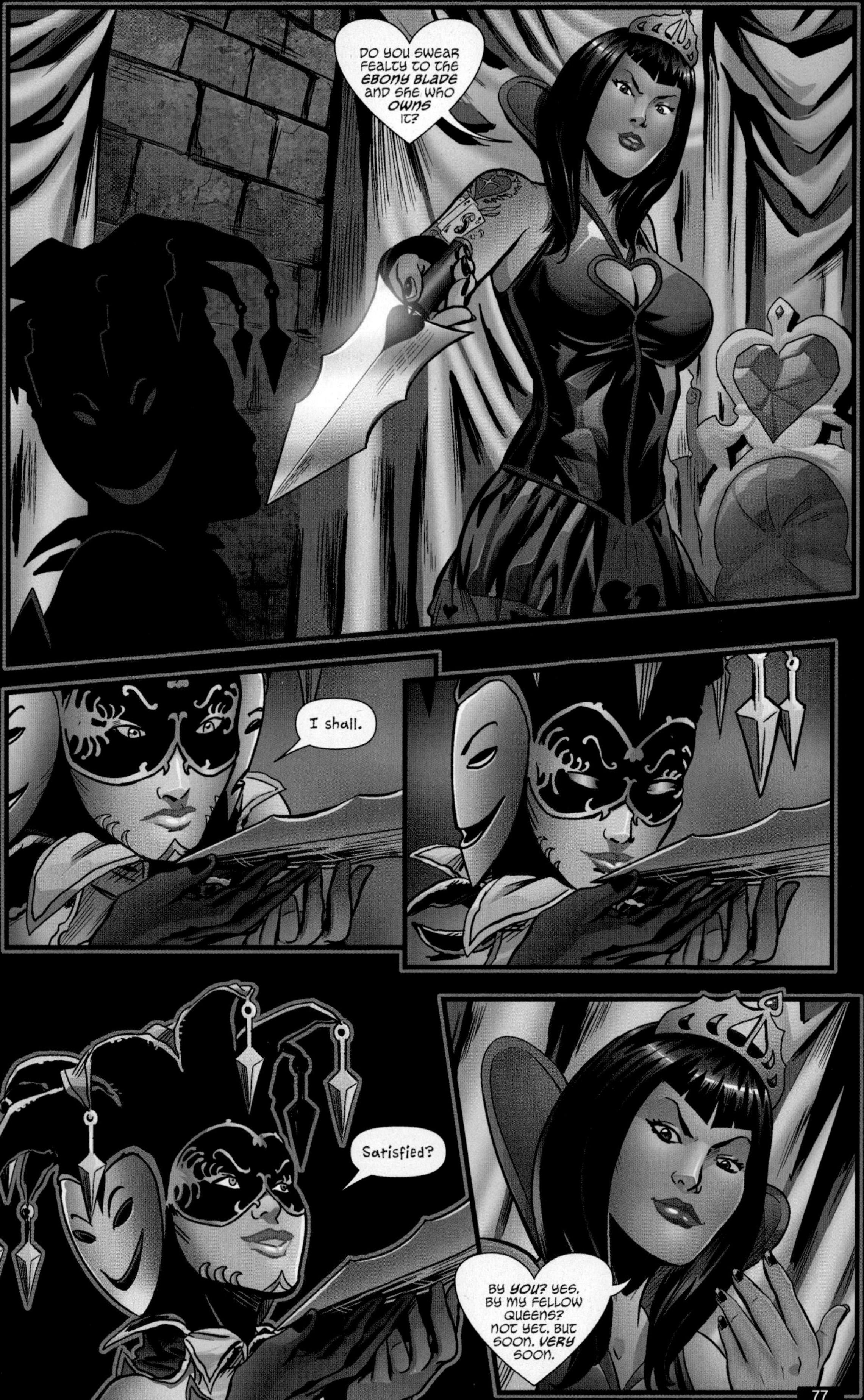
DO YOU SWEAR FEALTY TO THE EBONY BLADE AND SHE WHO OWNS IT?
I shall.
Satisfied?
BY YOU? YES. BY MY FELLOW QUEENS? NOT YET. BUT SOON. VERY SOON.

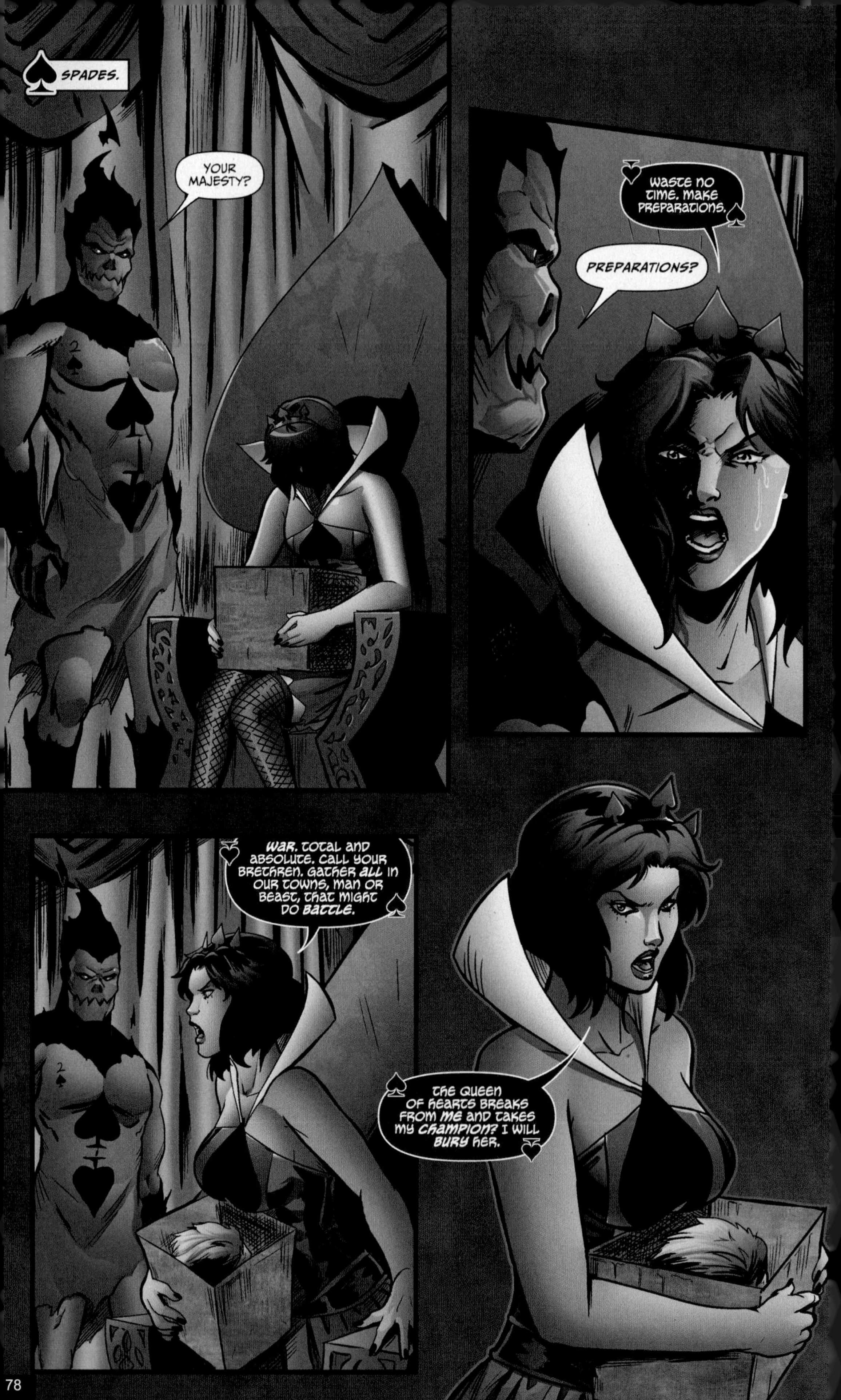
SPADES.
YOUR MAJESTY?
WASTE NO TIME. MAKE PREPARATIONS.
PREPARATIONS?
WAR. TOTAL AND ABSOLUTE. CALL YOUR BRETHREN. GATHER ALL IN OUR TOWNS, MAN OR BEAST, THAT MIGHT DO BATTLE.
THE QUEEN OF HEARTS BREAKS FROM ME AND TAKES MY CHAMPION? I WILL BURY HER.

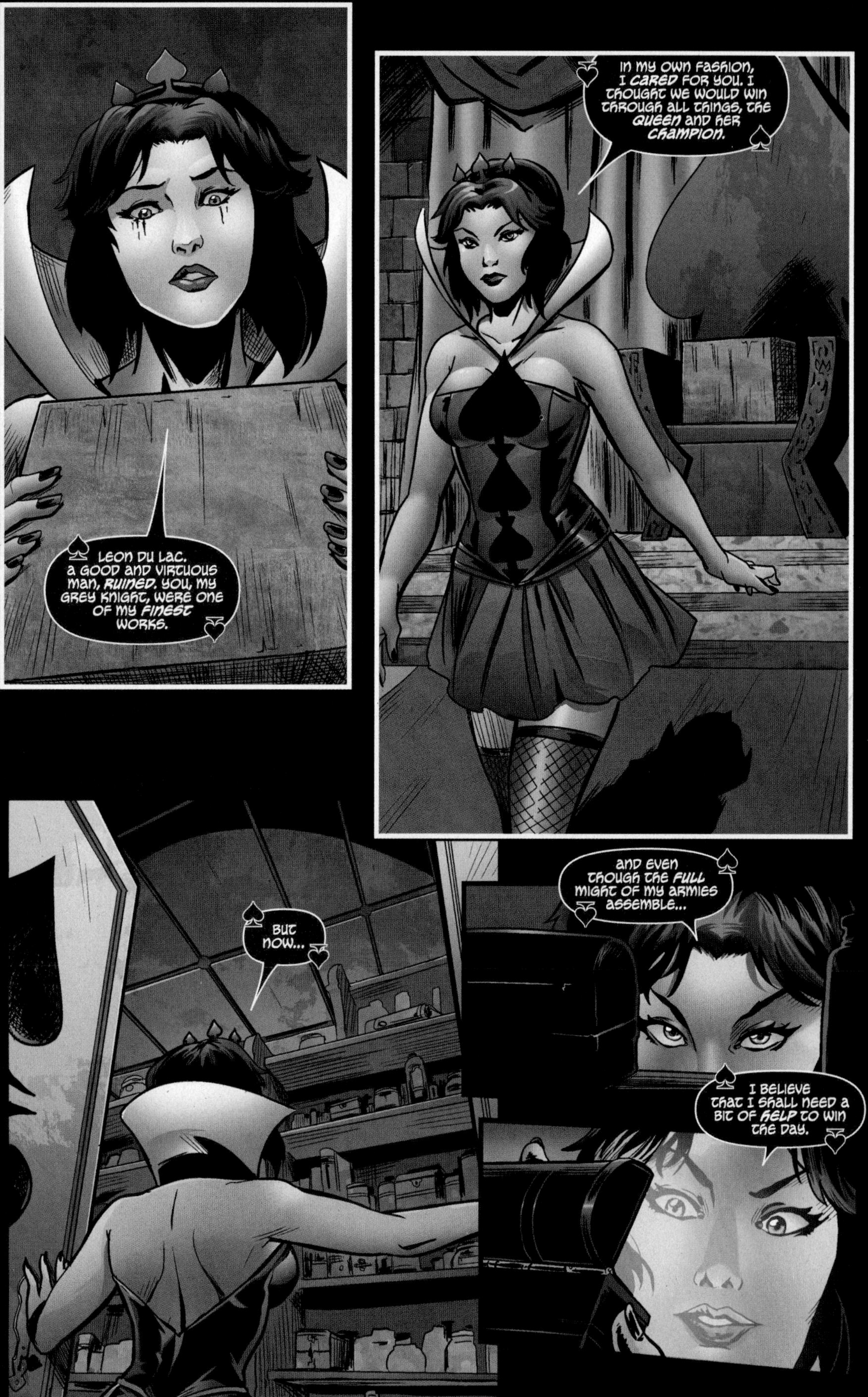
In my own fashion, I CARED for you. I thought we would win through all things, the QUEEN and her CHAMPION.
Leon du Lac. a good and virtuous man, RUINED. You, my grey knight, were one of my FINEST works.
But now...
and even though the FULL might of my armies assemble...
I believe that I shall need a bit of HELP to win the day.

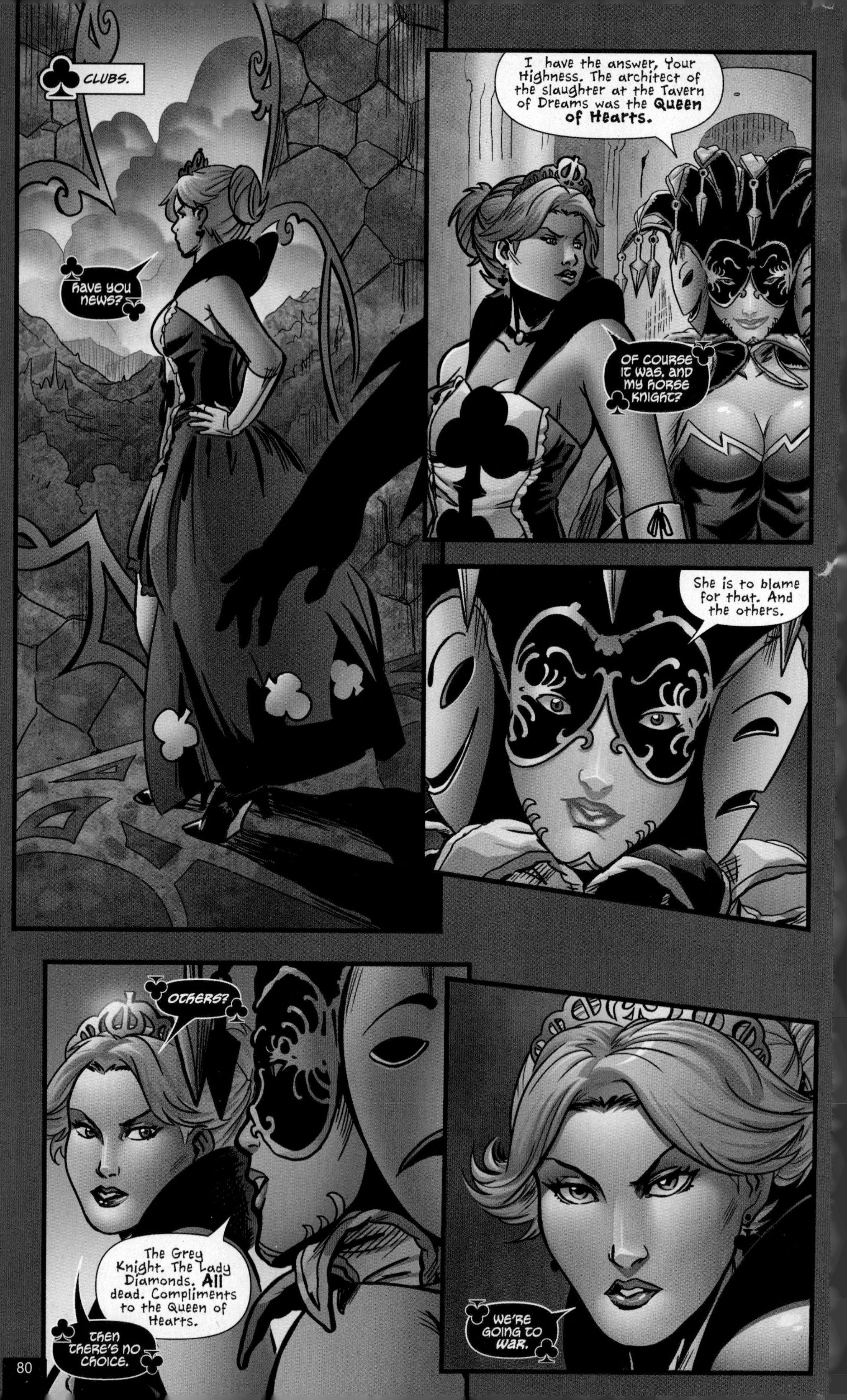
CLUBS.
HAVE YOU NEWS?
I have the answer, Your Highness. The architect of the slaughter at the Tavern of Dreams was the **Queen of Hearts.**
OF COURSE IT WAS. AND MY HORSE KNIGHT?
She is to blame for that. And the others.
OTHERS?
The Grey Knight. The Lady Diamonds. **All** dead. Compliments to the Queen of Hearts.
THEN THERE'S NO CHOICE.
WE'RE GOING TO *WAR.*

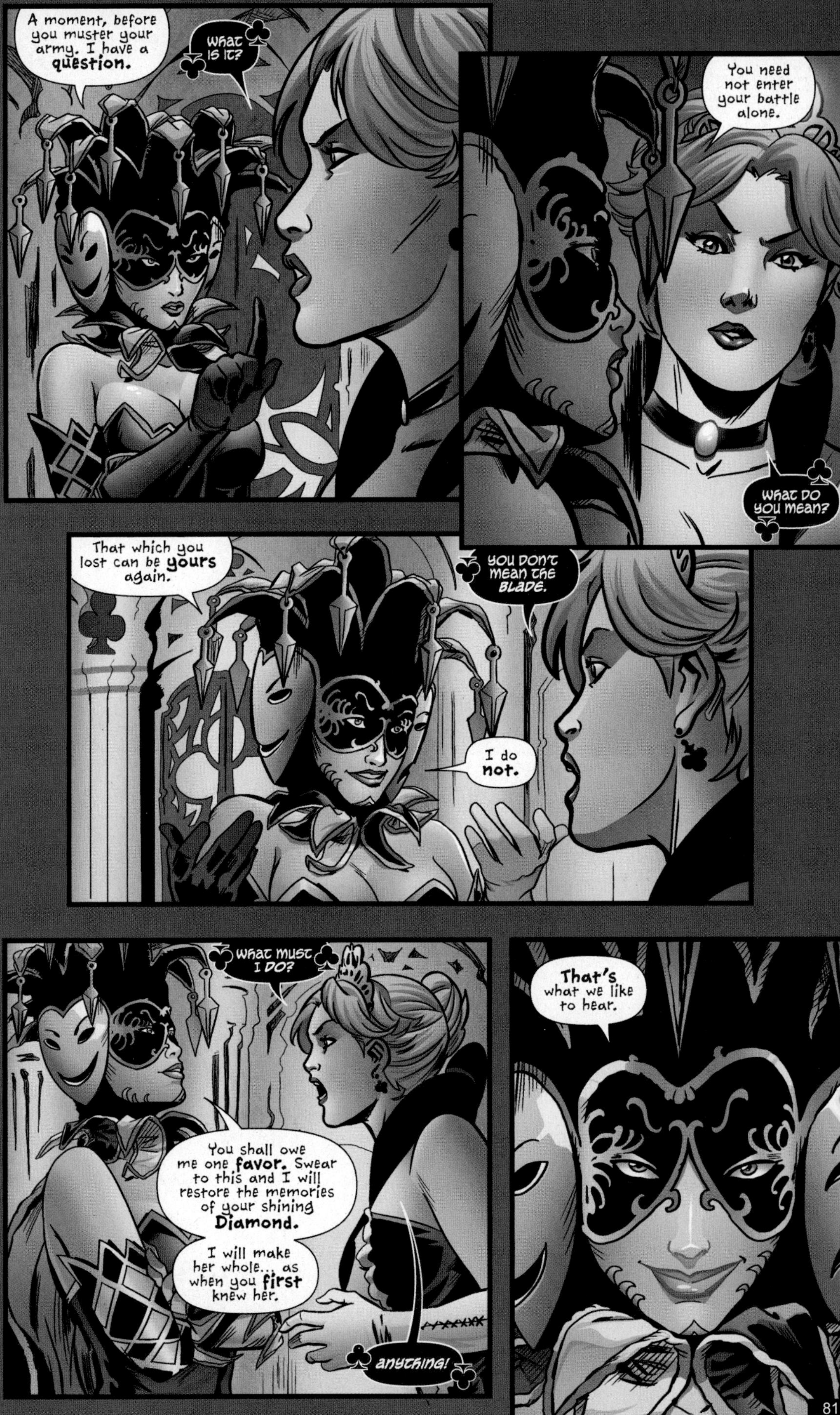
A moment, before you muster your army. I have a **question.**
WHAT IS IT?
You need not enter your battle alone.
WHAT DO YOU MEAN?
That which you lost can be **yours** again.
YOU DON'T MEAN THE *BLADE.*
I do **not.**
WHAT MUST I *DO?*
You shall owe me one **favor.** Swear to this and I will restore the memories of your shining **Diamond.**
I will make her whole... as when you **first** knew her.
ANYTHING!
That's what we like to hear.

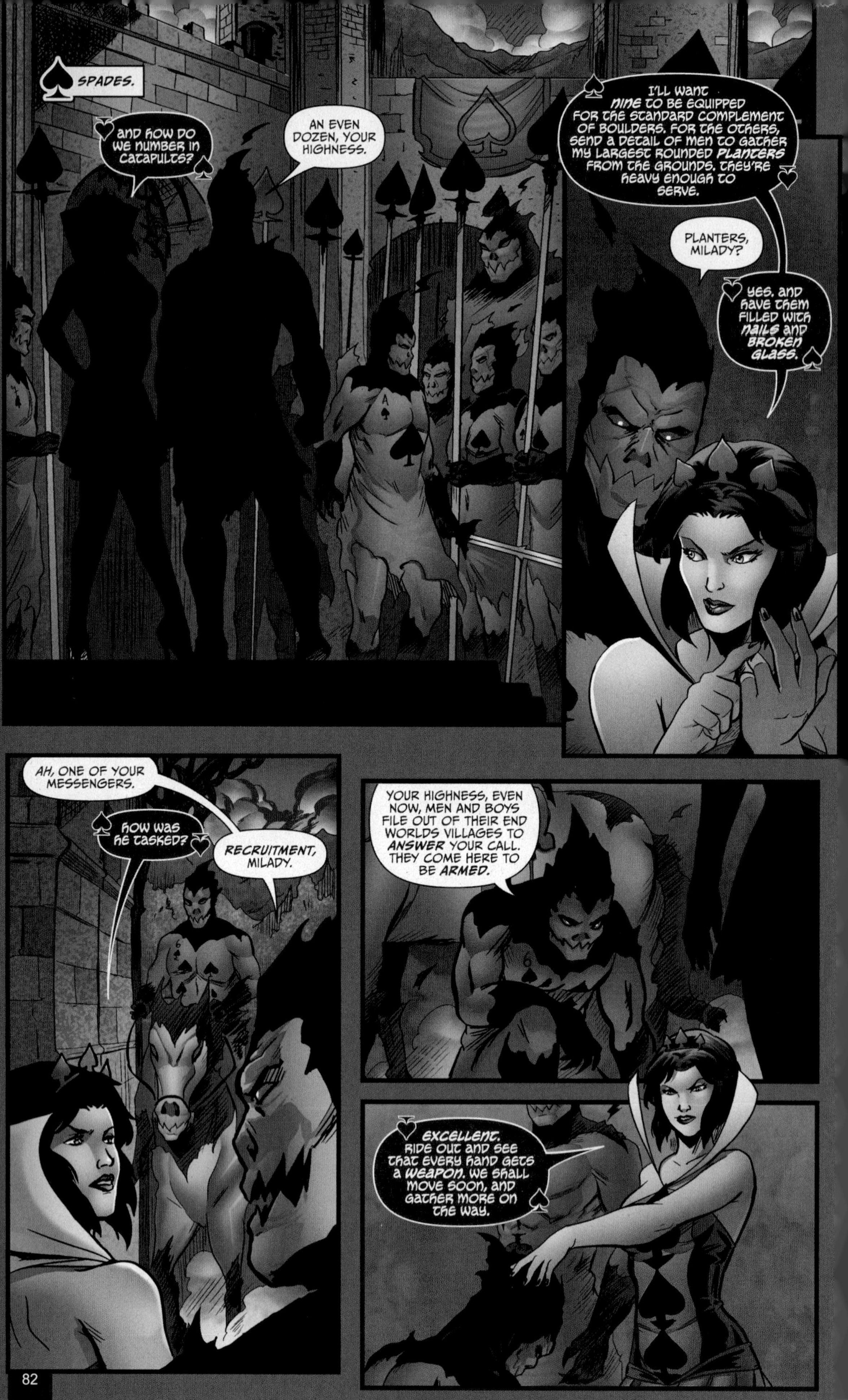
SPADES.
AND HOW DO WE NUMBER IN CATAPULTS?
AN EVEN DOZEN, YOUR HIGHNESS.
I'LL WANT NINE TO BE EQUIPPED FOR THE STANDARD COMPLEMENT OF BOULDERS. FOR THE OTHERS, SEND A DETAIL OF MEN TO GATHER MY LARGEST ROUNDED PLANTERS FROM THE GROUNDS. THEY'RE HEAVY ENOUGH TO SERVE.
PLANTERS, MILADY?
YES. AND HAVE THEM FILLED WITH NAILS AND BROKEN GLASS.
AH, ONE OF YOUR MESSENGERS.
HOW WAS HE TASKED?
RECRUITMENT, MILADY.
YOUR HIGHNESS, EVEN NOW, MEN AND BOYS FILE OUT OF THEIR END WORLDS VILLAGES TO ANSWER YOUR CALL. THEY COME HERE TO BE ARMED.
EXCELLENT. RIDE OUT AND SEE THAT EVERY HAND GETS A WEAPON. WE SHALL MOVE SOON, AND GATHER MORE ON THE WAY.

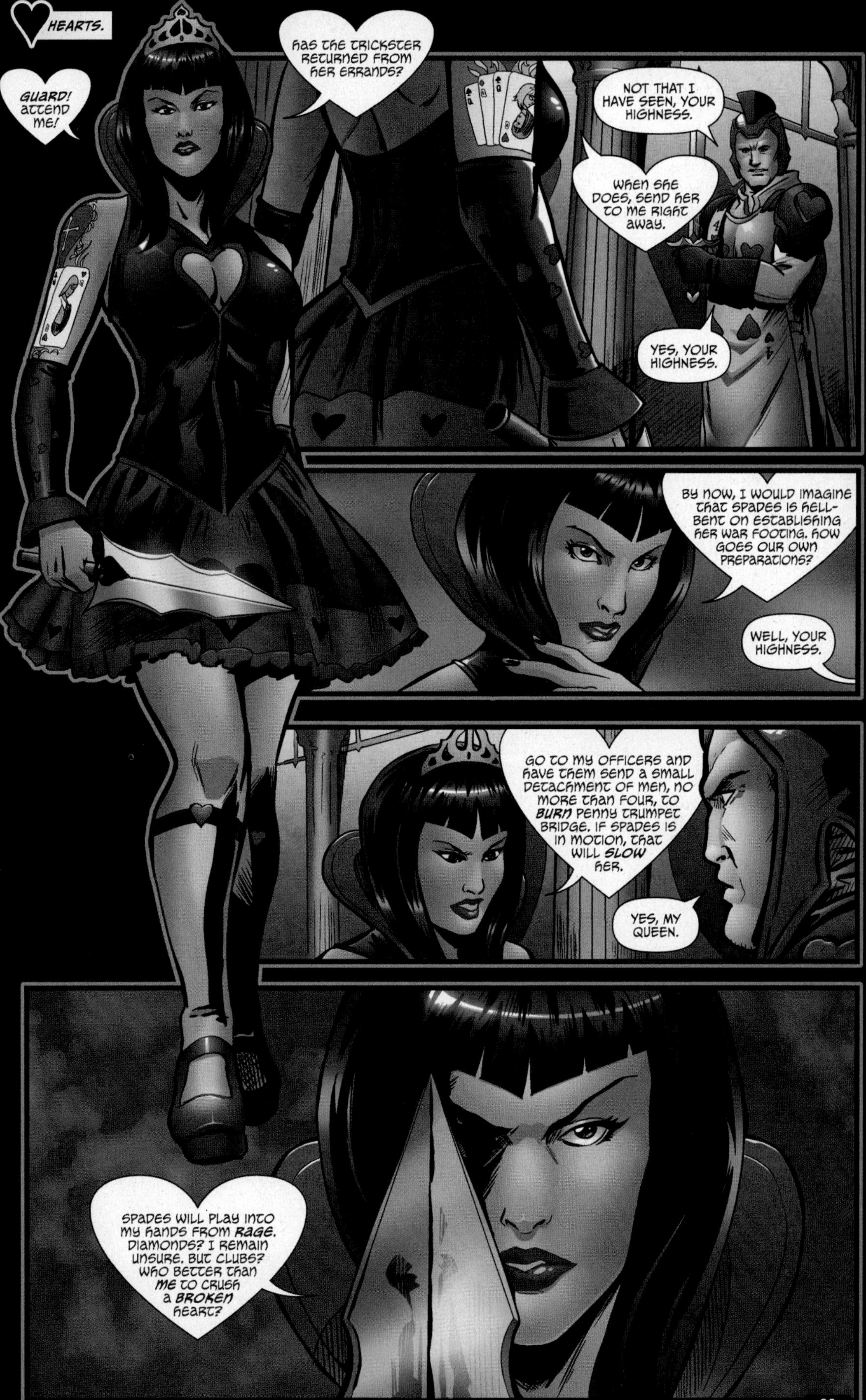
HEARTS.
GUARD! attend me!
has the trickster returned from her errands?
NOT THAT I HAVE SEEN, YOUR HIGHNESS.
when she does, send her to me right away.
YES, YOUR HIGHNESS.
By now, I would imagine that spades is hell-bent on establishing her war footing. how goes our own preparations?
WELL, YOUR HIGHNESS.
go to my officers and have them send a small detachment of men, no more than four, to BURN penny trumpet bridge. if spades is in motion, that will SLOW her.
YES, MY QUEEN.
spades will play into my hands from RAGE. diamonds? I remain unsure. but clubs? who better than ME to crush a BROKEN heart?

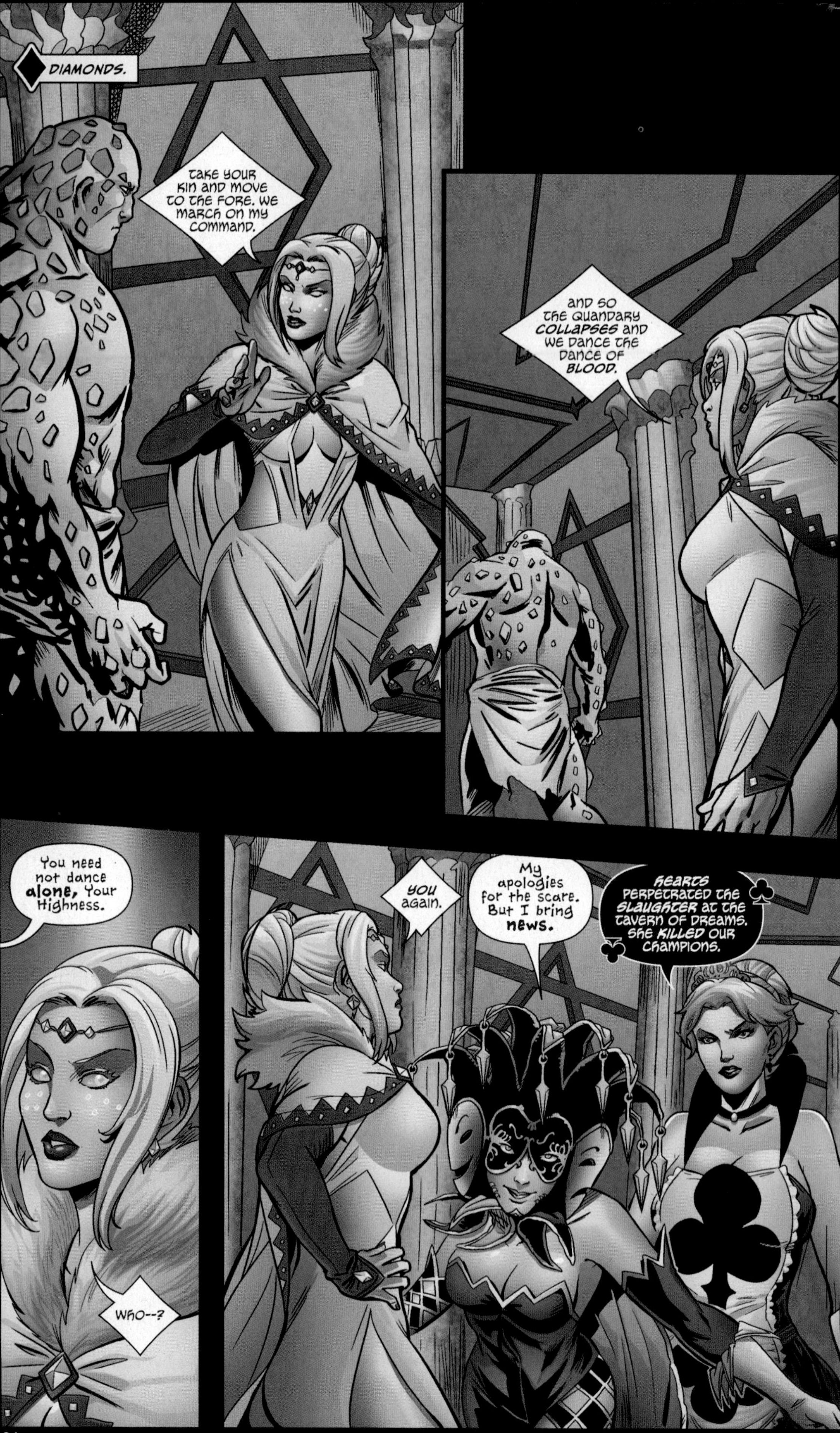
DIAMONDS.
TAKE YOUR KIN AND MOVE TO THE FORE. WE MARCH ON MY COMMAND.
AND SO THE QUANDARY COLLAPSES AND WE DANCE THE DANCE OF BLOOD.
You need not dance alone, Your Highness.
WHO--?
YOU again.
My apologies for the scare. But I bring news.
HEARTS PERPETRATED THE SLAUGHTER AT THE TAVERN OF DREAMS. SHE KILLED OUR CHAMPIONS.

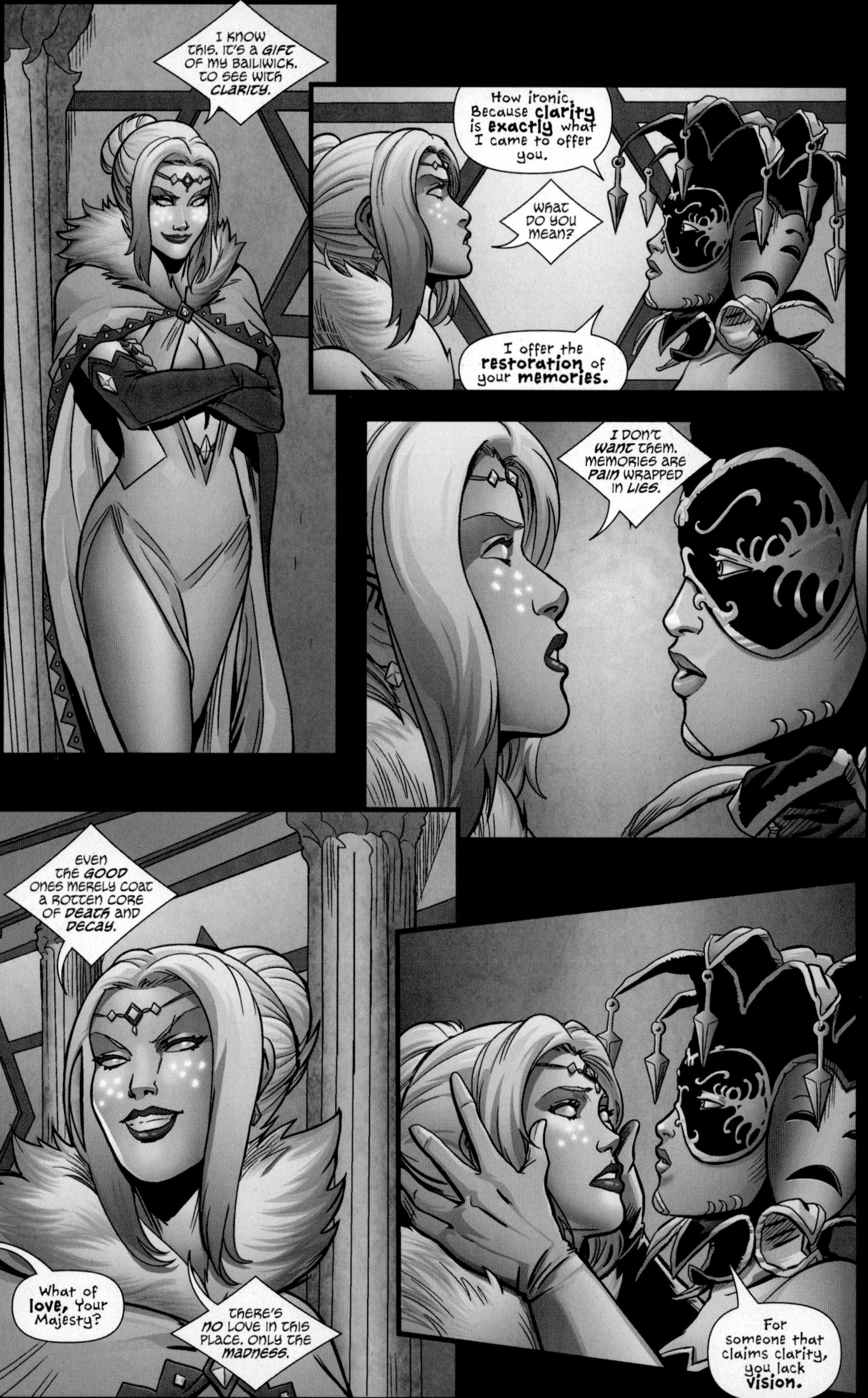

I KNOW THIS. IT'S A GIFT OF MY BAILIWICK. TO SEE WITH CLARITY.
How ironic. Because clarity is exactly what I came to offer you.
WHAT DO YOU MEAN?
I offer the restoration of your memories.
I DON'T WANT THEM. MEMORIES ARE PAIN WRAPPED IN LIES.
EVEN THE GOOD ONES MERELY COAT A ROTTEN CORE OF DEATH AND DECAY.
What of love, Your Majesty?
THERE'S NO LOVE IN THIS PLACE. ONLY THE MADNESS.
For someone that claims clarity, you lack vision.

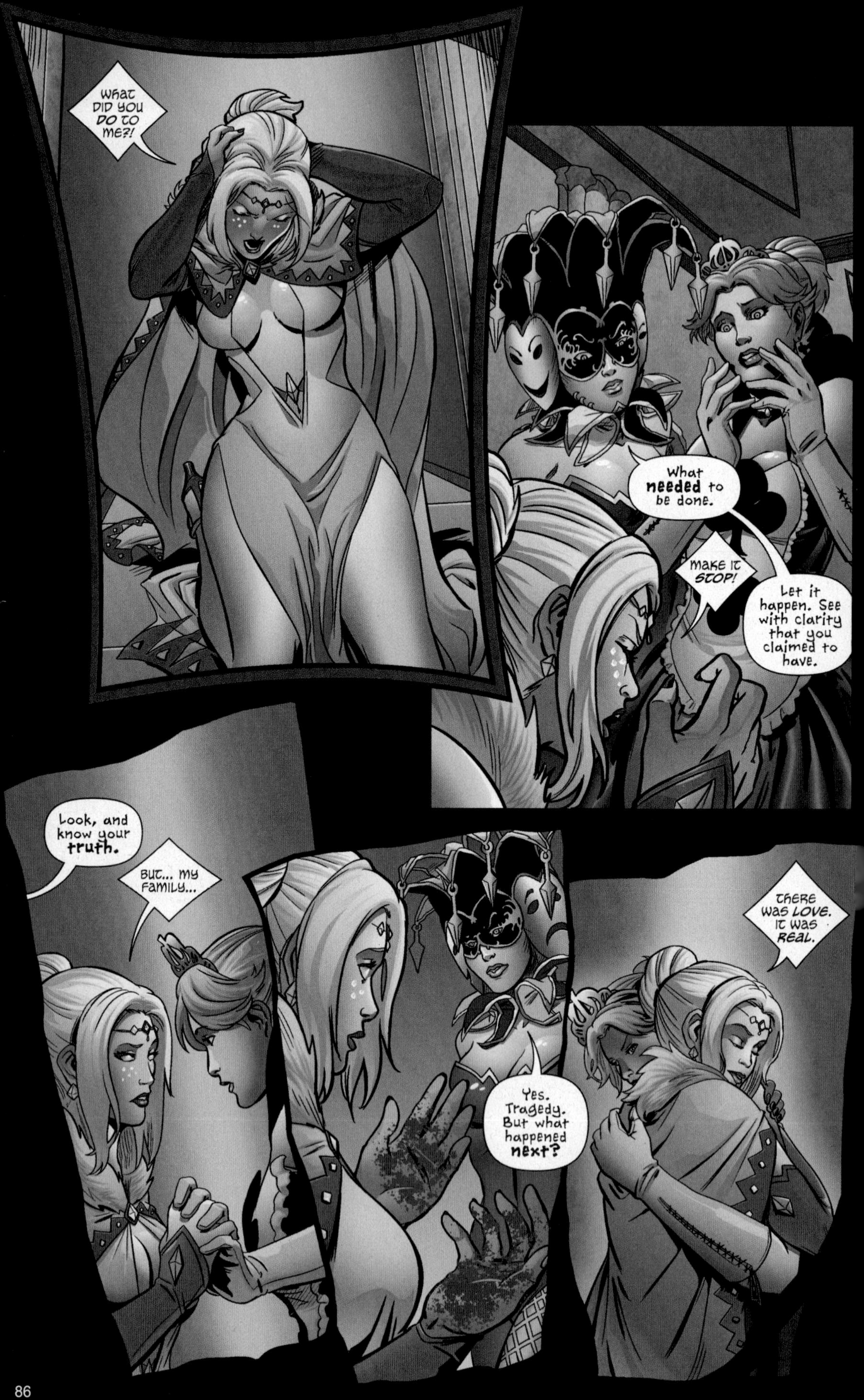
WHAT DID YOU DO TO ME?!
What needed to be done.
MAKE IT STOP!
Let it happen. See with clarity that you claimed to have.
Look, and know your truth.
BUT... MY FAMILY...
Yes. Tragedy. But what happened next?
THERE WAS LOVE. IT WAS REAL.

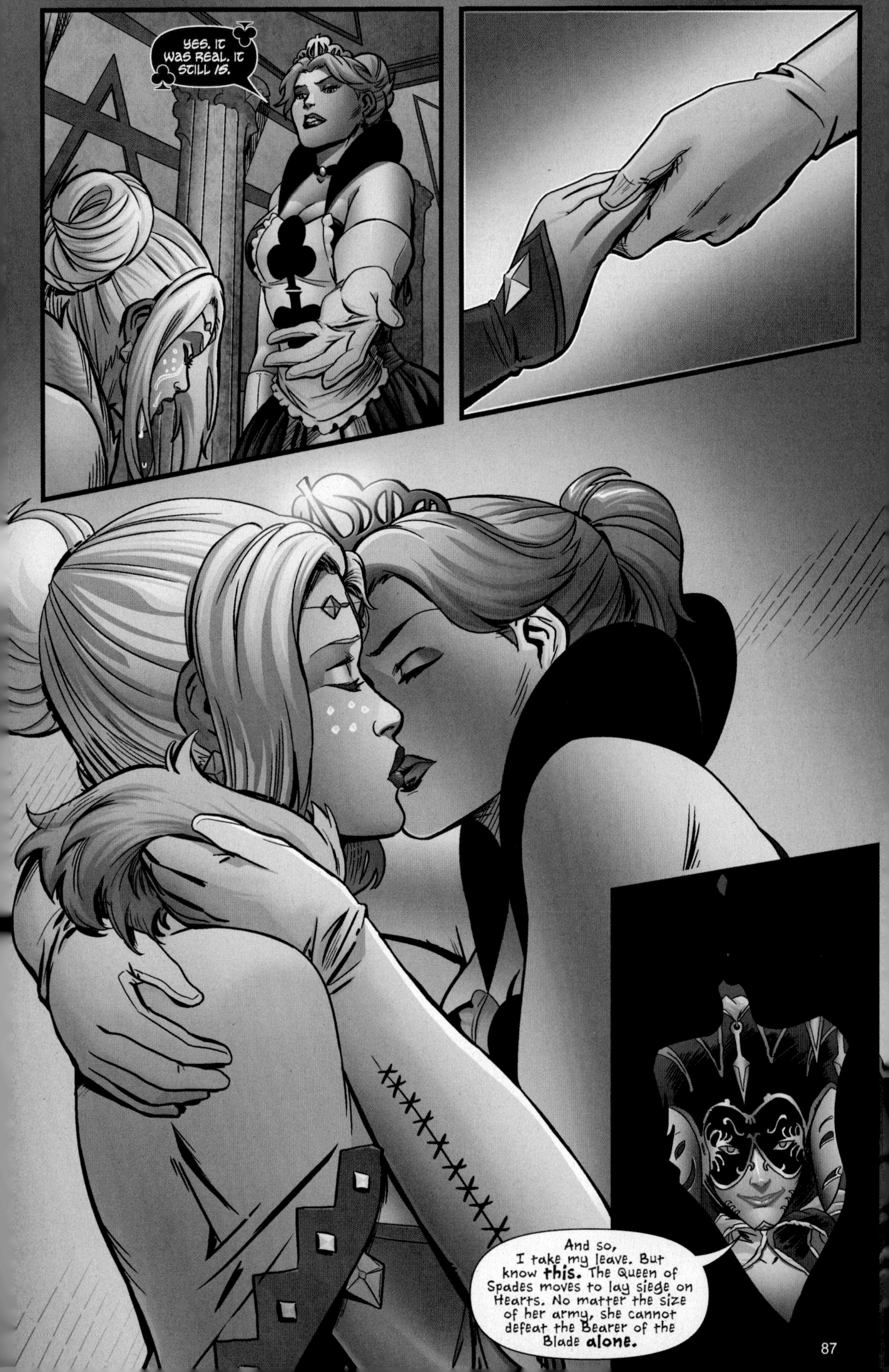

YES. IT WAS REAL. IT STILL IS.
And so, I take my leave. But know this. The Queen of Spades moves to lay siege on Hearts. No matter the size of her army, she cannot defeat the Bearer of the Blade alone.

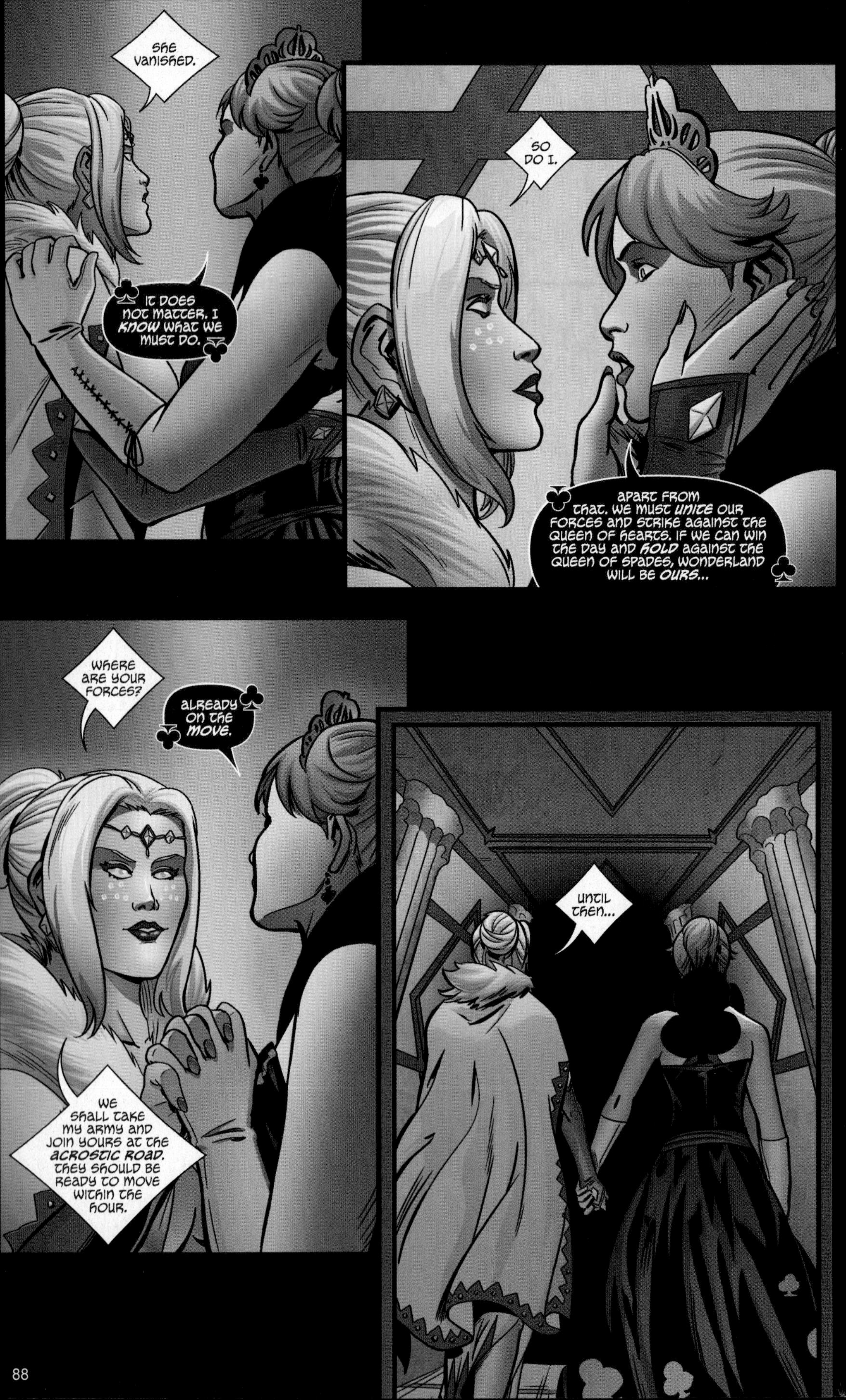
SHE VANISHED.
IT DOES NOT MATTER. I KNOW WHAT WE MUST DO.
SO DO I.
APART FROM THAT. WE MUST UNITE OUR FORCES AND STRIKE AGAINST THE QUEEN OF HEARTS. IF WE CAN WIN THE DAY AND HOLD AGAINST THE QUEEN OF SPADES, WONDERLAND WILL BE OURS...
WHERE ARE YOUR FORCES?
ALREADY ON THE MOVE.
WE SHALL TAKE MY ARMY AND JOIN YOURS AT THE ACROSTIC ROAD. THEY SHOULD BE READY TO MOVE WITHIN THE HOUR.
UNTIL THEN...

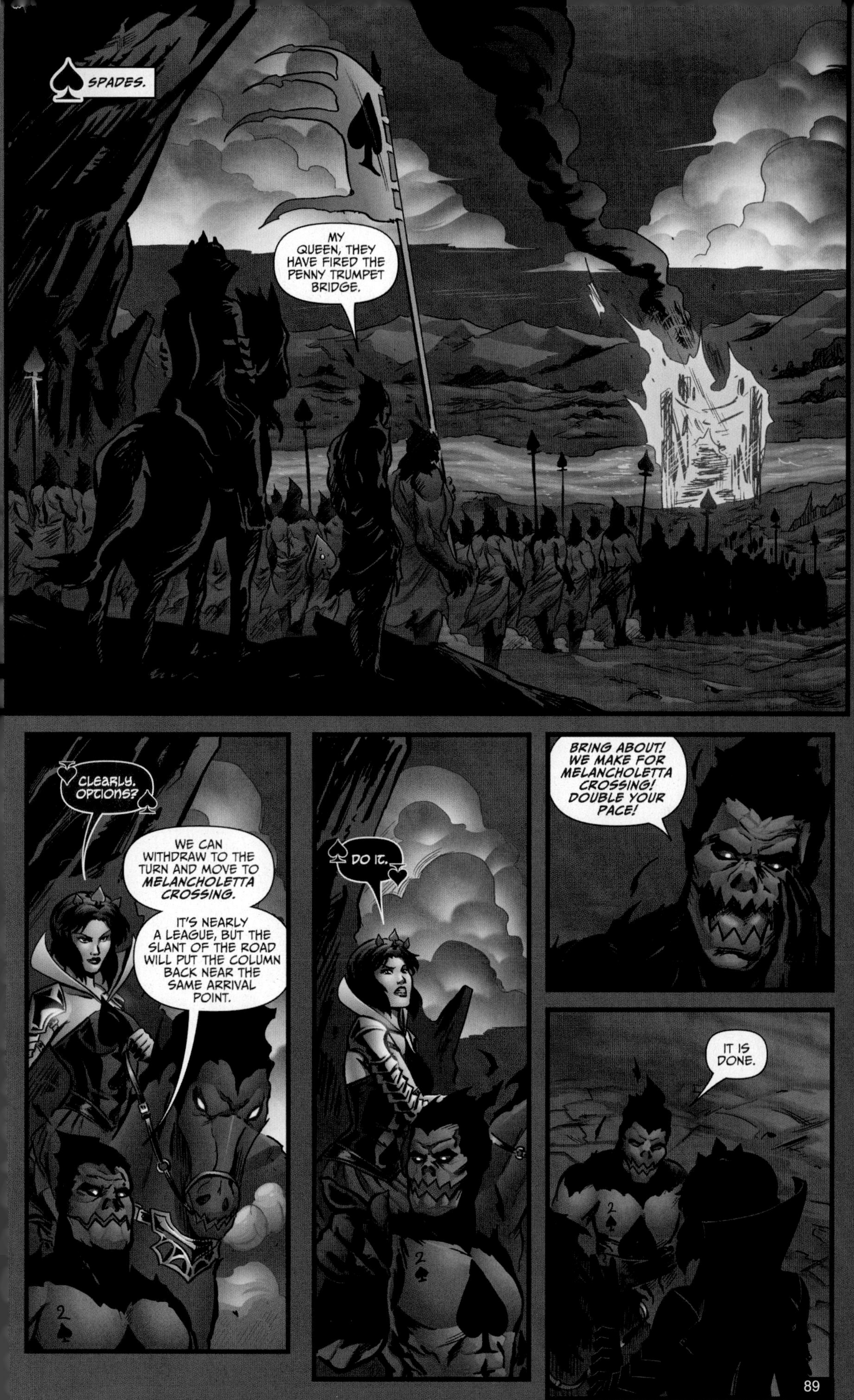
SPADES.
MY QUEEN, THEY HAVE FIRED THE PENNY TRUMPET BRIDGE.
CLEARLY. OPTIONS?
WE CAN WITHDRAW TO THE TURN AND MOVE TO MELANCHOLETTA CROSSING.
IT'S NEARLY A LEAGUE, BUT THE SLANT OF THE ROAD WILL PUT THE COLUMN BACK NEAR THE SAME ARRIVAL POINT.
DO IT.
BRING ABOUT! WE MAKE FOR MELANCHOLETTA CROSSING! DOUBLE YOUR PACE!
IT IS DONE.

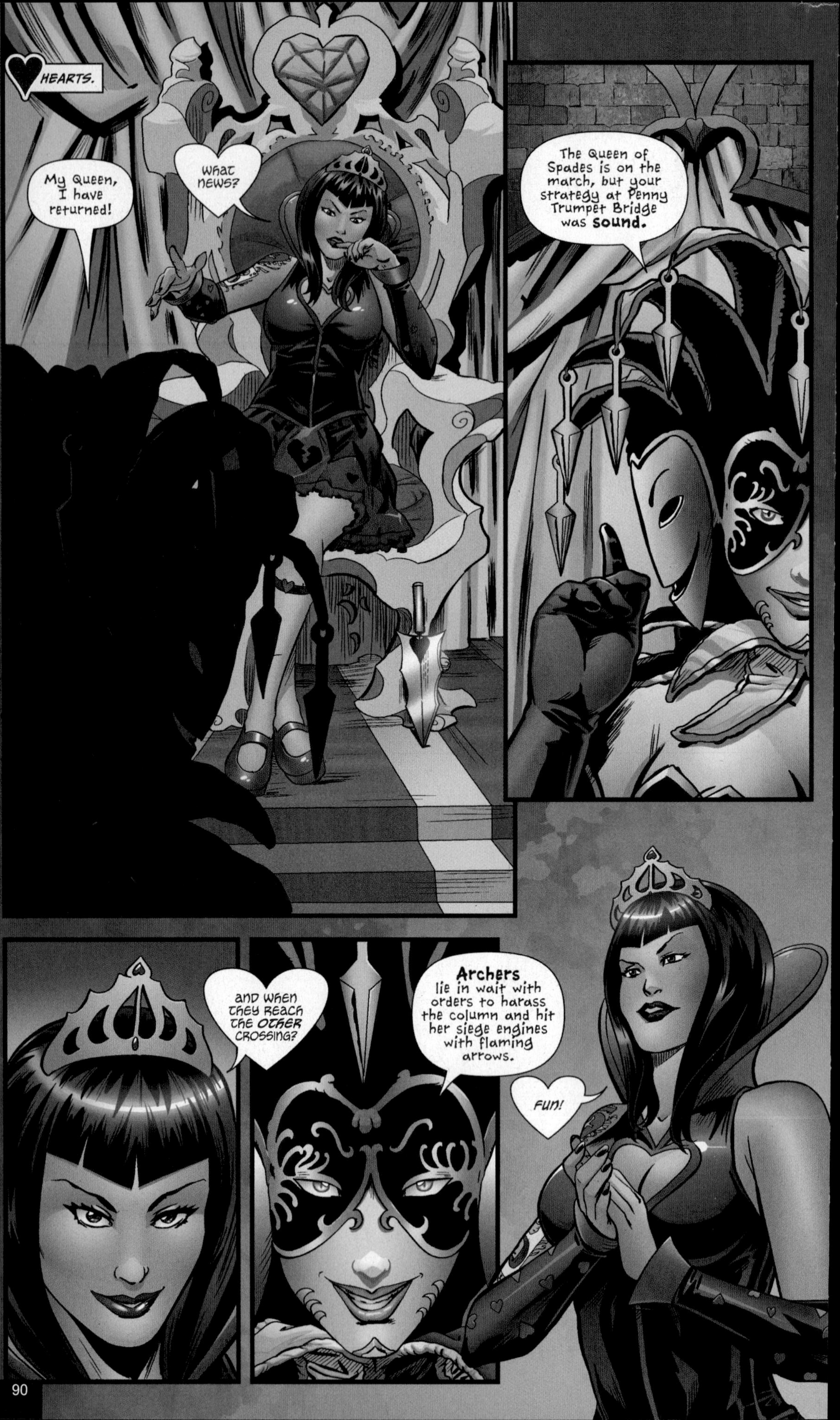
HEARTS.
My Queen, I have returned!
What news?
The Queen of Spades is on the march, but your strategy at Penny Trumpet Bridge was sound.
And when they reach the OTHER crossing?
Archers lie in wait with orders to harass the column and hit her siege engines with flaming arrows.
Fun!

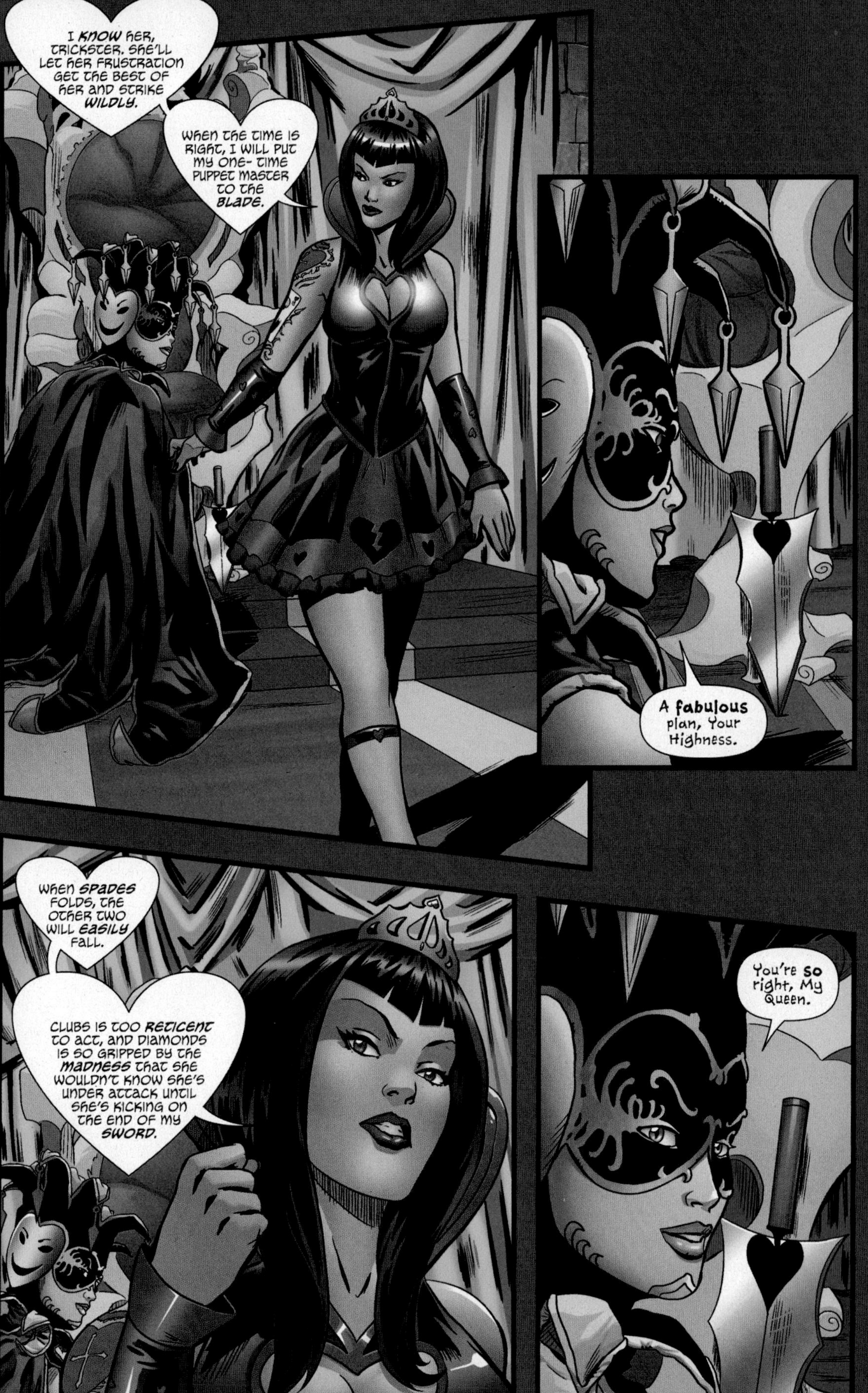
I KNOW HER, TRICKSTER. SHE'LL LET HER FRUSTRATION GET THE BEST OF HER AND STRIKE WILDLY.
WHEN THE TIME IS RIGHT, I WILL PUT MY ONE-TIME PUPPET MASTER TO THE BLADE.
A fabulous plan, Your Highness.
WHEN SPADES FOLDS, THE OTHER TWO WILL EASILY FALL.
CLUBS IS TOO RETICENT TO ACT, AND DIAMONDS IS SO GRIPPED BY THE MADNESS THAT SHE WOULDN'T KNOW SHE'S UNDER ATTACK UNTIL SHE'S KICKING ON THE END OF MY SWORD.
You're so right, My Queen.

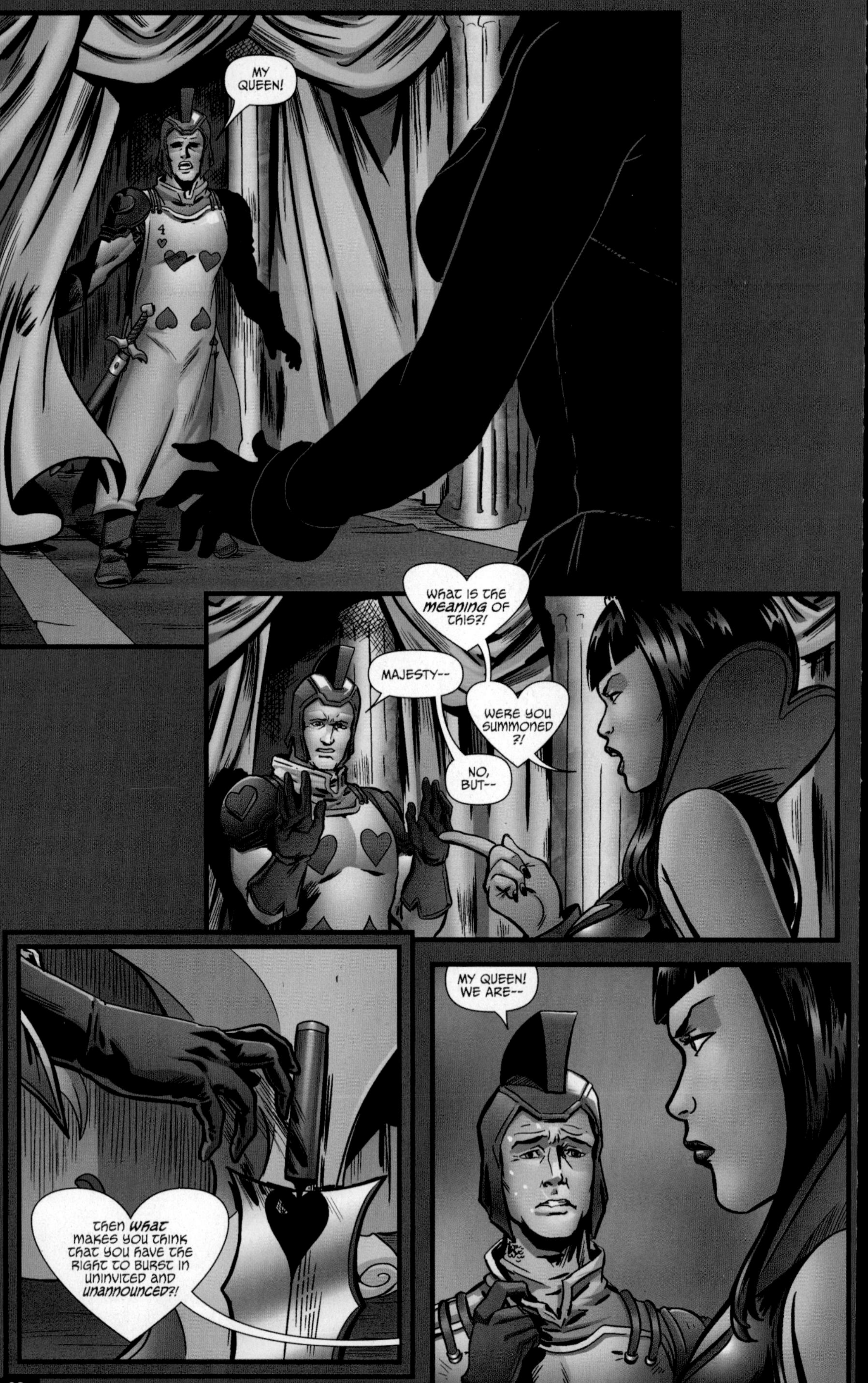
MY QUEEN!
WHAT IS THE MEANING OF THIS?!
MAJESTY--
WERE YOU SUMMONED ?!
NO, BUT--
THEN WHAT MAKES YOU THINK THAT YOU HAVE THE RIGHT TO BURST IN UNINVITED AND UNANNOUNCED?!
MY QUEEN! WE ARE--

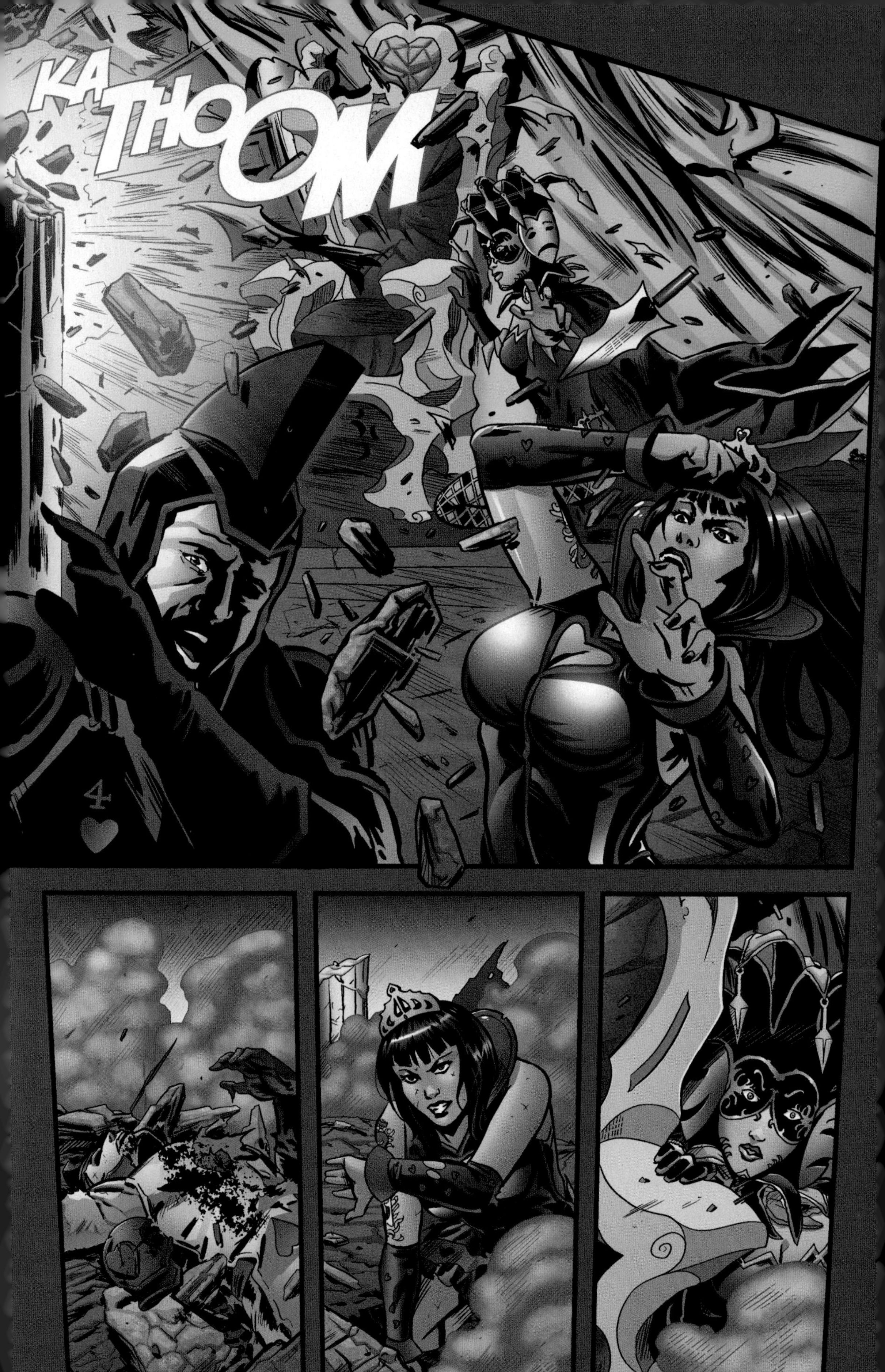
KA THOOM

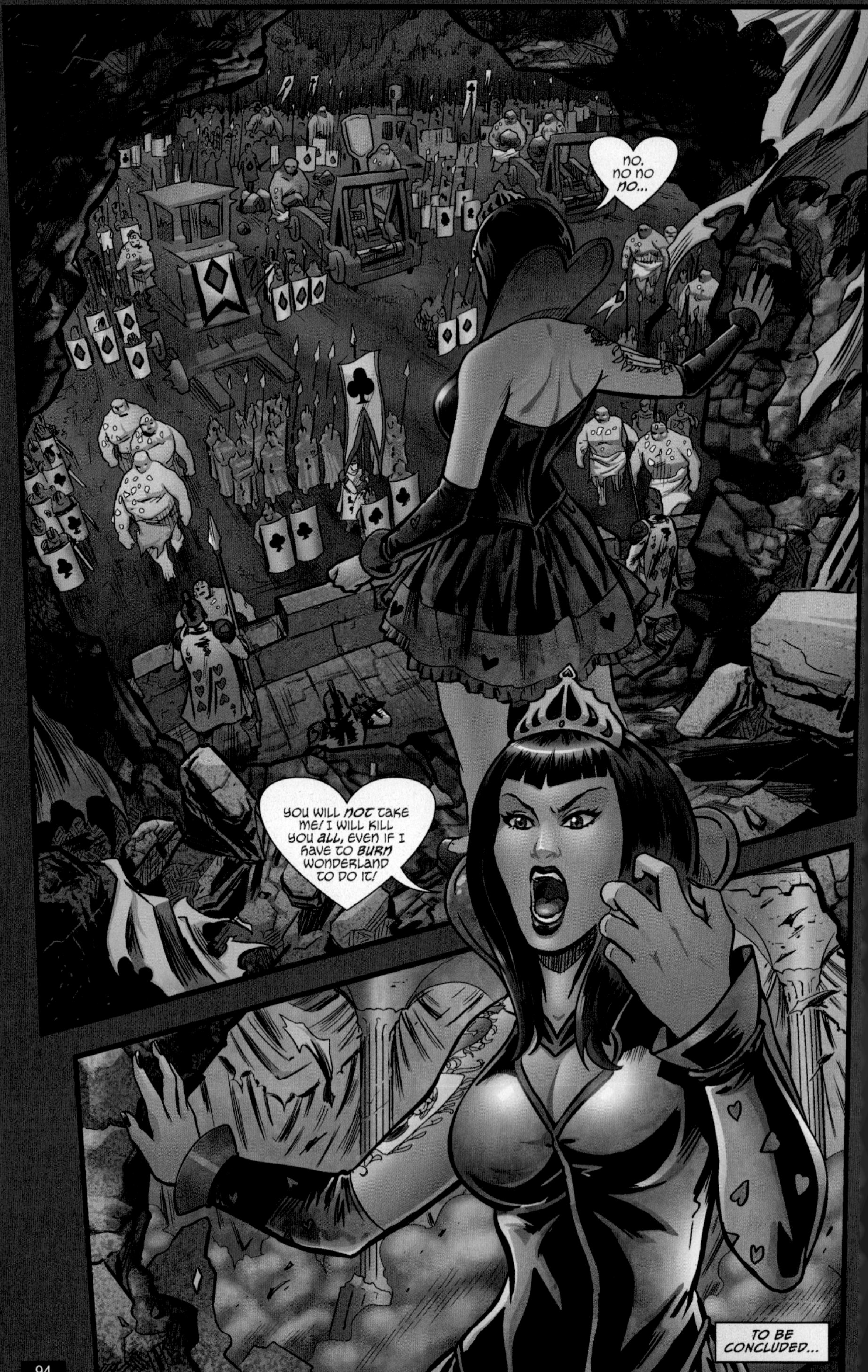
no.
no no
no...
you will not take me! I will kill you all, even if I have to burn wonderland to do it!
TO BE CONCLUDED...

Grimm Fairy Tales
presents

Wonderland

♠ ♥ **Clash of Queens** ♣ ♦

AGE OF DARKNESS

CHAPTER FIVE

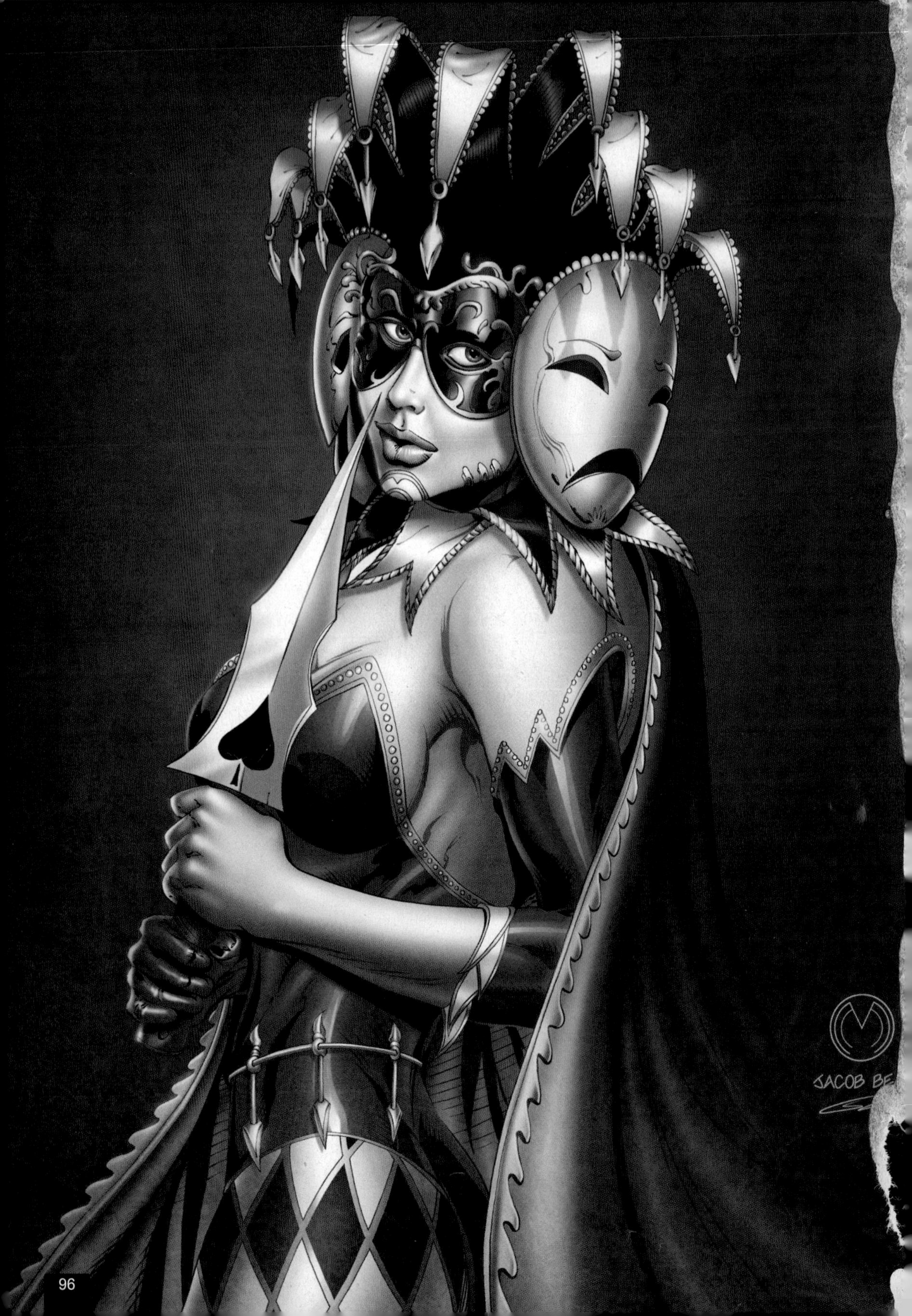

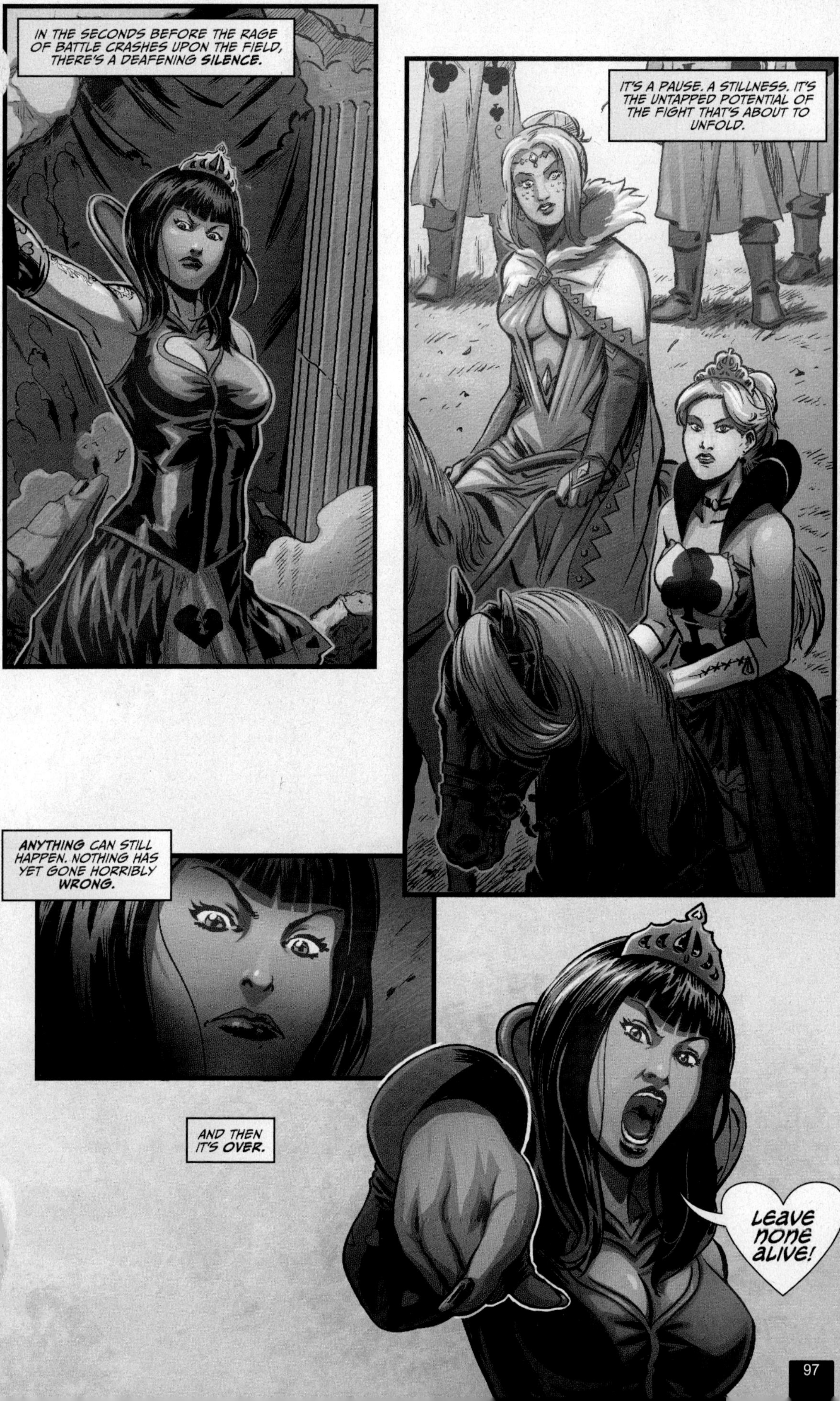
IN THE SECONDS BEFORE THE RAGE OF BATTLE CRASHES UPON THE FIELD, THERE'S A DEAFENING SILENCE.
IT'S A PAUSE. A STILLNESS. IT'S THE UNTAPPED POTENTIAL OF THE FIGHT THAT'S ABOUT TO UNFOLD.
ANYTHING CAN STILL HAPPEN. NOTHING HAS YET GONE HORRIBLY WRONG.
AND THEN IT'S OVER.
LEAVE NONE ALIVE!

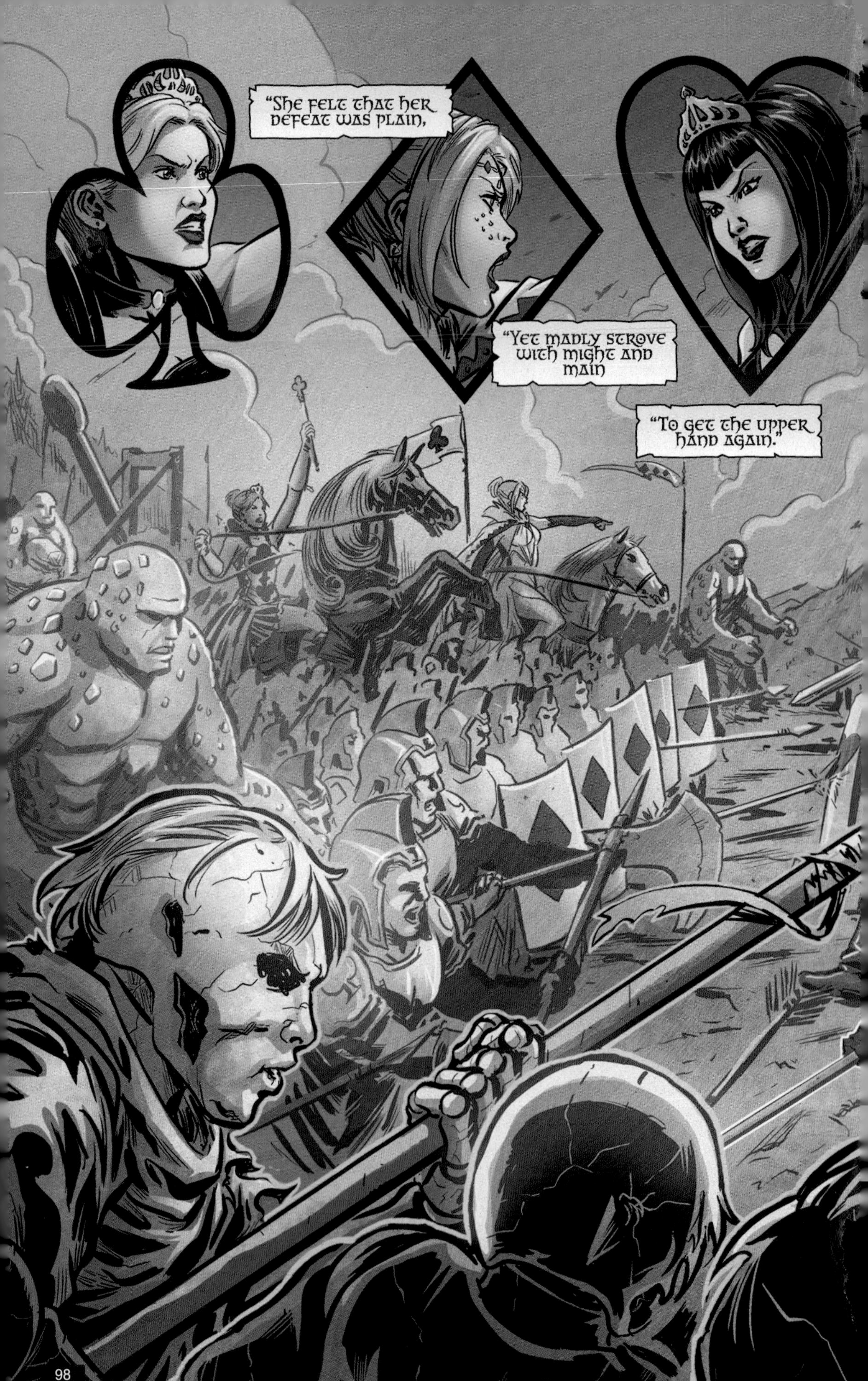
"She felt that her defeat was plain,
"Yet madly strove with might and main
"To get the upper hand again."

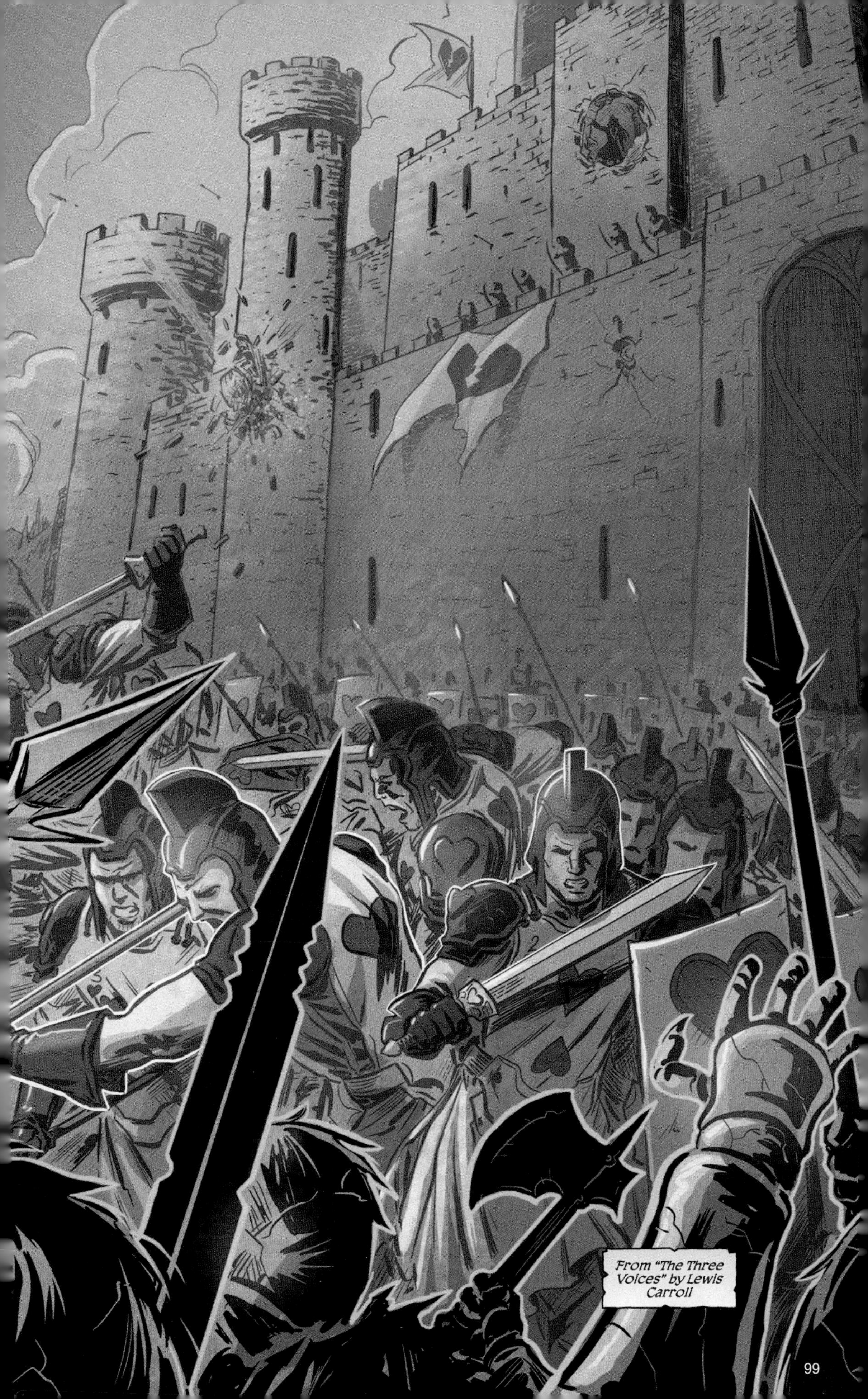
From "The Three Voices" by Lewis Carroll

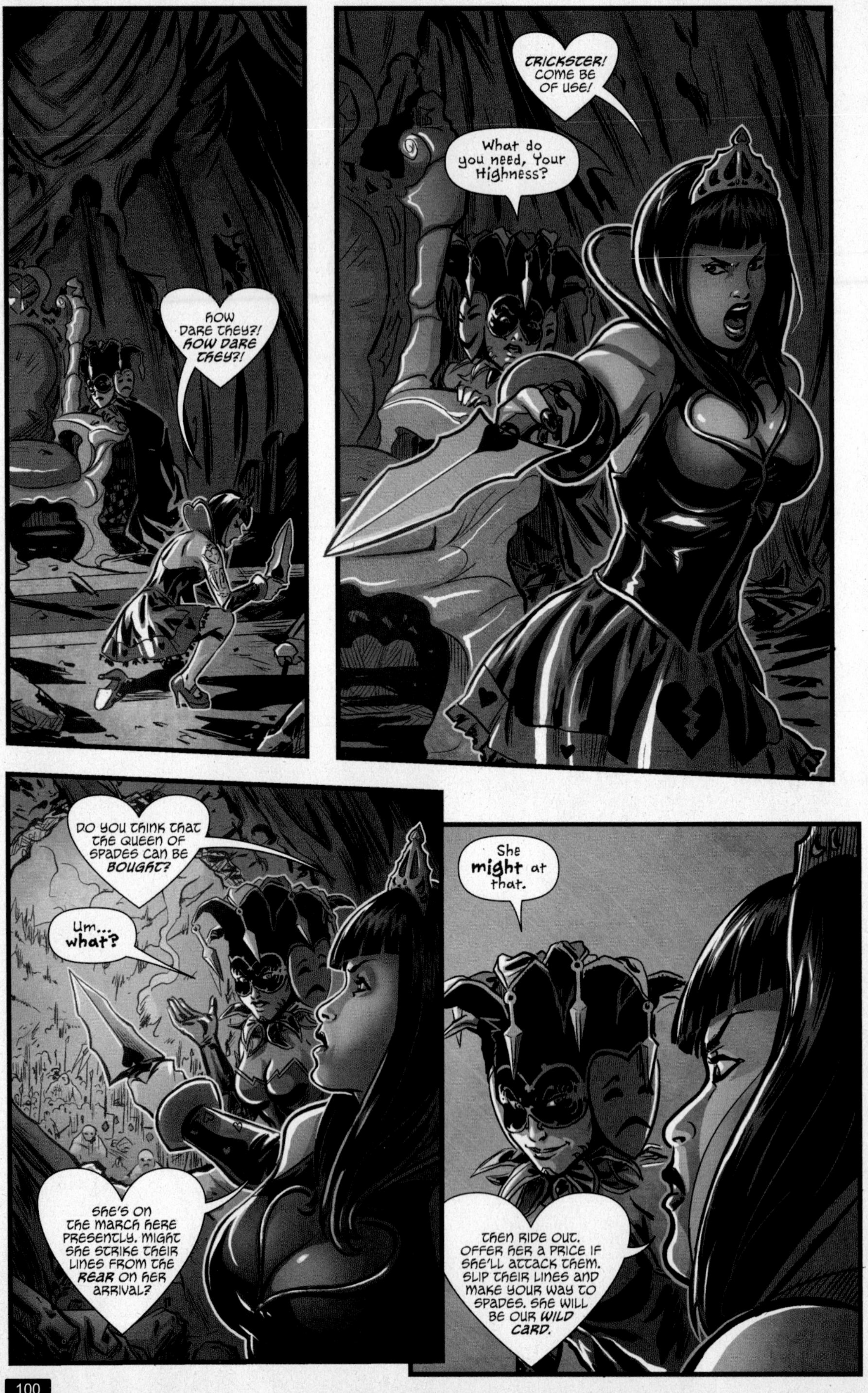
HOW DARE THEY?! HOW DARE THEY?!
TRICKSTER! COME BE OF USE!
What do you need, Your Highness?
DO YOU THINK THAT THE QUEEN OF SPADES CAN BE BOUGHT?
Um... what?
SHE'S ON THE MARCH HERE PRESENTLY. MIGHT SHE STRIKE THEIR LINES FROM THE REAR ON HER ARRIVAL?
She might at that.
THEN RIDE OUT. OFFER HER A PRICE IF SHE'LL ATTACK THEM. SLIP THEIR LINES AND MAKE YOUR WAY TO SPADES. SHE WILL BE OUR WILD CARD.

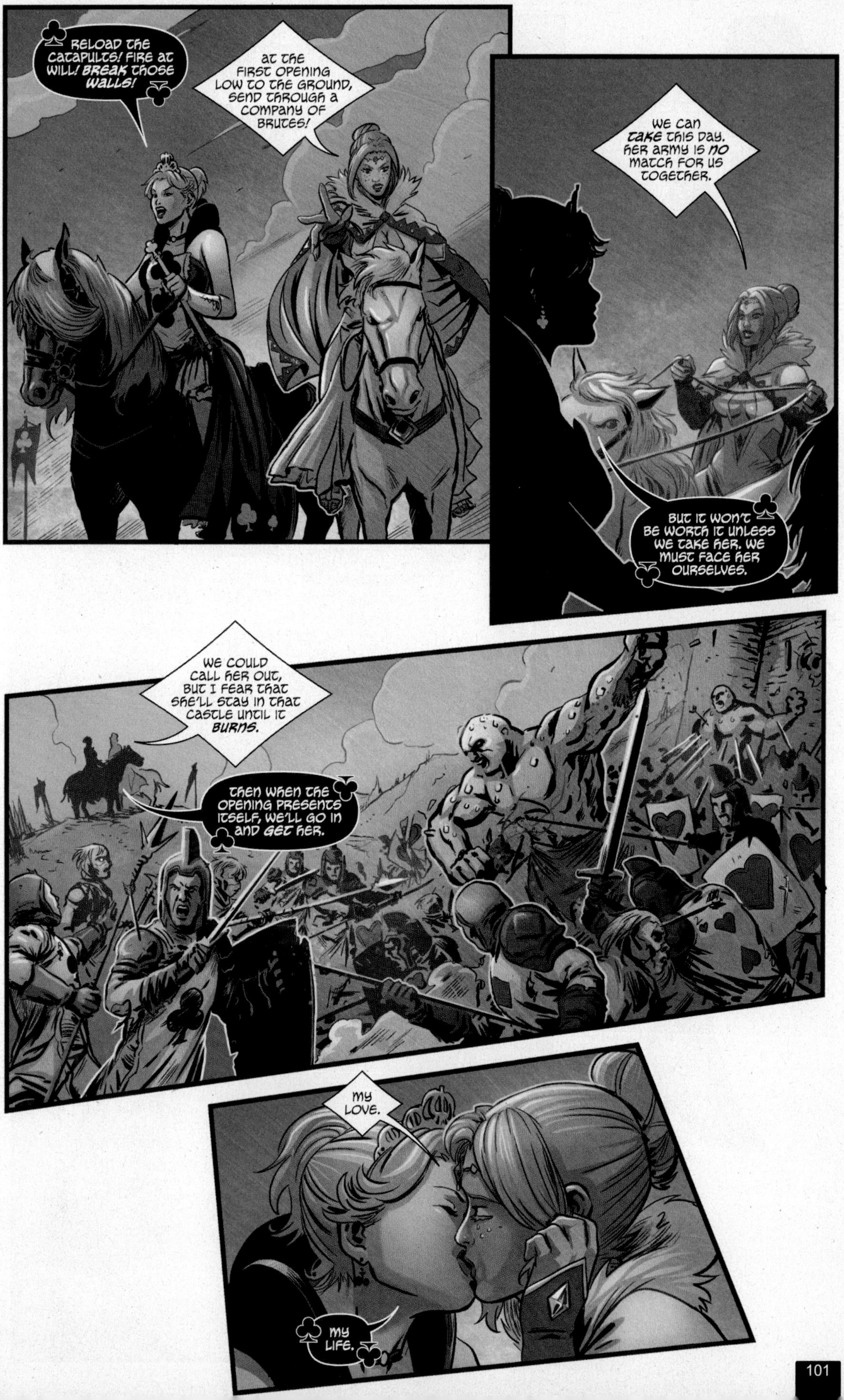

RELOAD THE CATAPULTS! FIRE AT WILL! BREAK THOSE WALLS!
AT THE FIRST OPENING LOW TO THE GROUND, SEND THROUGH A COMPANY OF BRUTES!
WE CAN TAKE THIS DAY. HER ARMY IS NO MATCH FOR US TOGETHER.
BUT IT WON'T BE WORTH IT UNLESS WE TAKE HER. WE MUST FACE HER OURSELVES.
WE COULD CALL HER OUT, BUT I FEAR THAT SHE'LL STAY IN THAT CASTLE UNTIL IT BURNS.
THEN WHEN THE OPENING PRESENTS ITSELF, WE'LL GO IN AND GET HER.
MY LOVE.
MY LIFE.

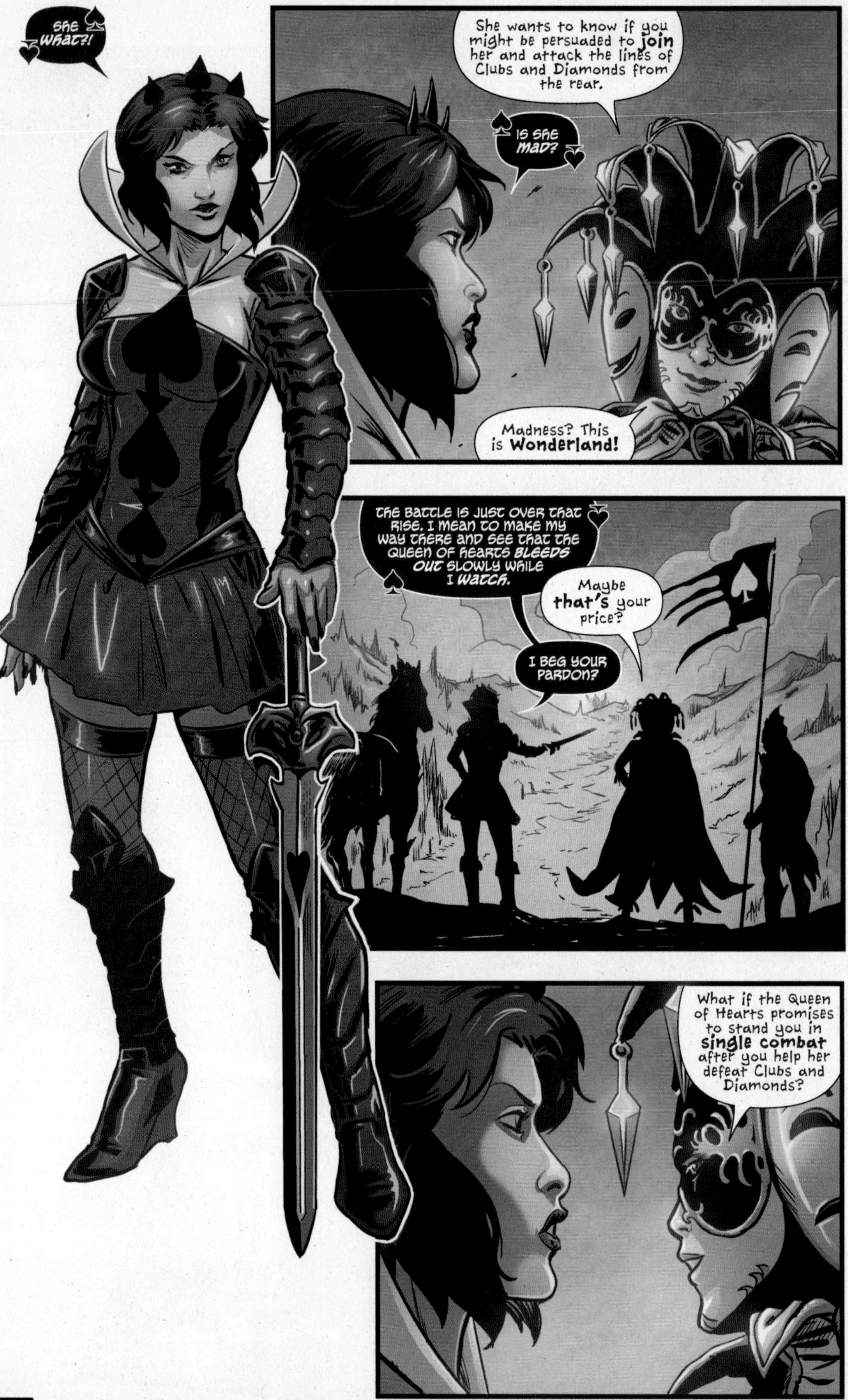
SHE WHAT?!
She wants to know if you might be persuaded to join her and attack the lines of Clubs and Diamonds from the rear.
IS SHE MAD?
Madness? This is Wonderland!
THE BATTLE IS JUST OVER THAT RISE. I MEAN TO MAKE MY WAY THERE AND SEE THAT THE QUEEN OF HEARTS BLEEDS OUT SLOWLY WHILE I WATCH.
Maybe that's your price?
I BEG YOUR PARDON?
What if the Queen of Hearts promises to stand you in single combat after you help her defeat Clubs and Diamonds?

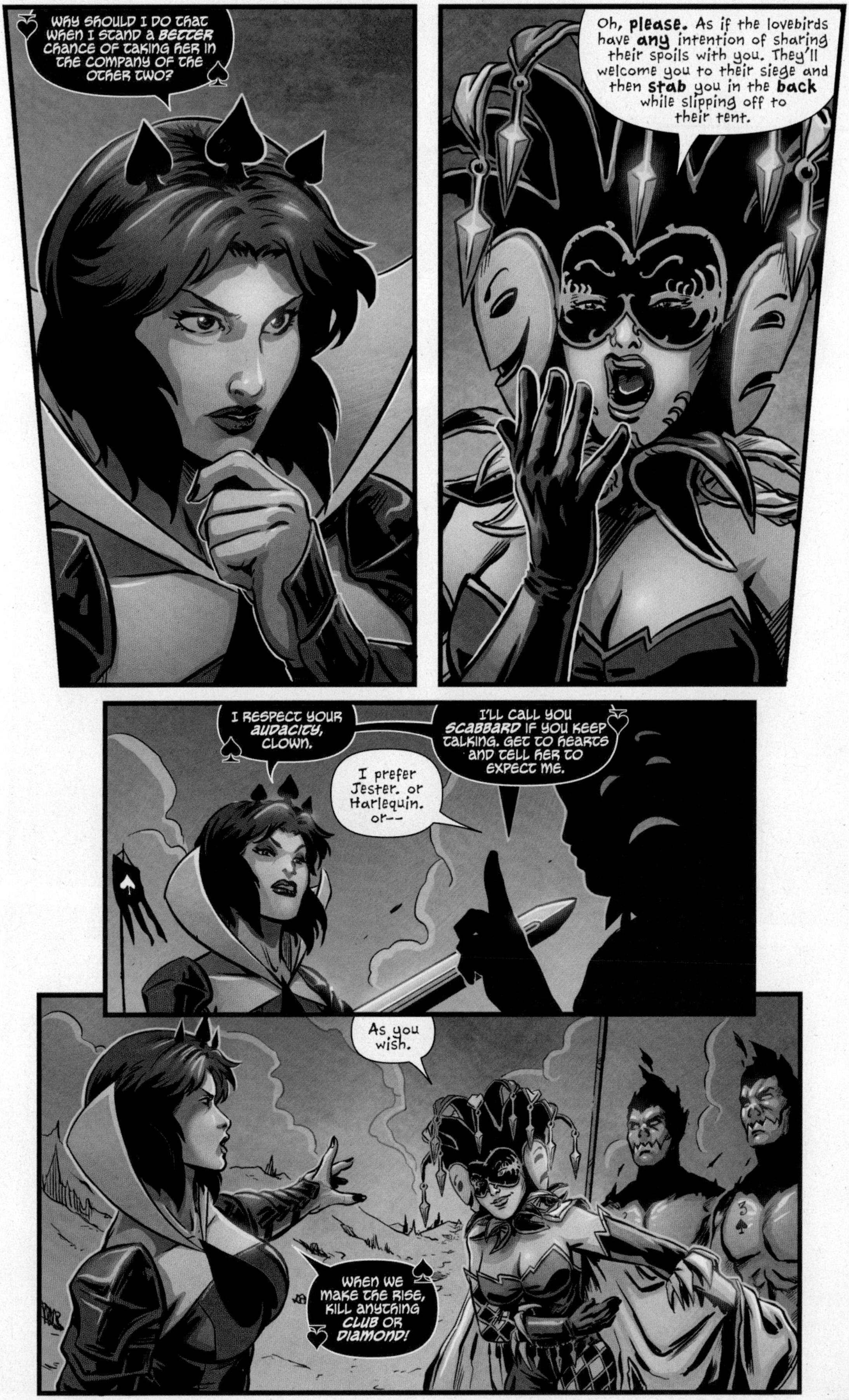

WHY SHOULD I DO THAT WHEN I STAND A BETTER CHANCE OF TAKING HER IN THE COMPANY OF THE OTHER TWO?
Oh, please. As if the lovebirds have any intention of sharing their spoils with you. They'll welcome you to their siege and then stab you in the back while slipping off to their tent.
I RESPECT YOUR AUDACITY, CLOWN.
I prefer Jester. or Harlequin. or--
I'LL CALL YOU SCABBARD IF YOU KEEP TALKING. GET TO HEARTS AND TELL HER TO EXPECT ME.
As you wish.
WHEN WE MAKE THE RISE, KILL ANYTHING CLUB OR DIAMOND!

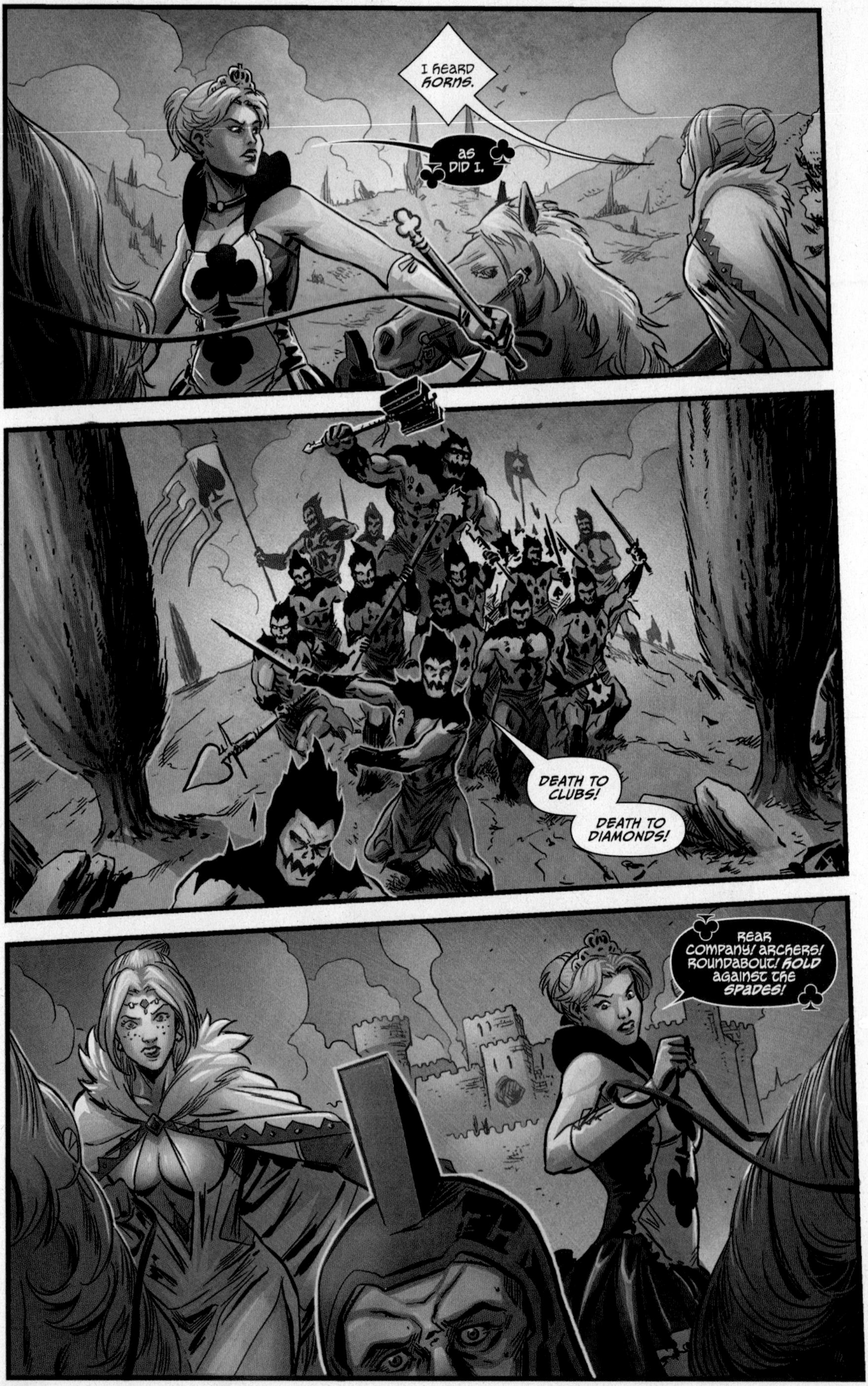
I HEARD HORNS.
AS DID I.
DEATH TO CLUBS!
DEATH TO DIAMONDS!
REAR COMPANY! ARCHERS! ROUNDABOUT! HOLD AGAINST THE SPADES!

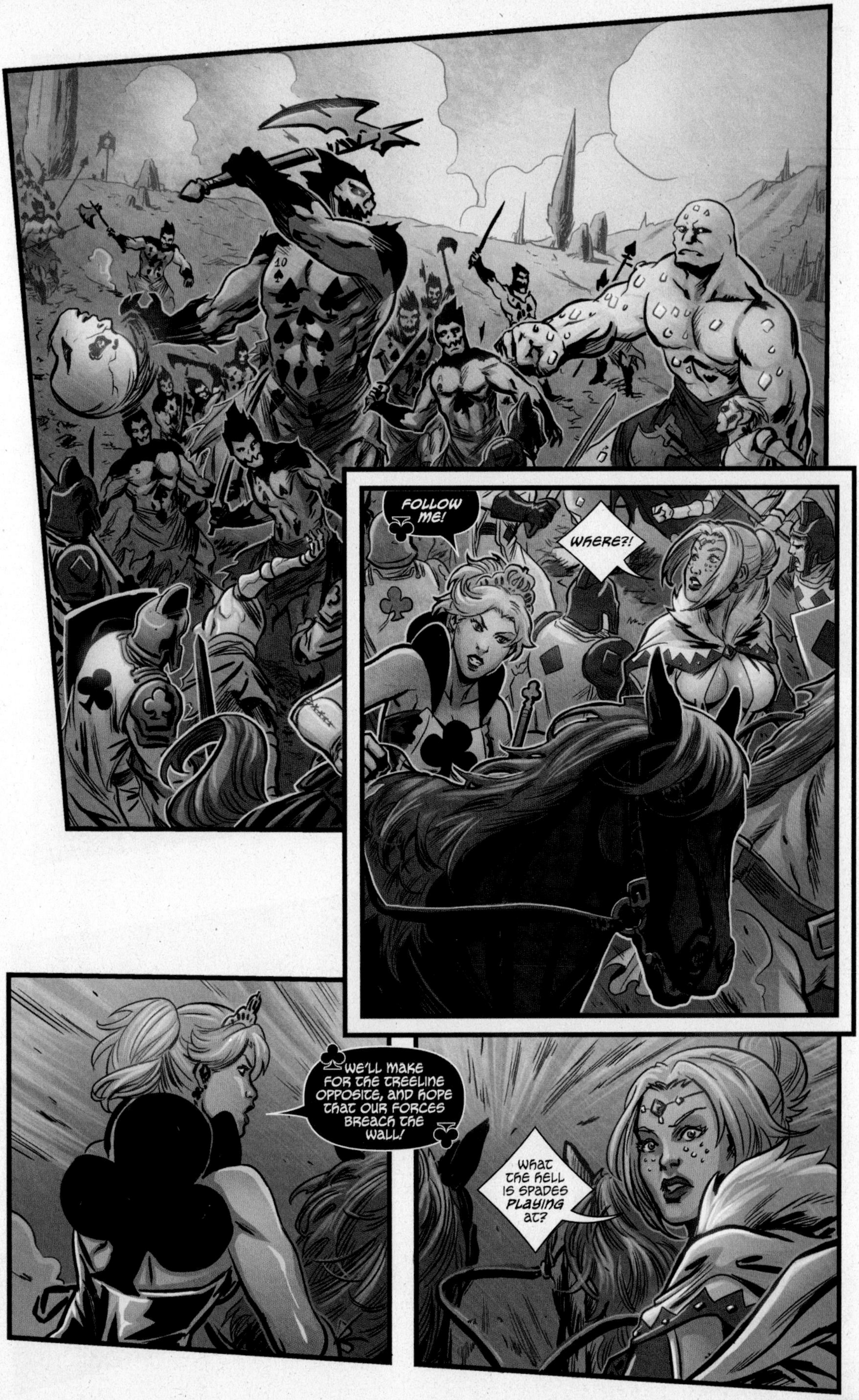
FOLLOW ME!
WHERE?!
WE'LL MAKE FOR THE TREELINE OPPOSITE, AND HOPE THAT OUR FORCES BREACH THE WALL!
WHAT THE HELL IS SPADES PLAYING AT?

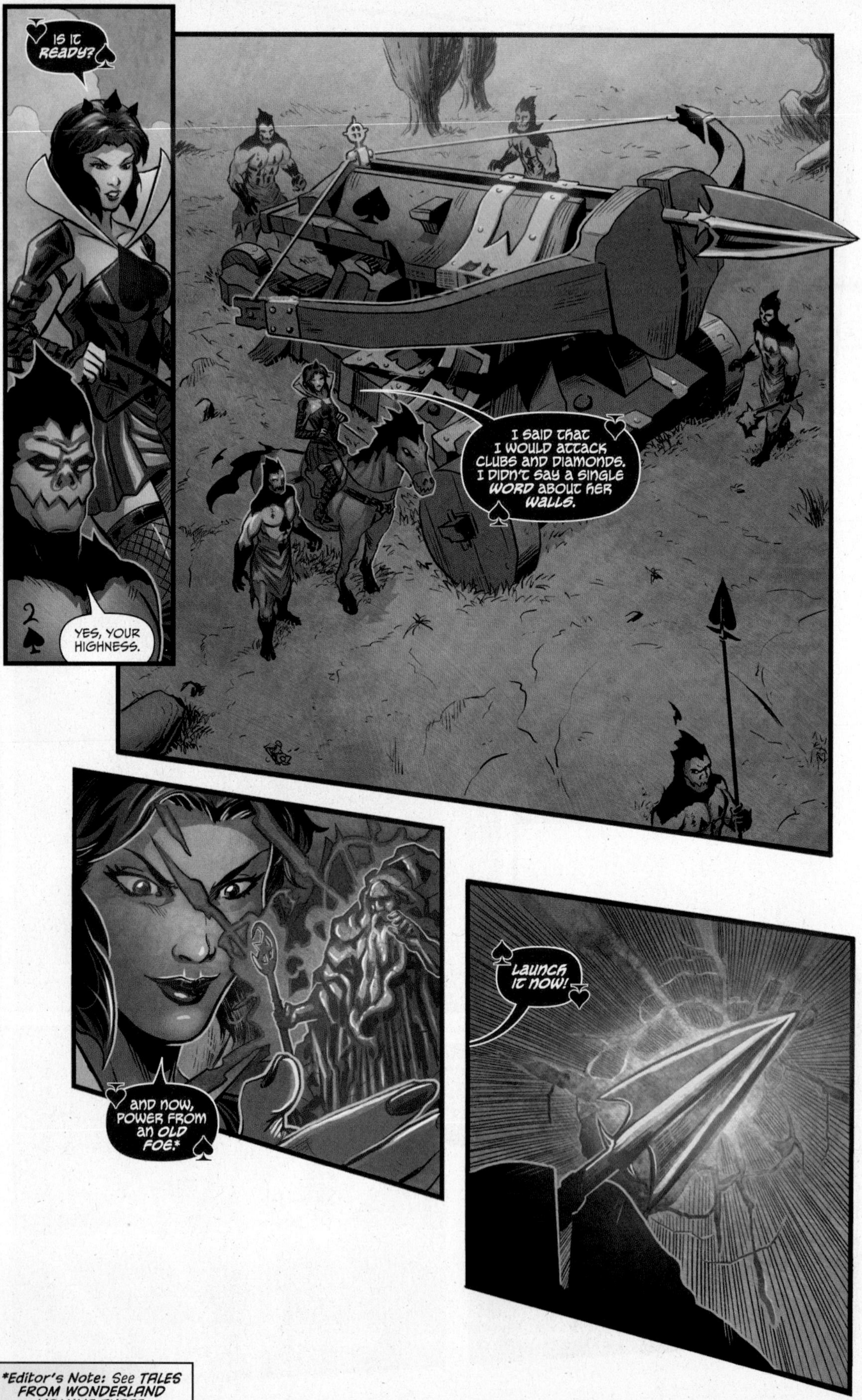
Is it ready?
Yes, your highness.
I said that I would attack clubs and diamonds. I didn't say a single word about her walls.
And now, power from an old foe.*
Launch it now!

*Editor's Note: See TALES FROM WONDERLAND VOLUME THREE.

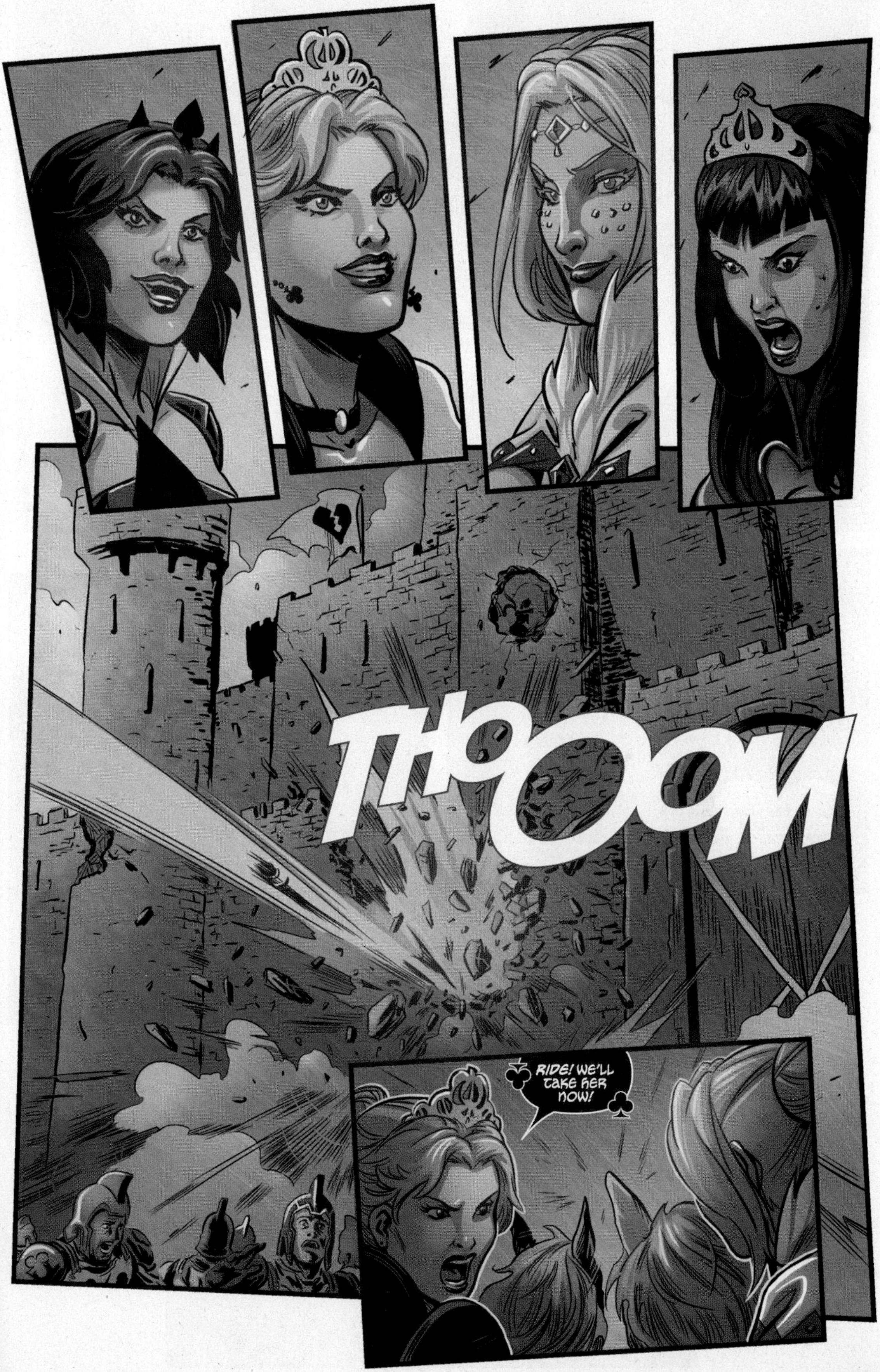
THOOM
RIDE! WE'LL TAKE HER NOW!

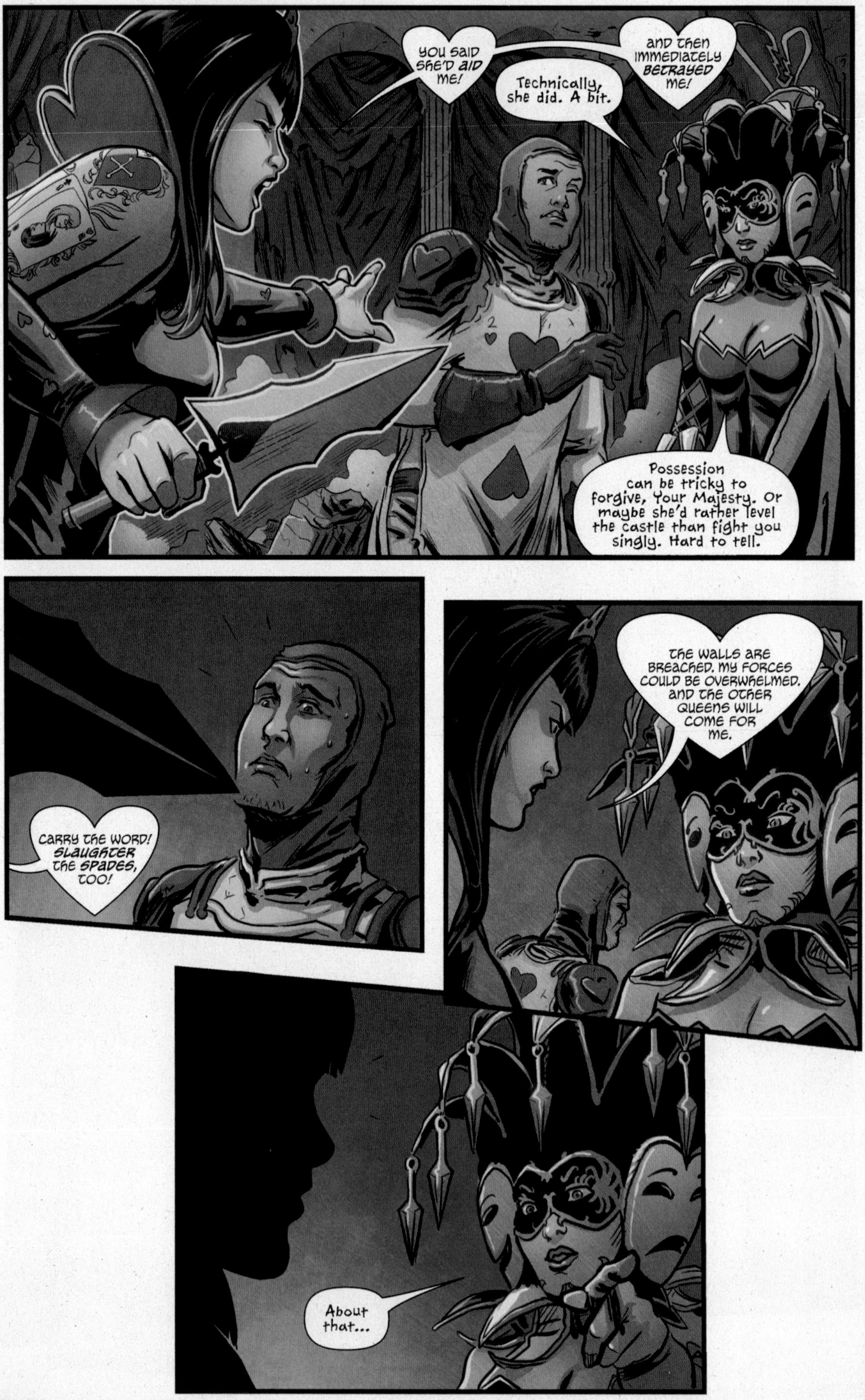
YOU SAID SHE'D AID ME!
Technically, she did. A bit.
AND THEN IMMEDIATELY BETRAYED ME!
Possession can be tricky to forgive, Your Majesty. Or maybe she'd rather level the castle than fight you singly. Hard to tell.
CARRY THE WORD! SLAUGHTER THE SPADES, TOO!
THE WALLS ARE BREACHED. MY FORCES COULD BE OVERWHELMED. AND THE OTHER QUEENS WILL COME FOR ME.
About that...

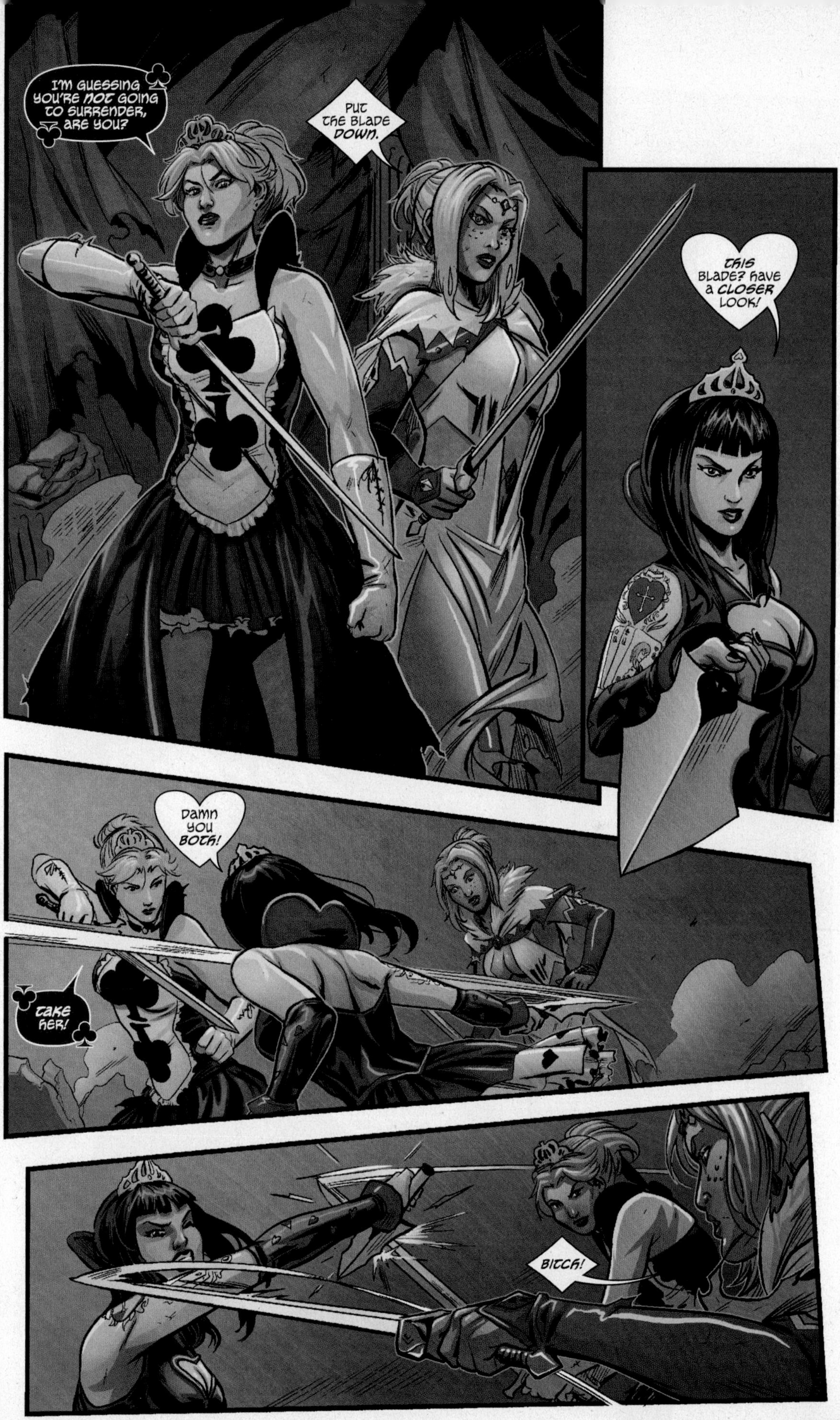

I'M GUESSING YOU'RE NOT GOING TO SURRENDER, ARE YOU?
PUT THE BLADE DOWN.
THIS BLADE? HAVE A CLOSER LOOK!
DAMN YOU BOTH!
TAKE HER!
BITCH!

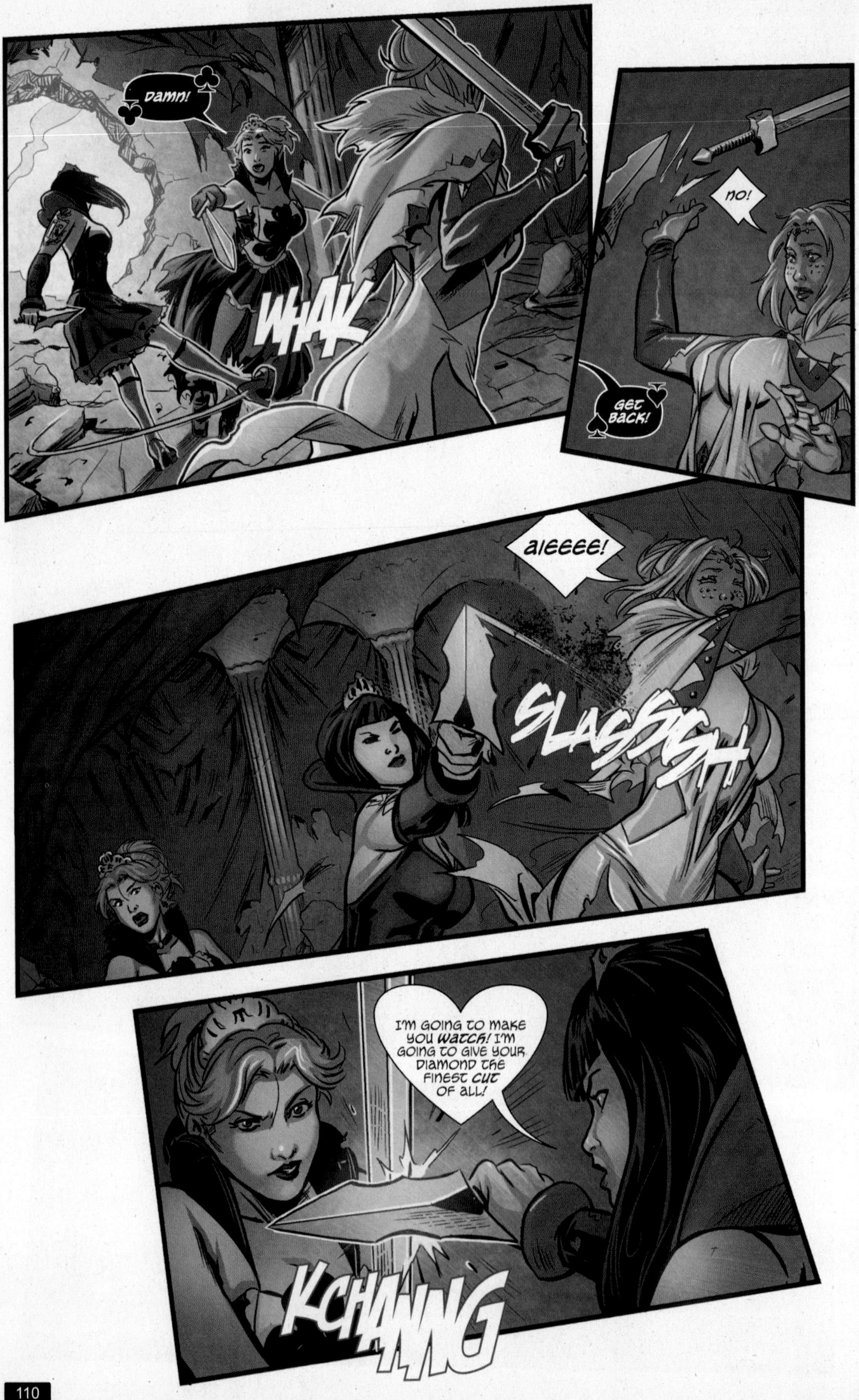
Damn!
WHAK
no!
GET BACK!
aleeee!
SLASSSH
I'M GOING TO MAKE YOU WATCH! I'M GOING TO GIVE YOUR DIAMOND THE FINEST CUT OF ALL!
KCHANNG

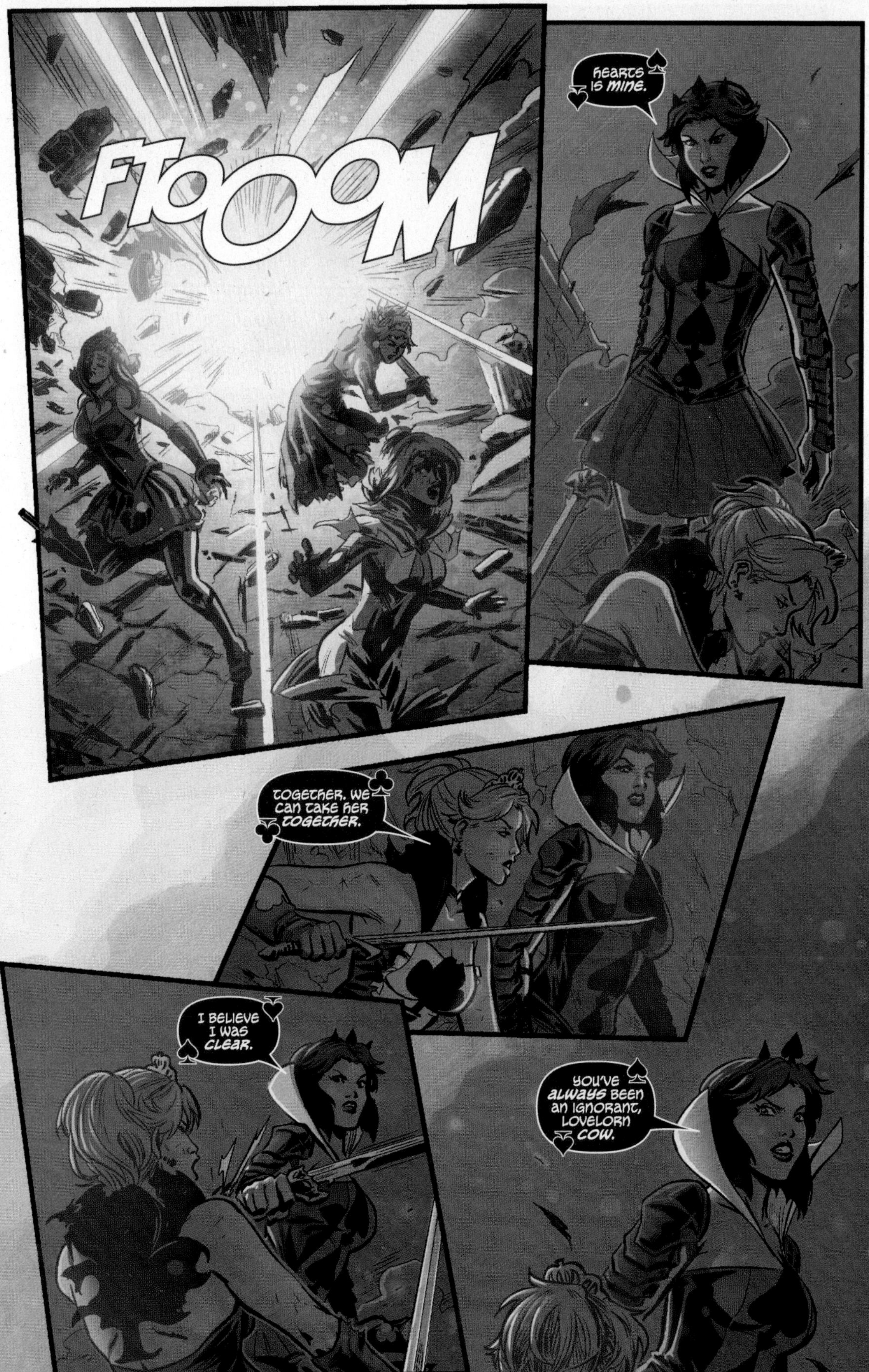
FTOOOM
HEARTS IS MINE.
TOGETHER. WE CAN TAKE HER TOGETHER.
I BELIEVE I WAS CLEAR.
YOU'VE ALWAYS BEEN AN IGNORANT, LOVELORN COW.

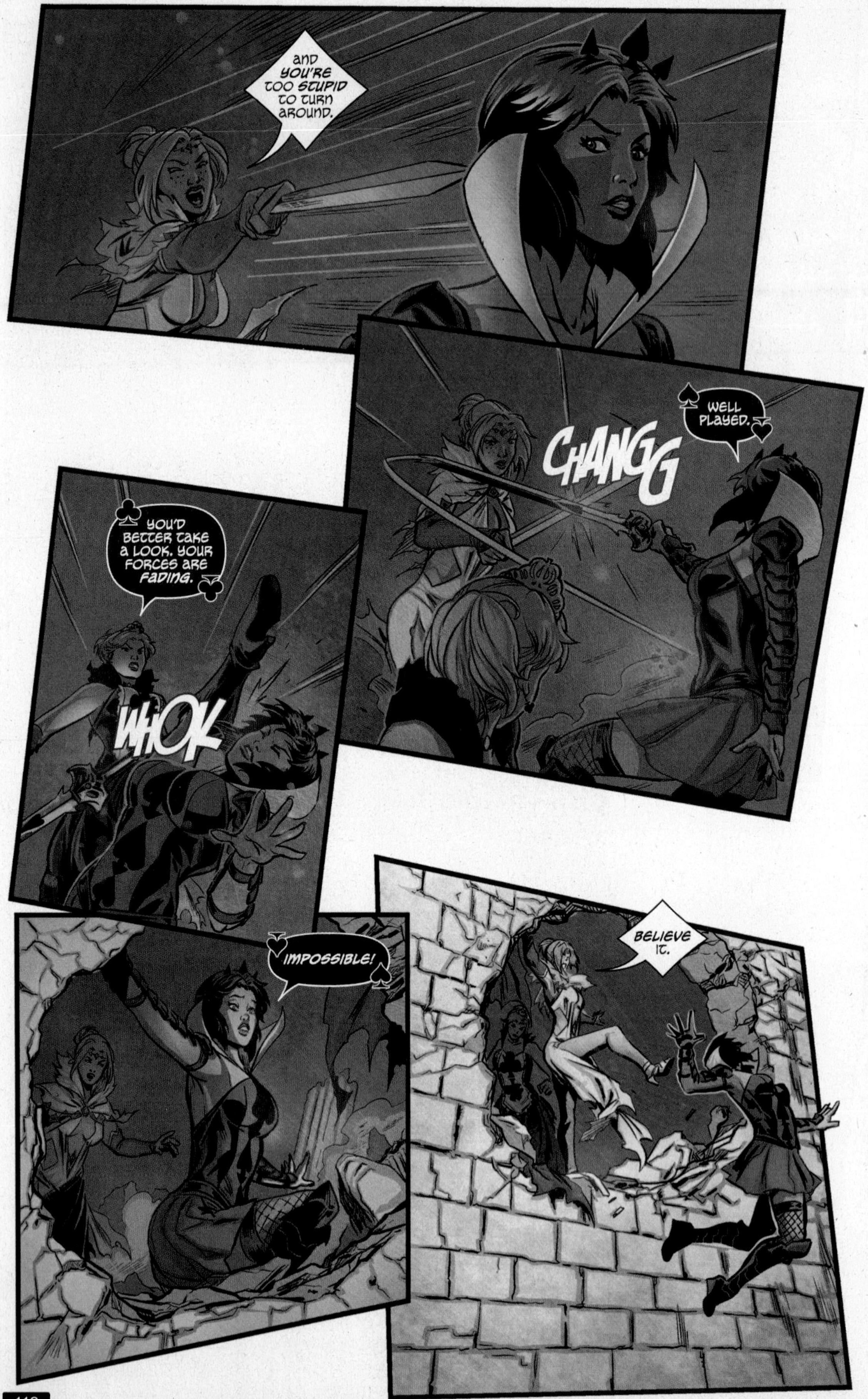
and you're too stupid to turn around.
CHANGG
WELL PLAYED.
YOU'D BETTER TAKE A LOOK. YOUR FORCES ARE FADING.
WHOK
IMPOSSIBLE!
BELIEVE IT.

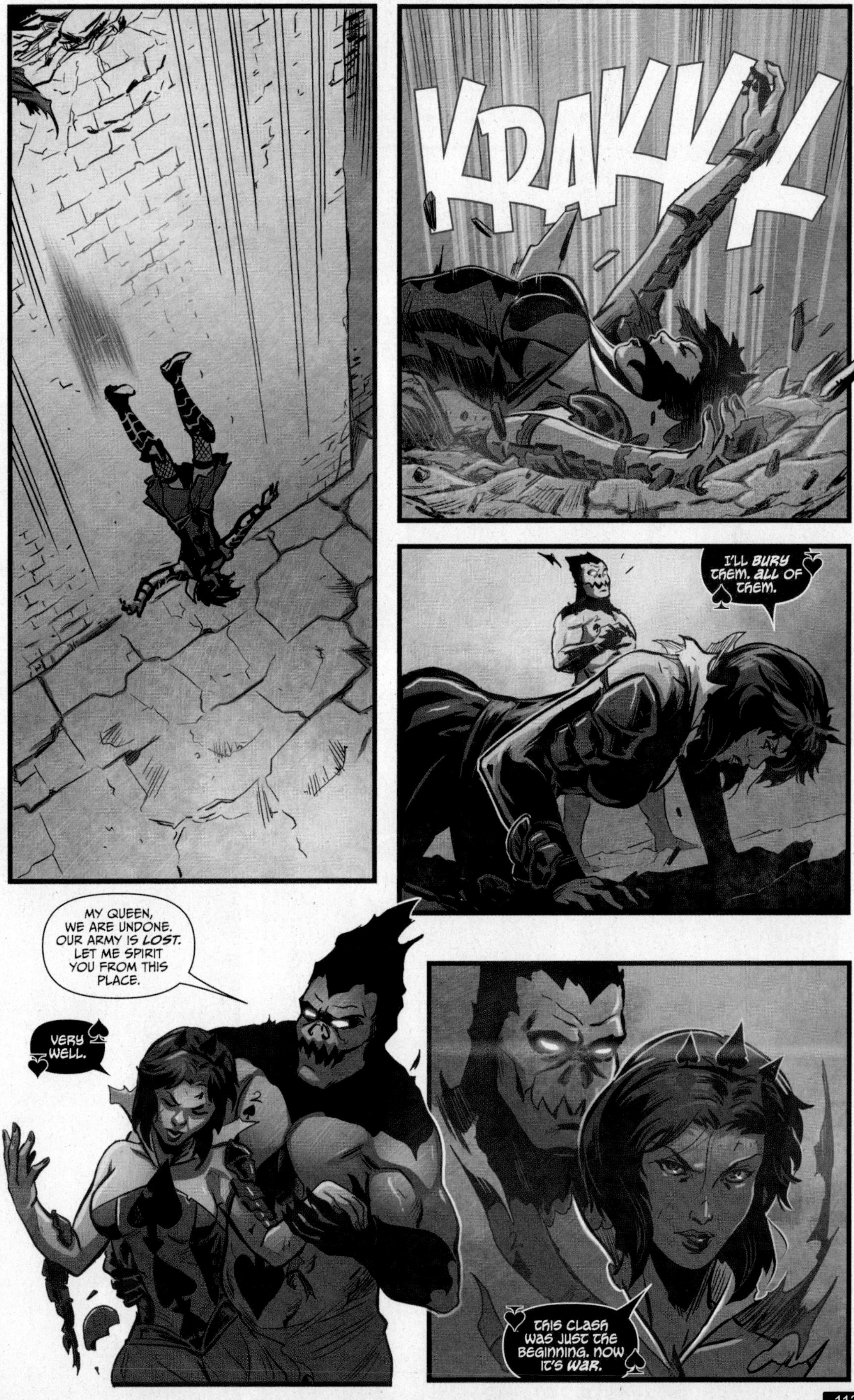
KRAKKL
I'LL BURY THEM. ALL OF THEM.
MY QUEEN, WE ARE UNDONE. OUR ARMY IS LOST. LET ME SPIRIT YOU FROM THIS PLACE.
VERY WELL.
THIS CLASH WAS JUST THE BEGINNING. NOW IT'S WAR.

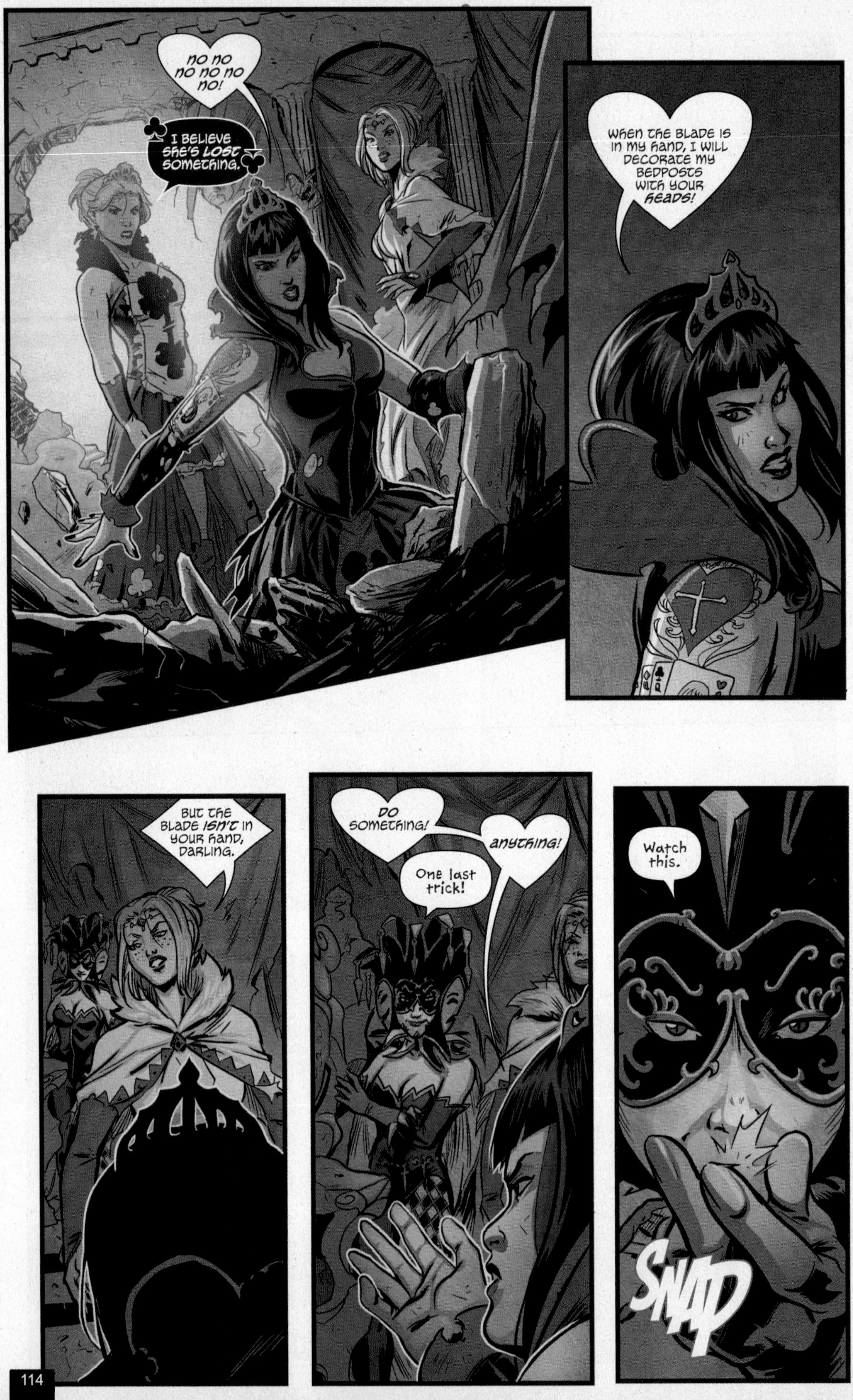
no no no no no no!
I BELIEVE SHE'S LOST SOMETHING.
WHEN THE BLADE IS IN MY HAND, I WILL DECORATE MY BEDPOSTS WITH YOUR HEADS!
BUT THE BLADE ISN'T IN YOUR HAND, DARLING.
DO SOMETHING!
ANYTHING!
One last trick!
Watch this.
SNAP

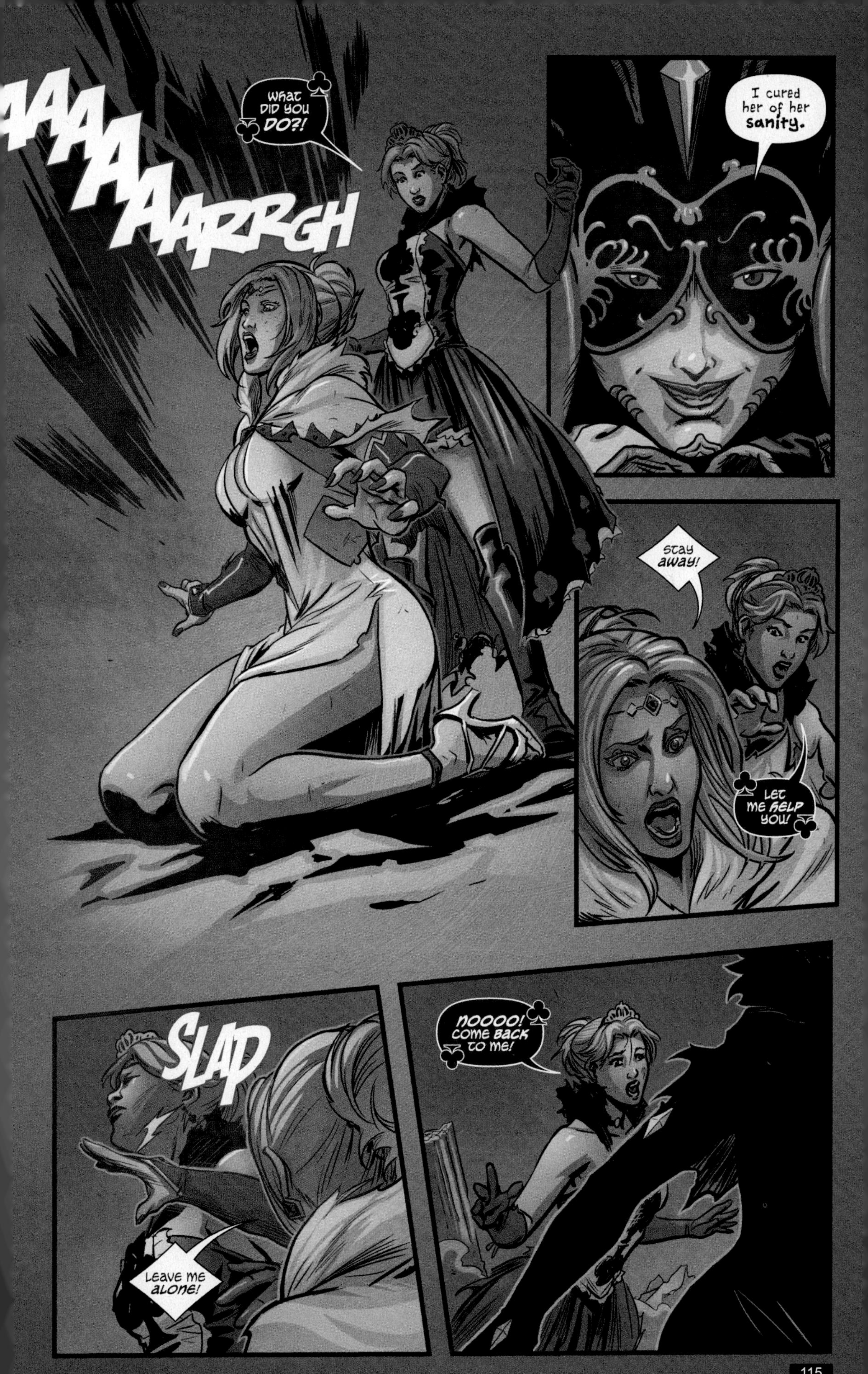
AAAAAAARRGH
WHAT DID YOU DO?!
I cured her of her sanity.
STAY away!
LET ME HELP YOU!
SLAP
LEAVE ME alone!
NOOOO! COME BACK TO ME!

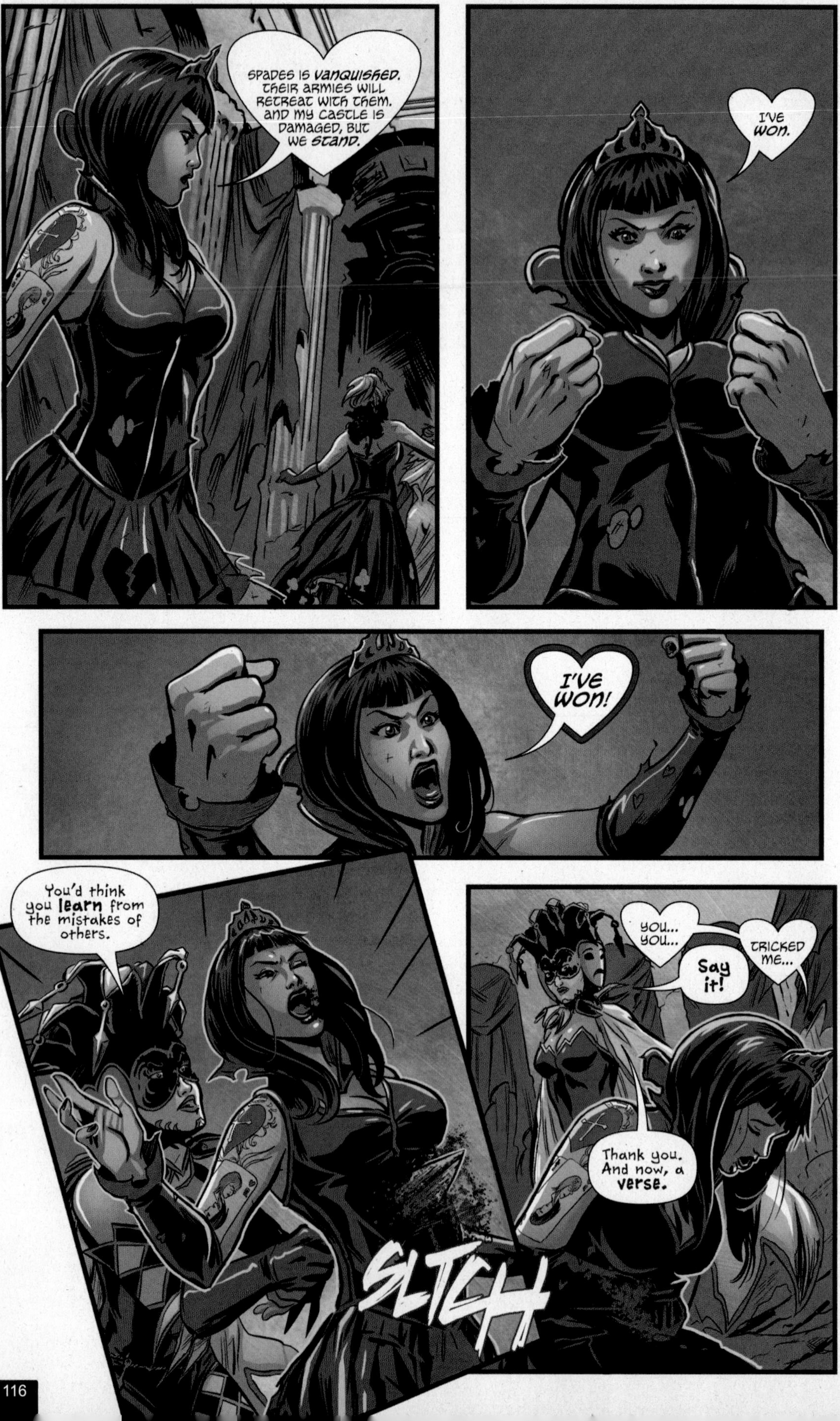
SPADES IS VANQUISHED. THEIR ARMIES WILL RETREAT WITH THEM. AND MY CASTLE IS DAMAGED, BUT WE STAND.
I'VE WON.
I'VE WON!
You'd think you learn from the mistakes of others.
SLTCH
YOU... YOU...
TRICKED ME...
Say it!
Thank you. And now, a verse.

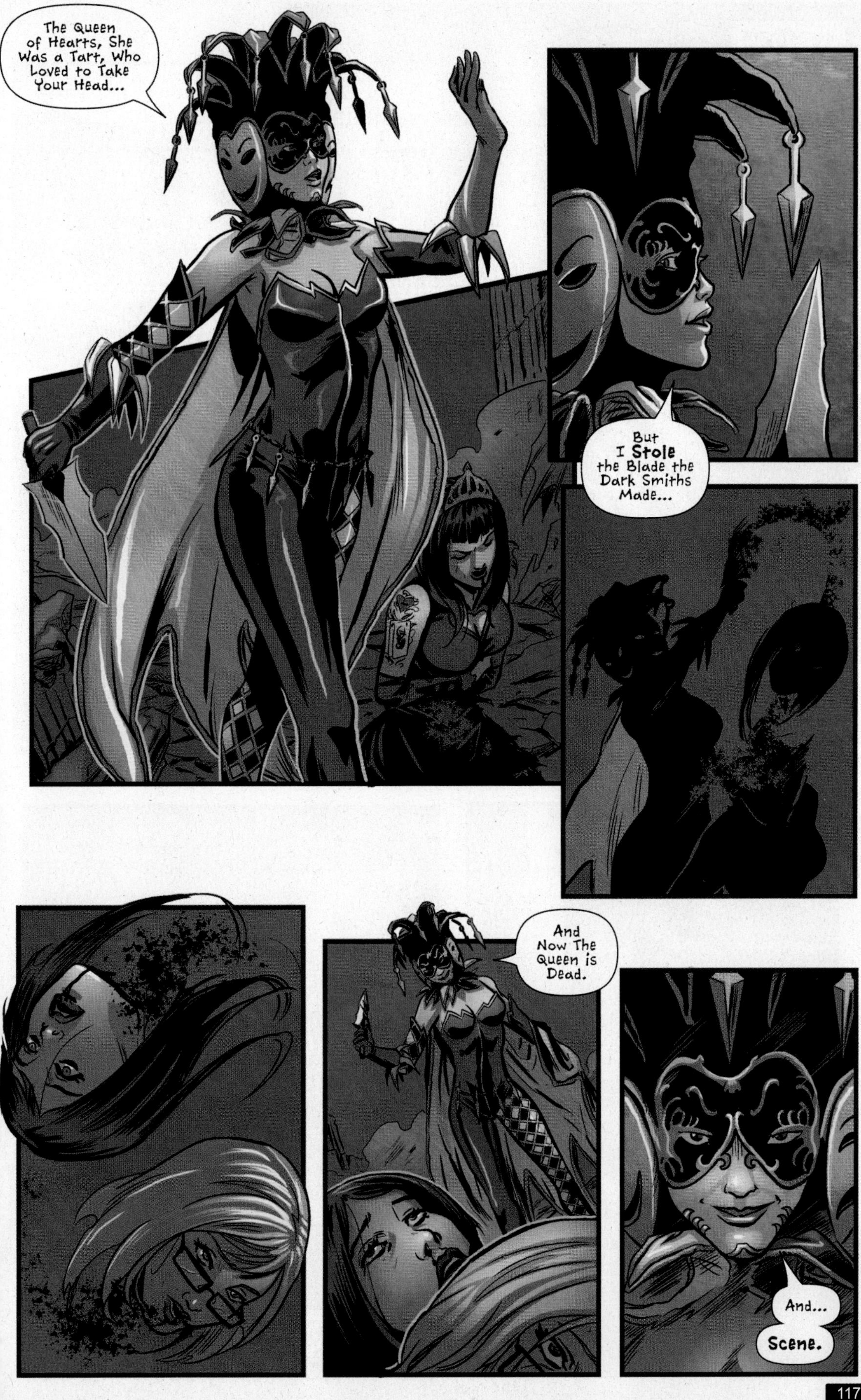
The Queen of Hearts, She Was a Tart, Who Loved to Take Your Head...
But I Stole the Blade the Dark Smiths Made...
And Now The Queen is Dead.
And...
Scene.

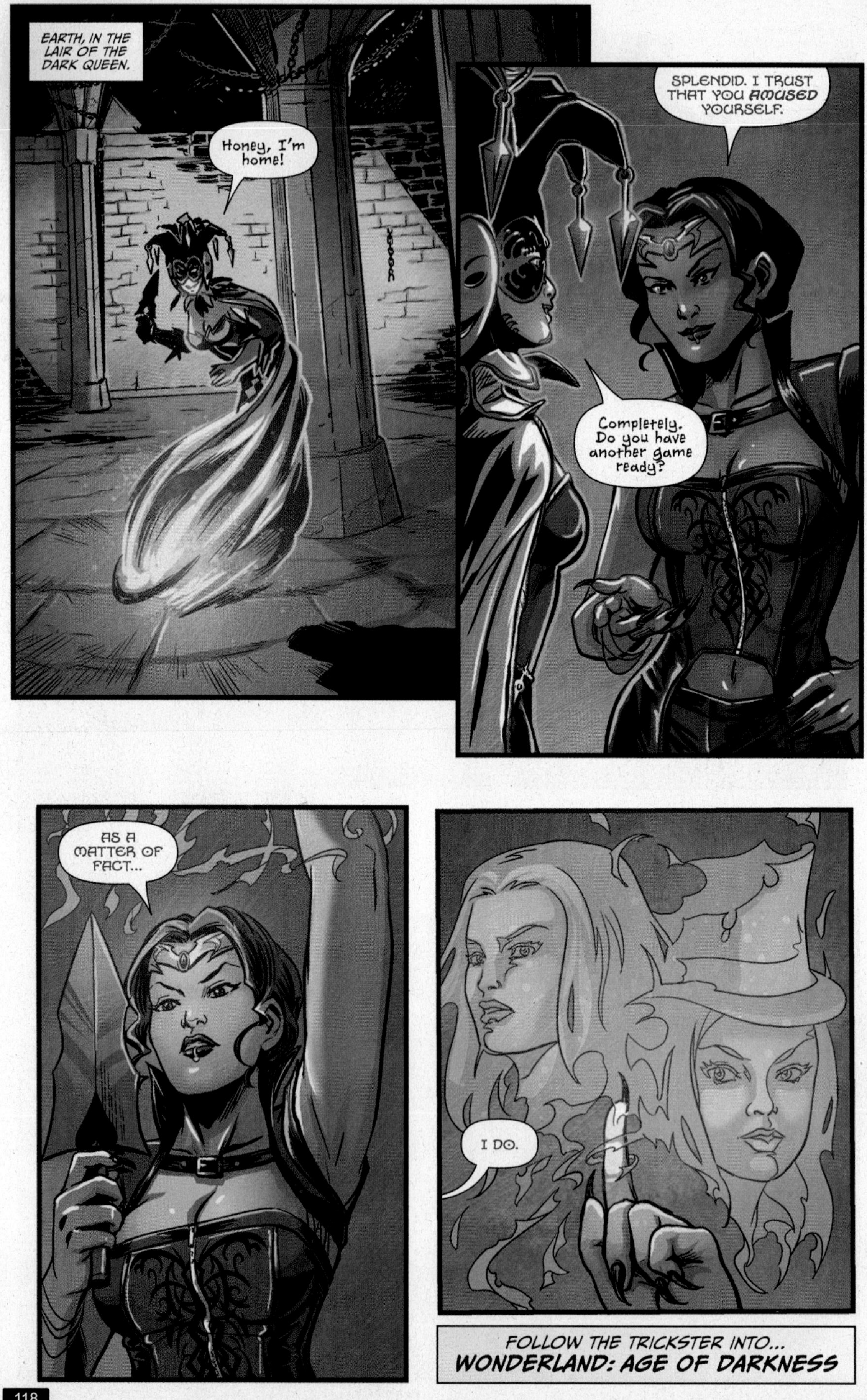
EARTH, IN THE LAIR OF THE DARK QUEEN.
Honey, I'm home!
SPLENDID. I TRUST THAT YOU AMUSED YOURSELF.
Completely. Do you have another game ready?
AS A MATTER OF FACT...
I DO.
FOLLOW THE TRICKSTER INTO...
WONDERLAND: AGE OF DARKNESS

Grimm Fairy Tales presents

Wonderland

Clash of Queens

Age of Darkness

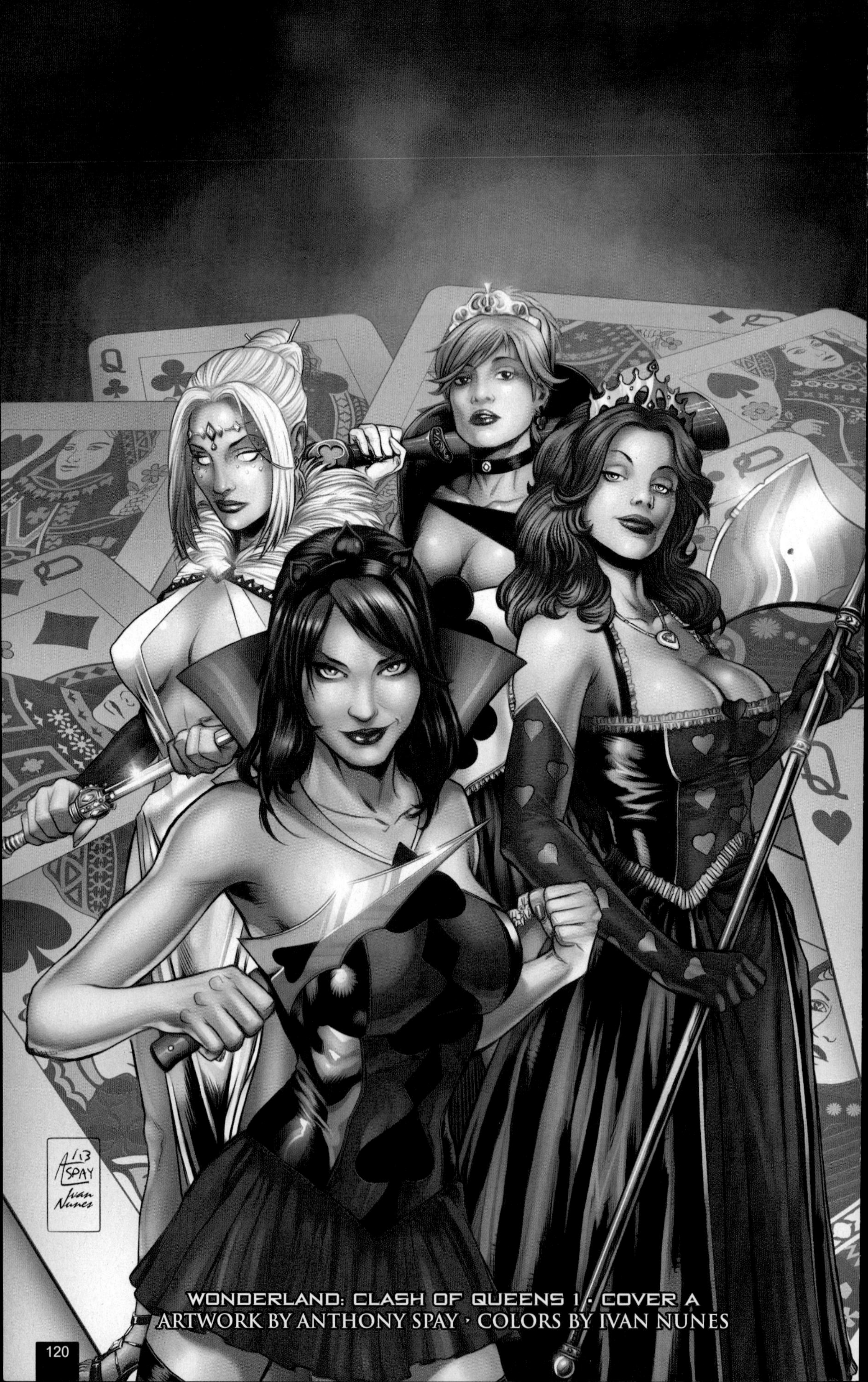
A 13
SPAY
Ivan
Nunes

WONDERLAND: CLASH OF QUEENS 1 · COVER A
ARTWORK BY ANTHONY SPAY · COLORS BY IVAN NUNES

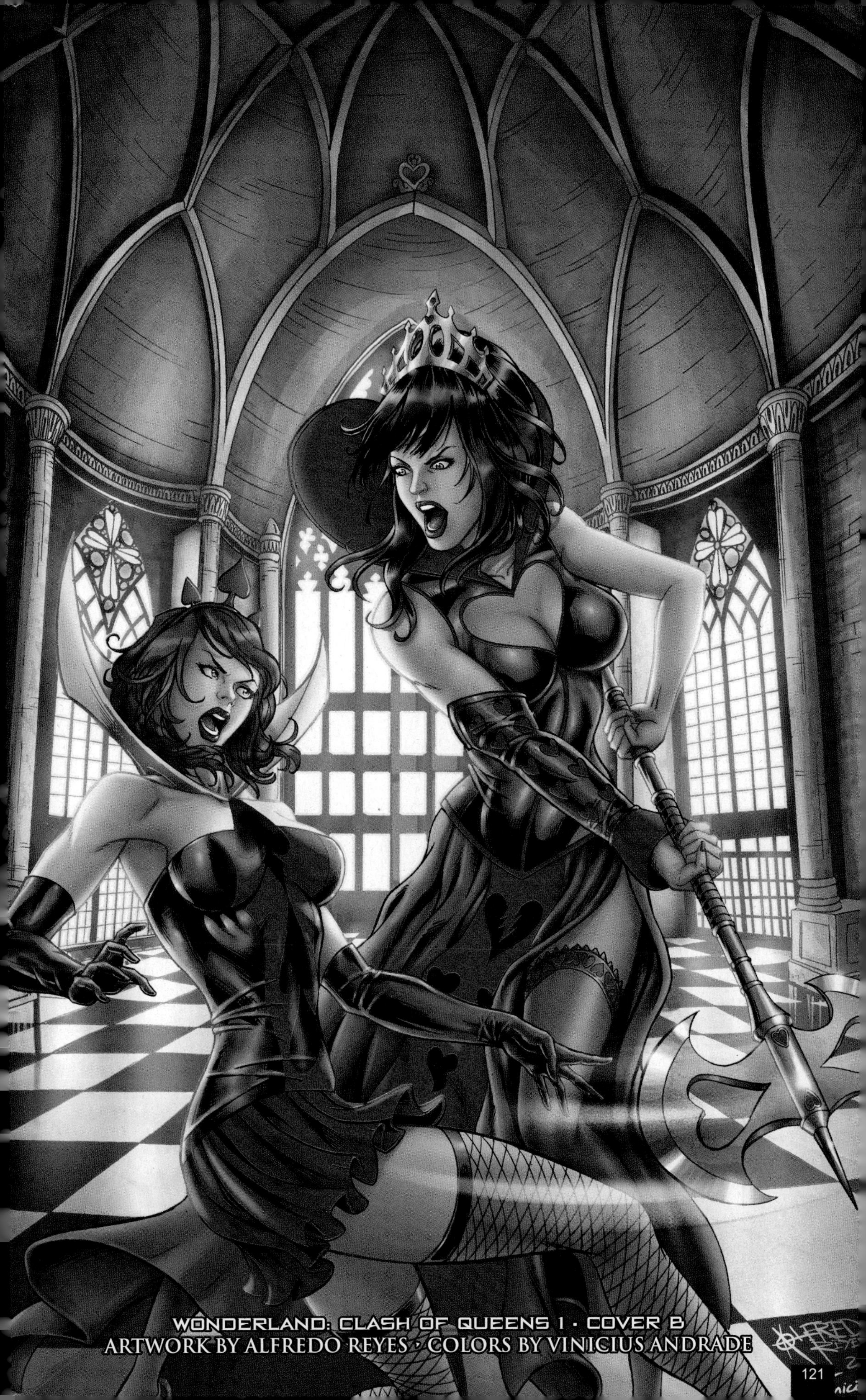

WONDERLAND: CLASH OF QUEENS 1 · COVER B
ARTWORK BY ALFREDO REYES · COLORS BY VINICIUS ANDRADE

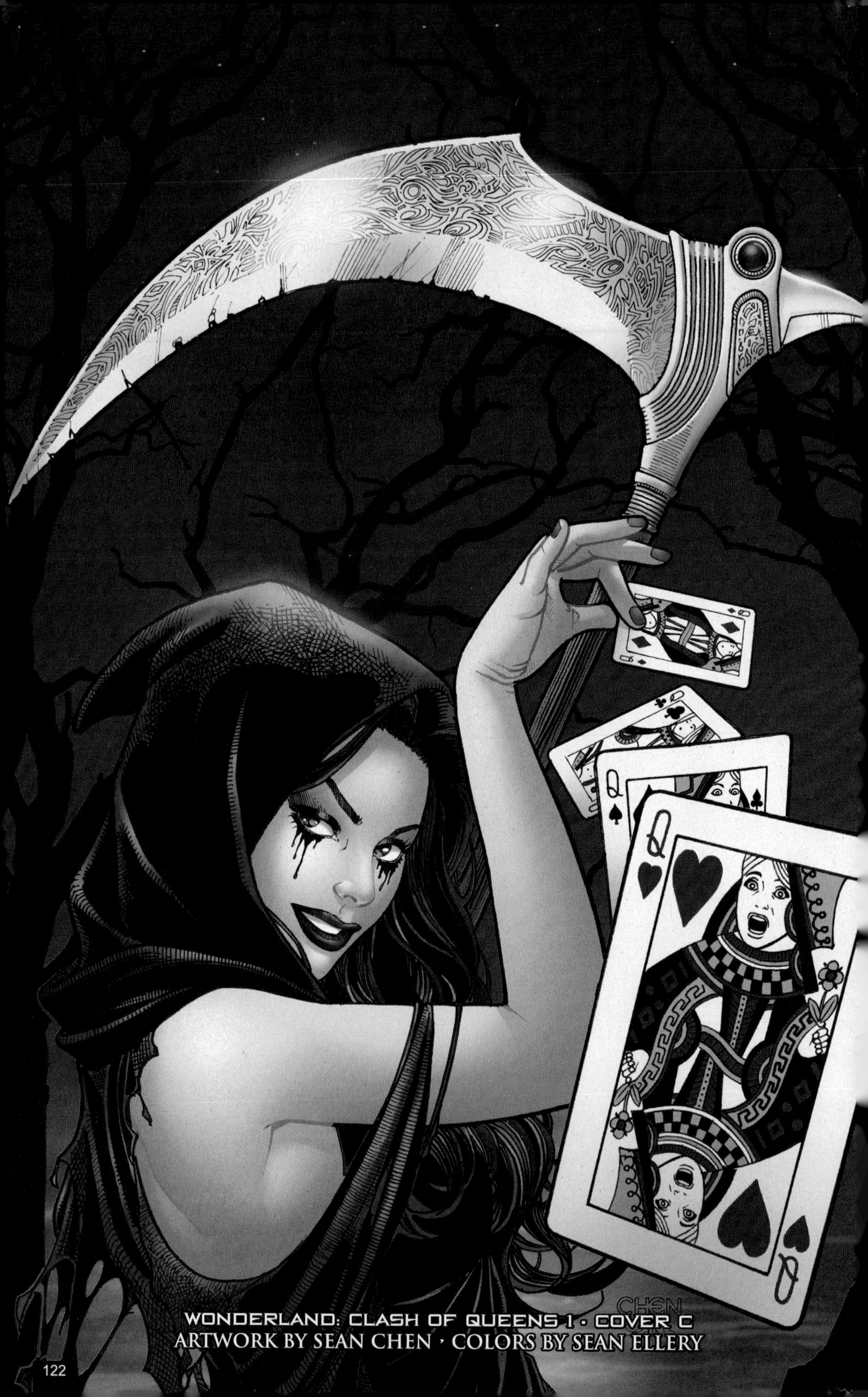
CHEN

WONDERLAND: CLASH OF QUEENS 1 · COVER C
ARTWORK BY SEAN CHEN · COLORS BY SEAN ELLERY

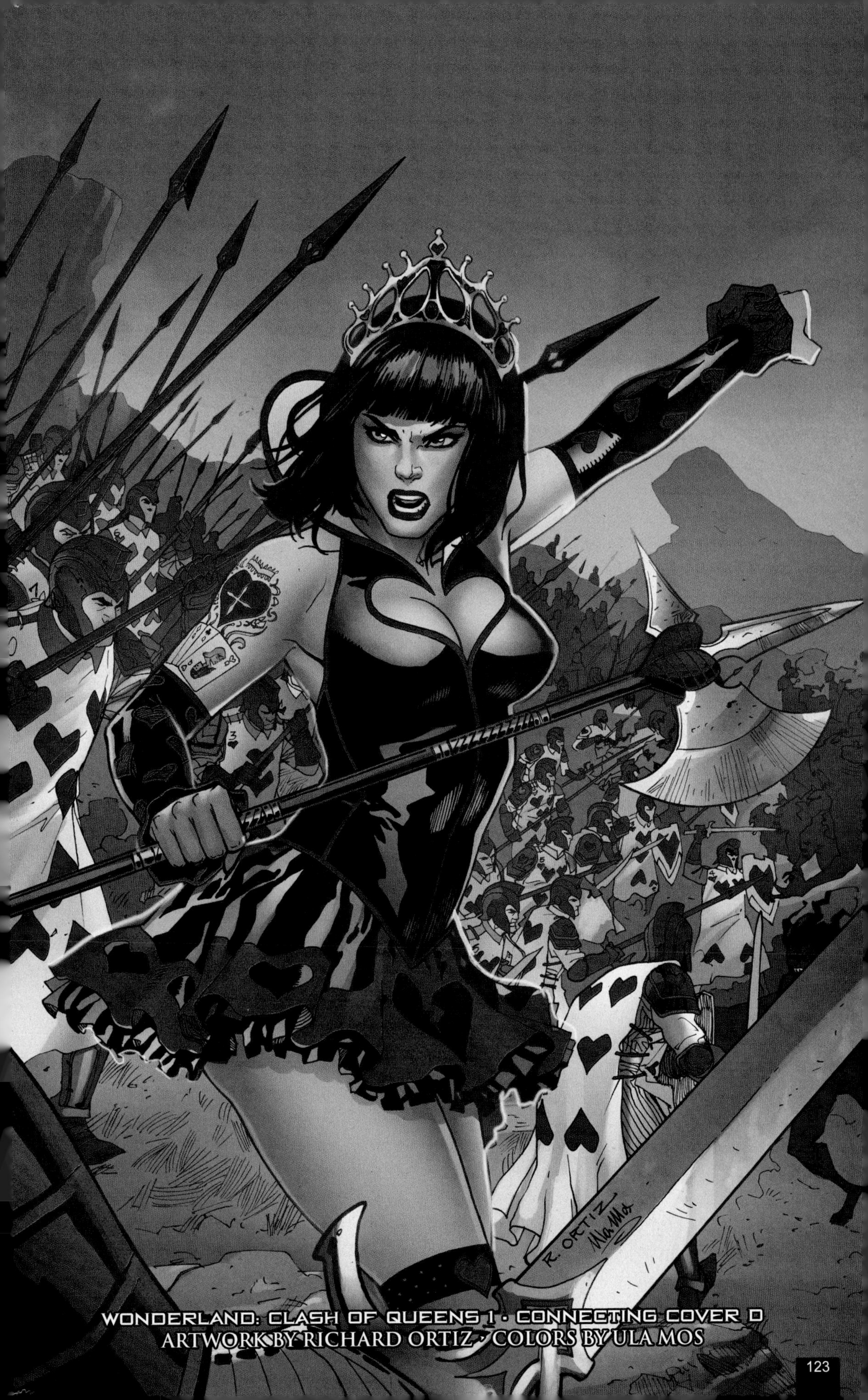
R. ORTIZ

WONDERLAND: CLASH OF QUEENS 1 · CONNECTING COVER D
ARTWORK BY RICHARD ORTIZ · COLORS BY ULA MOS

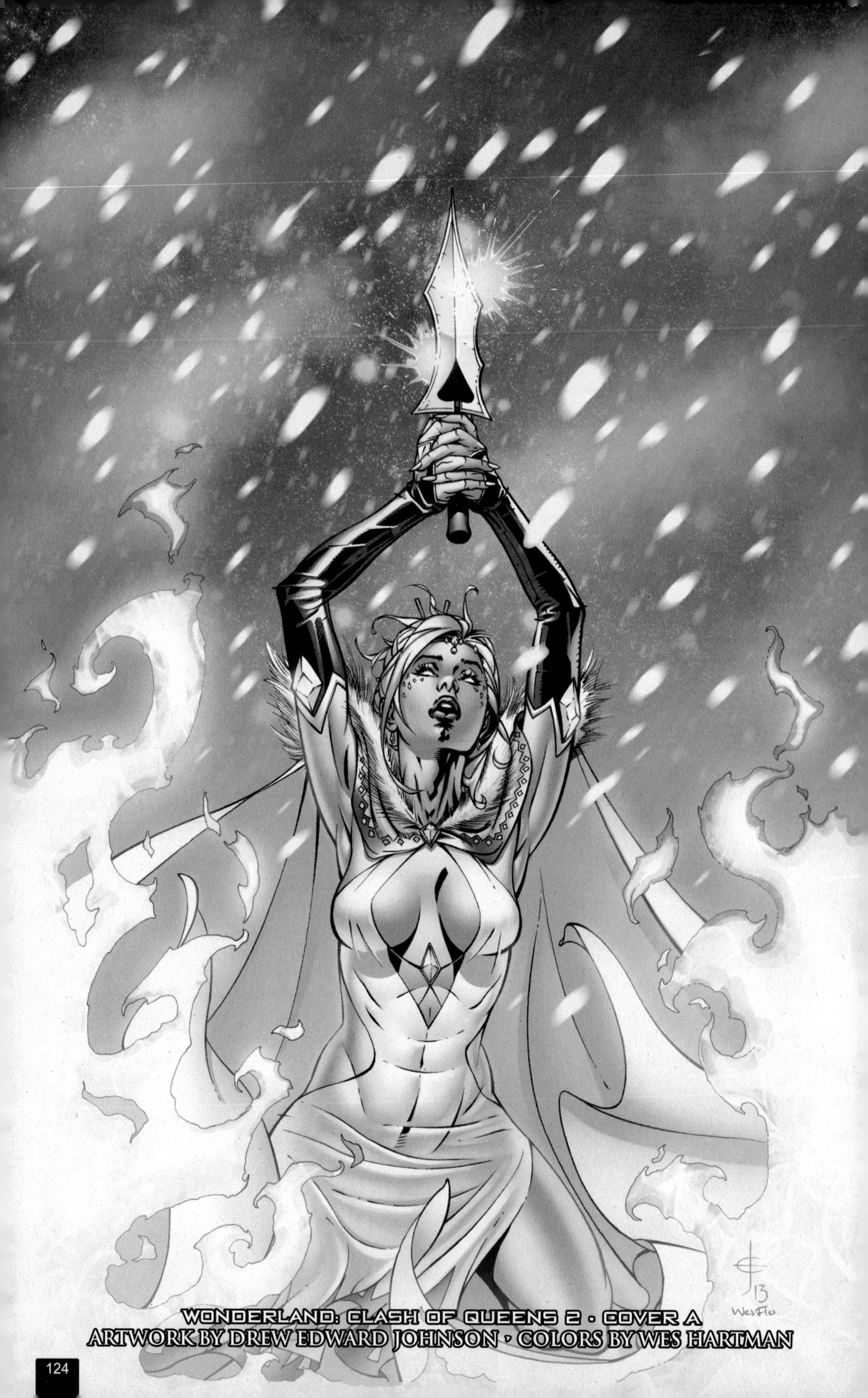

WONDERLAND: CLASH OF QUEENS 2 • COVER A
ARTWORK BY DREW EDWARD JOHNSON • COLORS BY WES HARTMAN

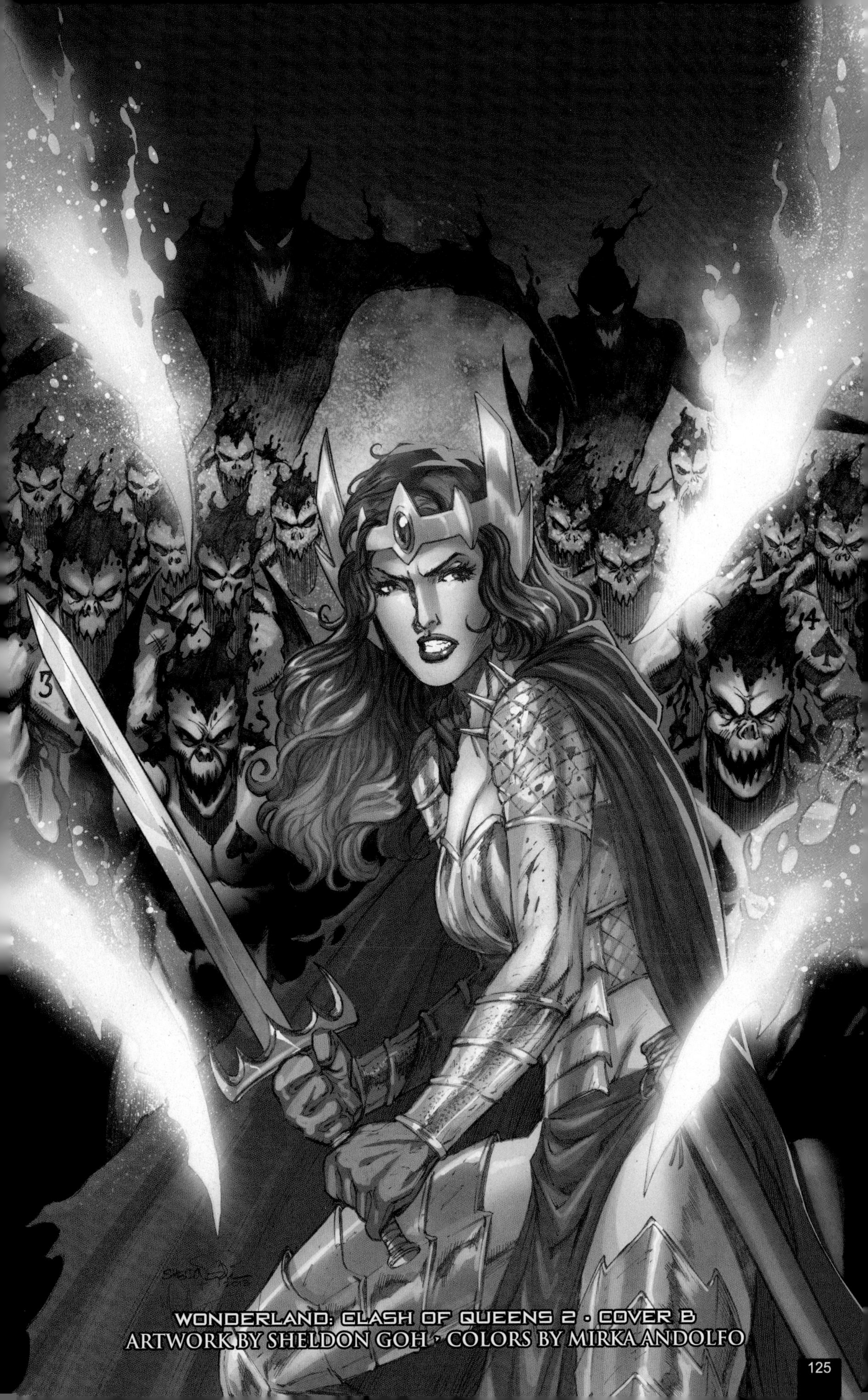

WONDERLAND: CLASH OF QUEENS 2 • COVER B
ARTWORK BY SHELDON GOH • COLORS BY MIRKA ANDOLFO

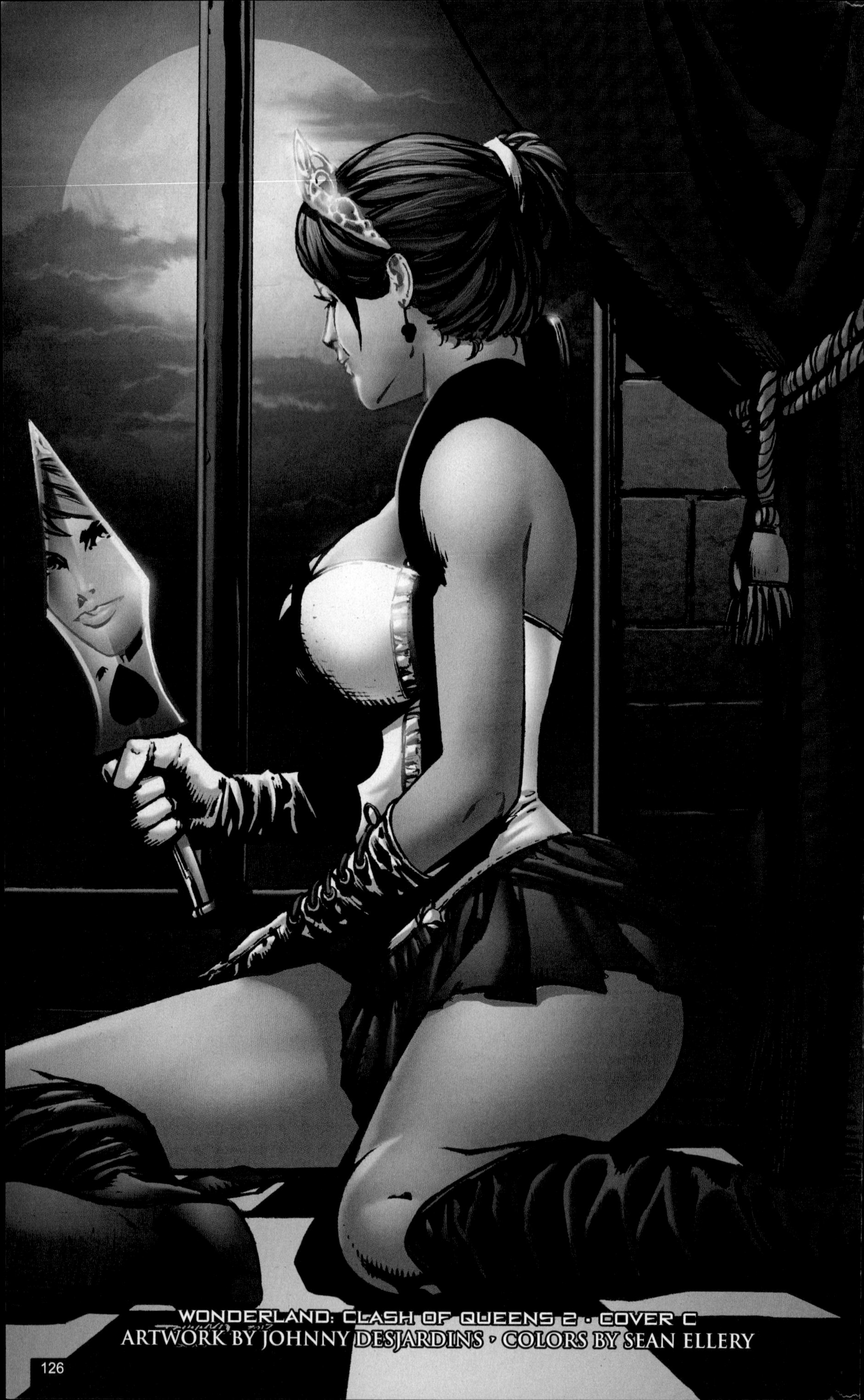

WONDERLAND: CLASH OF QUEENS 2 • COVER C
ARTWORK BY JOHNNY DESJARDINS • COLORS BY SEAN ELLERY

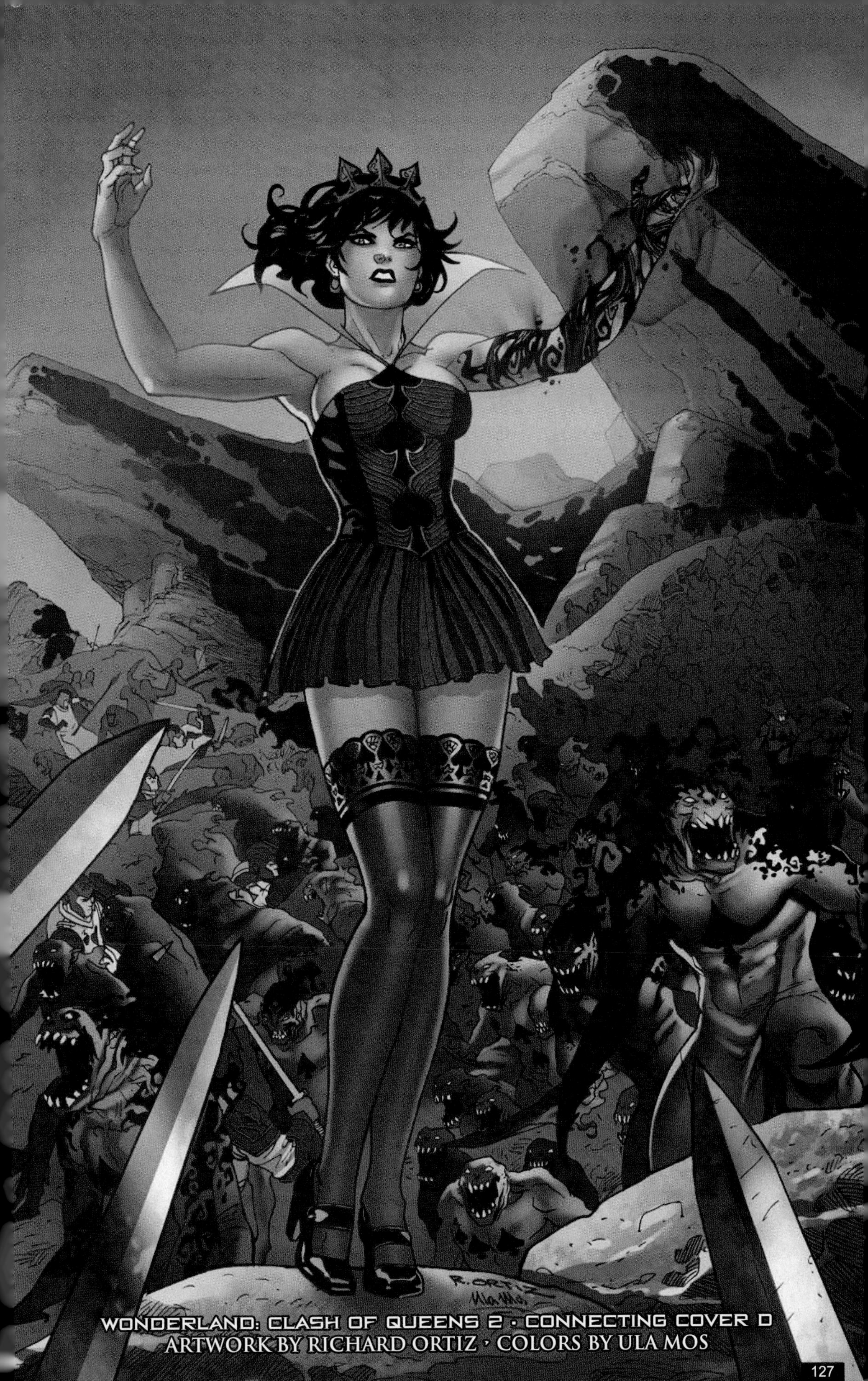
R.ORTIZ

WONDERLAND: CLASH OF QUEENS 2 · CONNECTING COVER D
ARTWORK BY RICHARD ORTIZ · COLORS BY ULA MOS

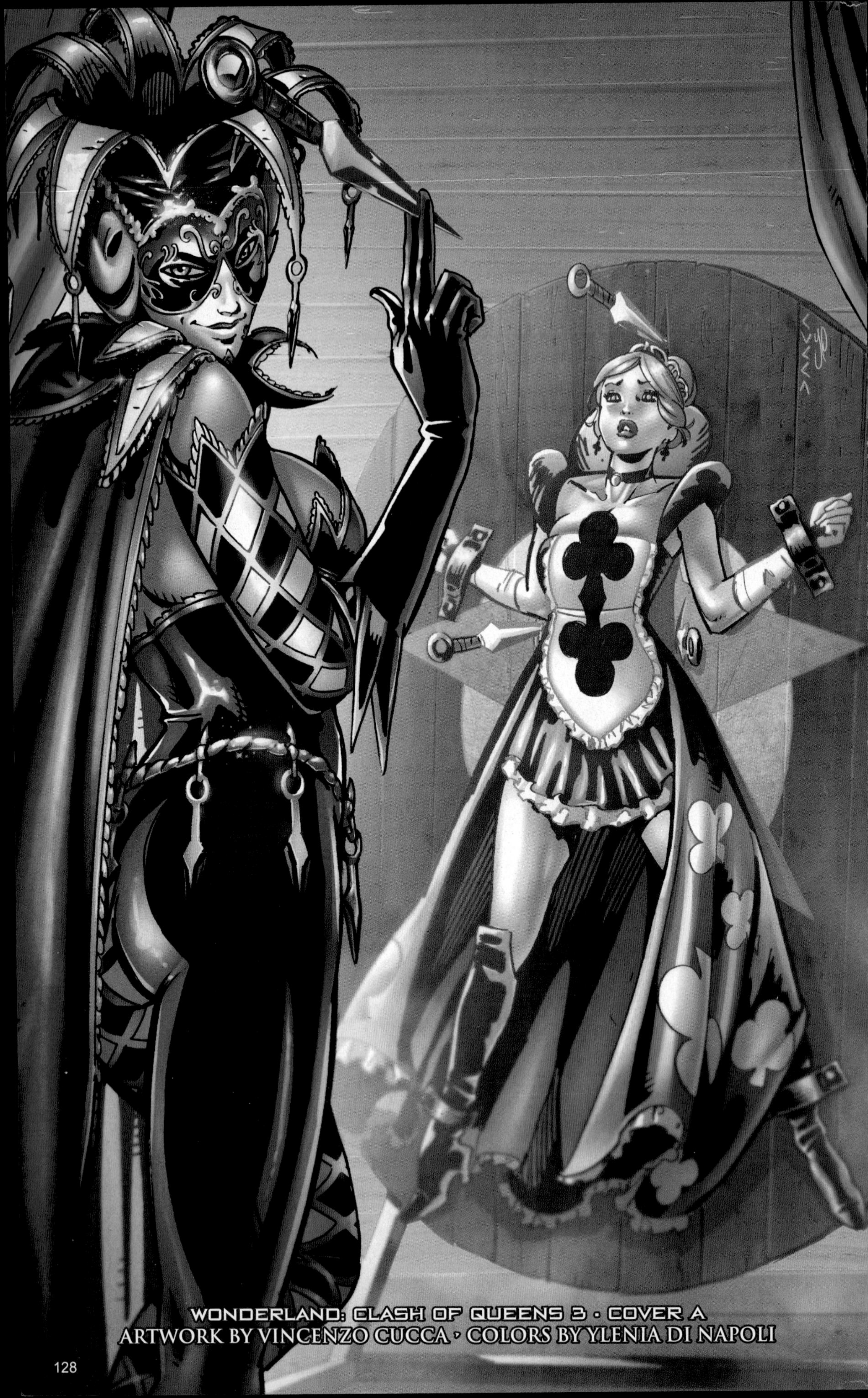

WONDERLAND: CLASH OF QUEENS 3 • COVER A
ARTWORK BY VINCENZO CUCCA • COLORS BY YLENIA DI NAPOLI

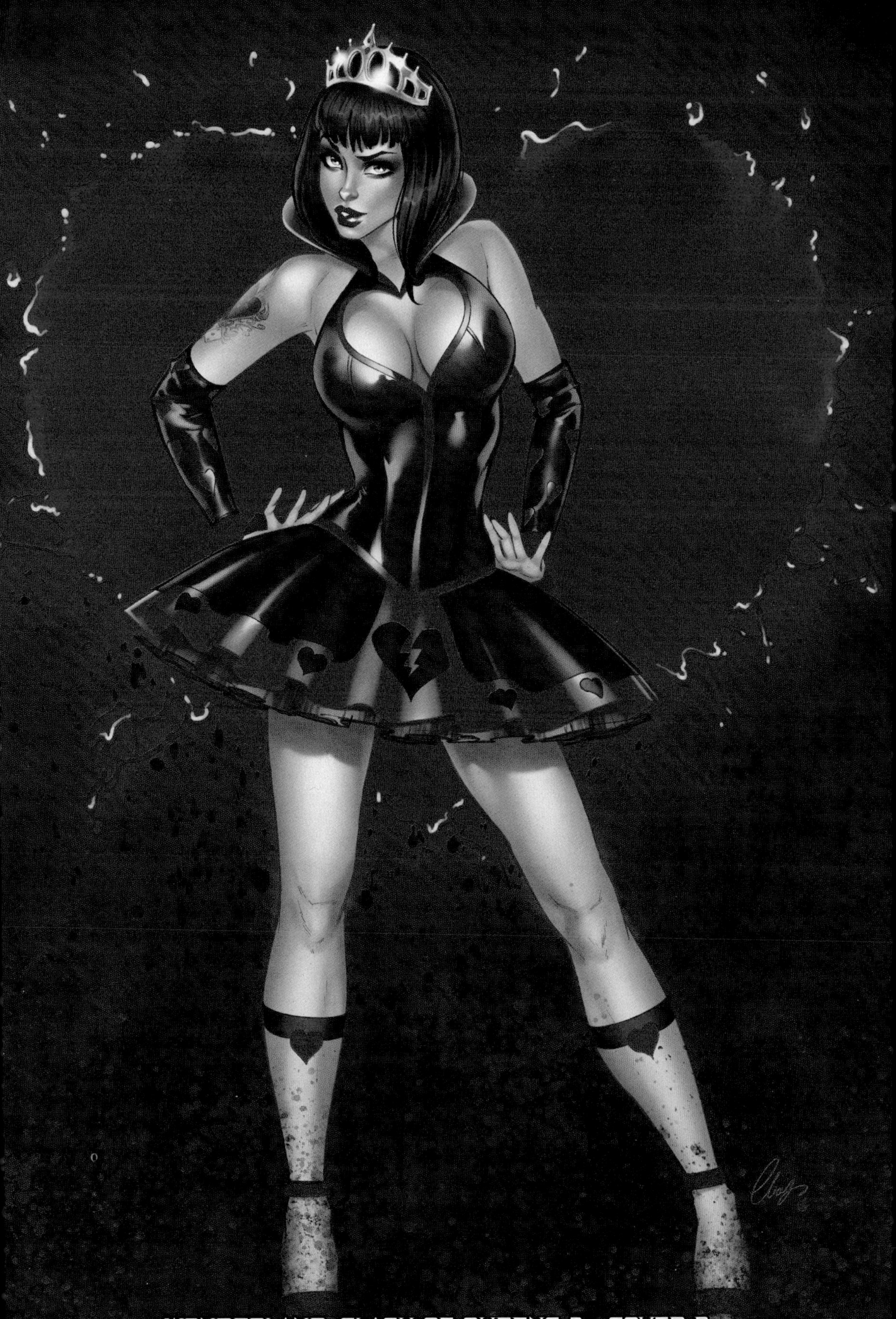

WONDERLAND: CLASH OF QUEENS 3 · COVER B
ARTWORK BY ELIAS CHATZOUDIS

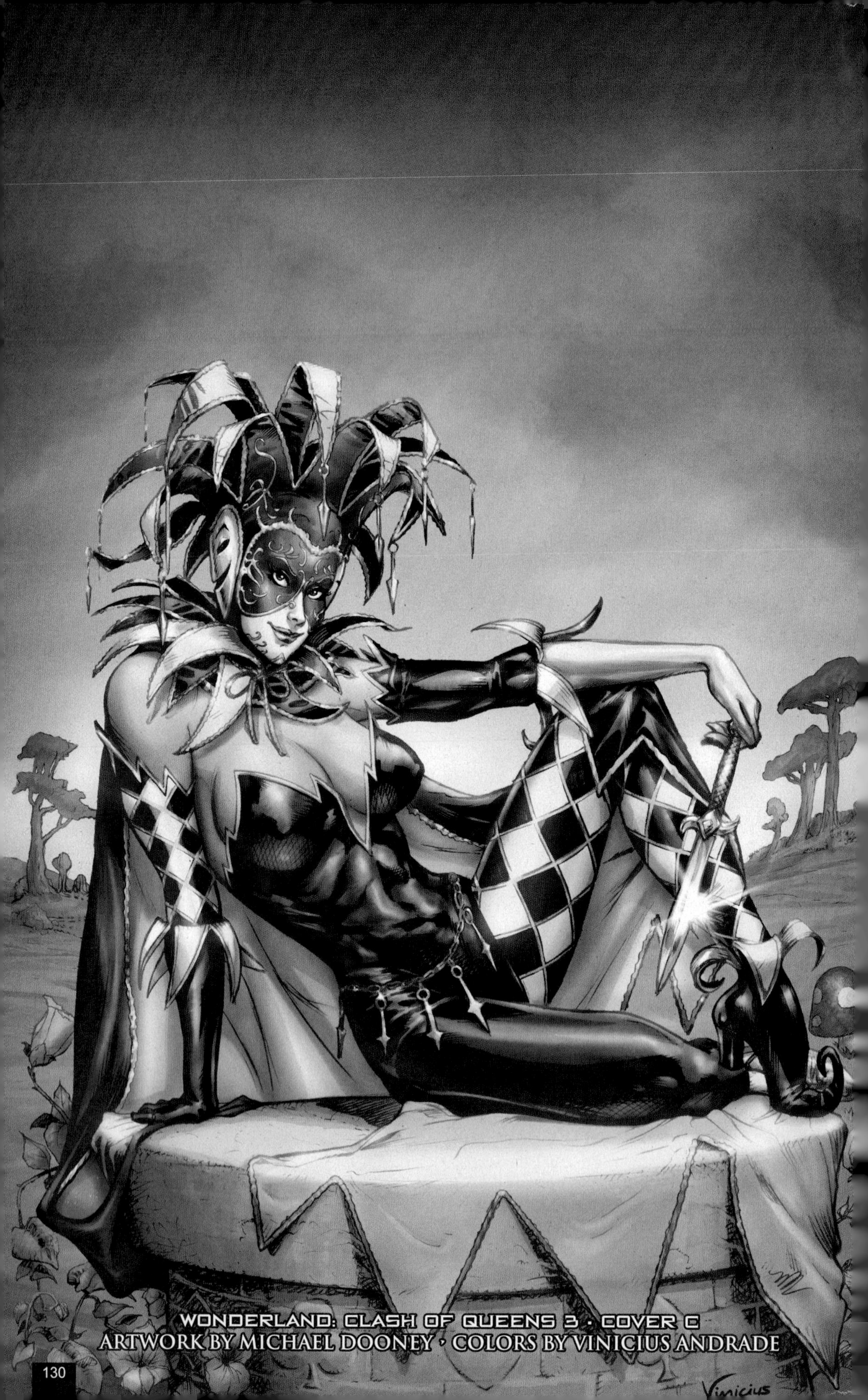
Vinicius

WONDERLAND: CLASH OF QUEENS 3 · COVER C
ARTWORK BY MICHAEL DOONEY › COLORS BY VINICIUS ANDRADE

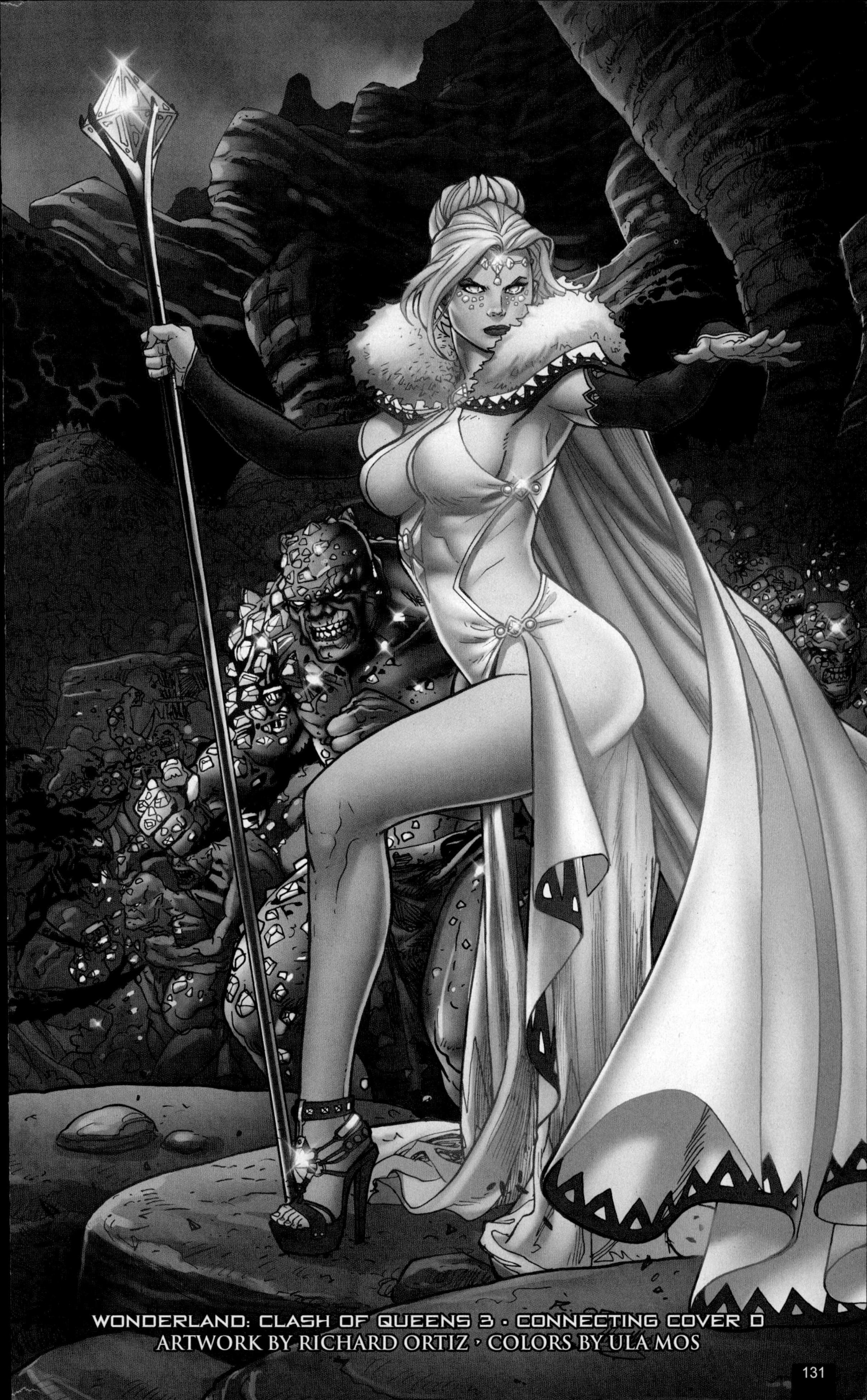

WONDERLAND: CLASH OF QUEENS 3 • CONNECTING COVER D
ARTWORK BY RICHARD ORTIZ • COLORS BY ULA MOS

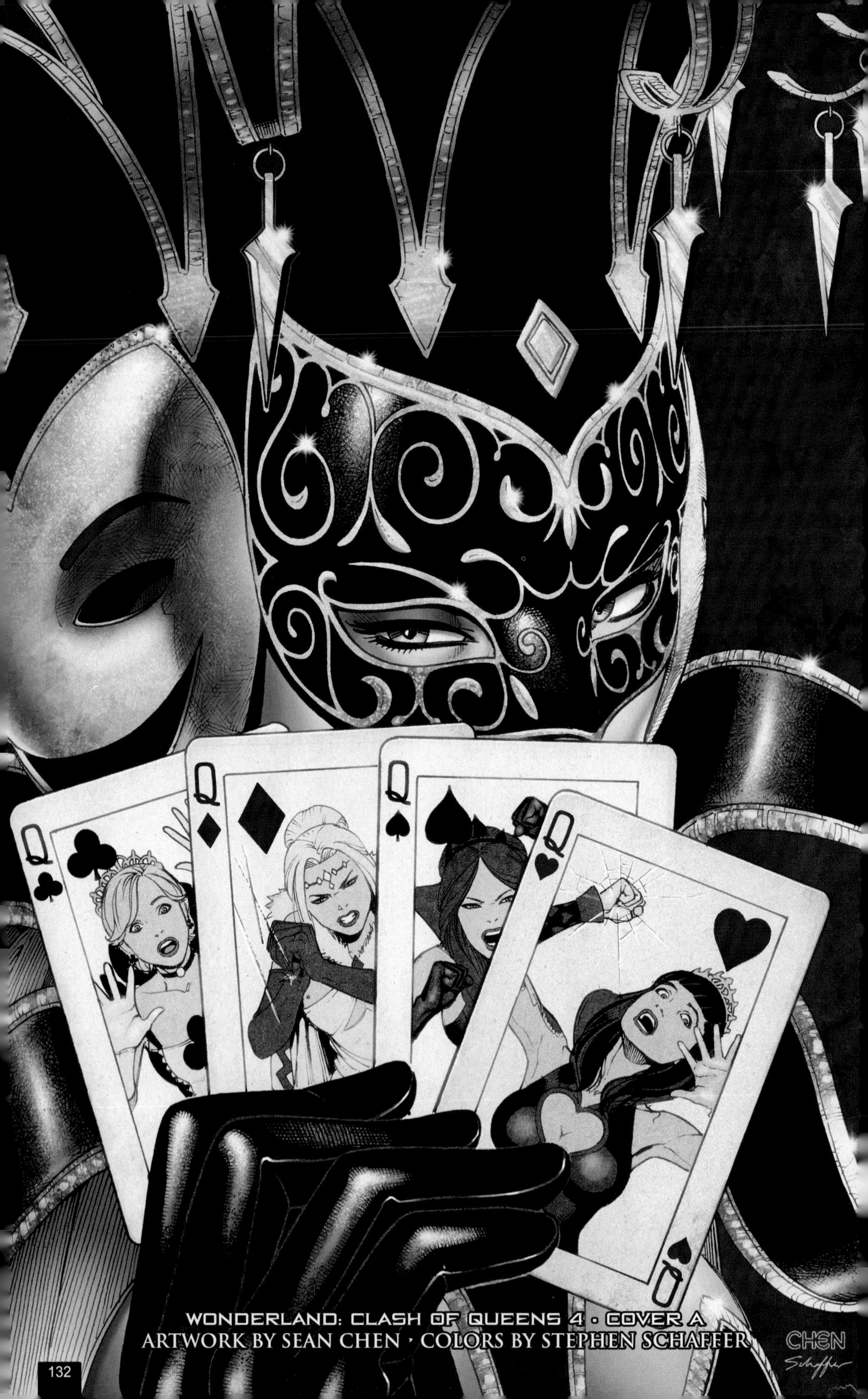
CHEN
Schaffer

WONDERLAND: CLASH OF QUEENS 4 · COVER A
ARTWORK BY SEAN CHEN · COLORS BY STEPHEN SCHAFFER

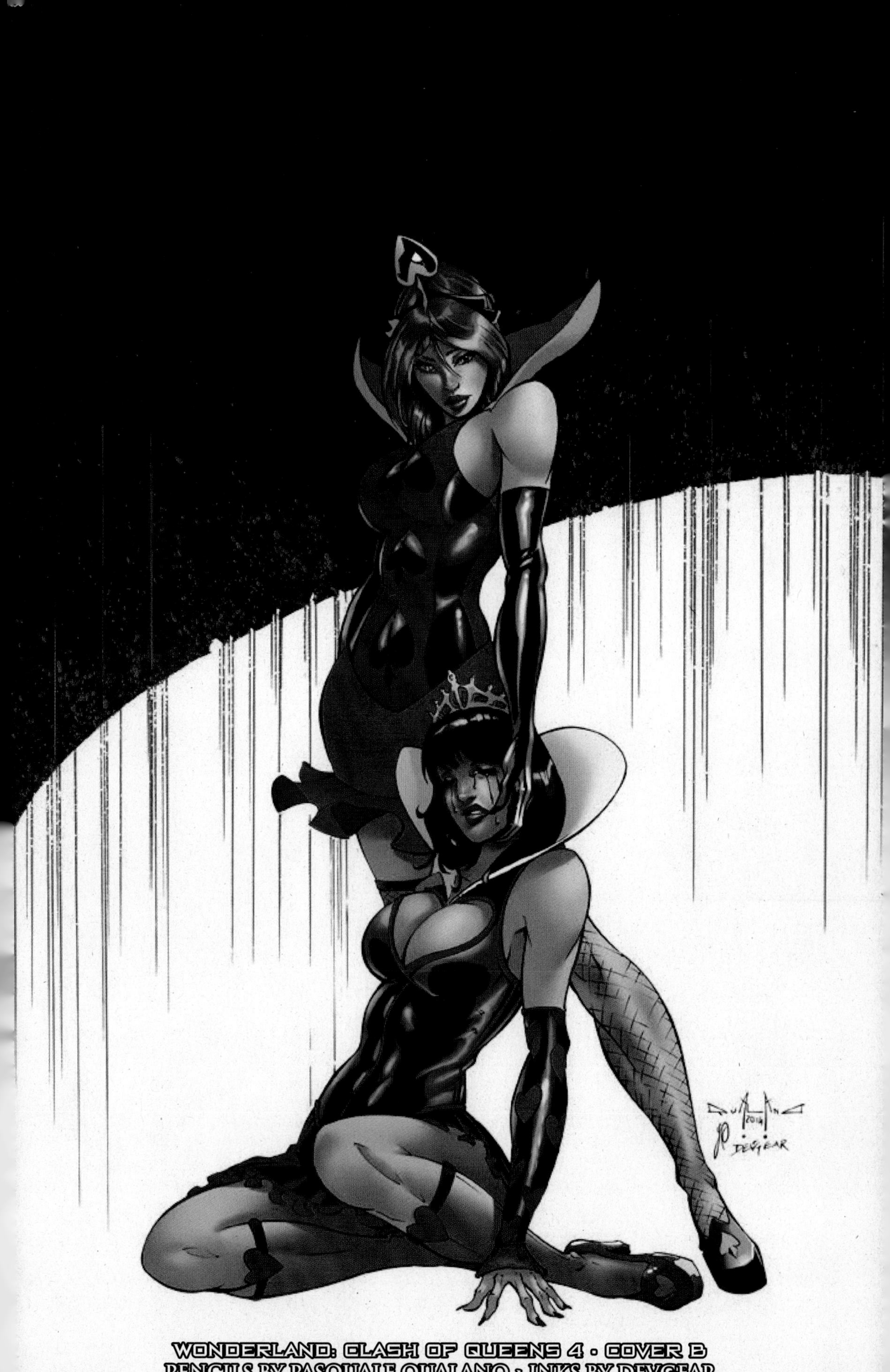

WONDERLAND: CLASH OF QUEENS 4 • COVER B
PENCILS BY PASQUALE QUALANO • INKS BY DEVGEAR
COLORS BY YLENIA DI NAPOLI

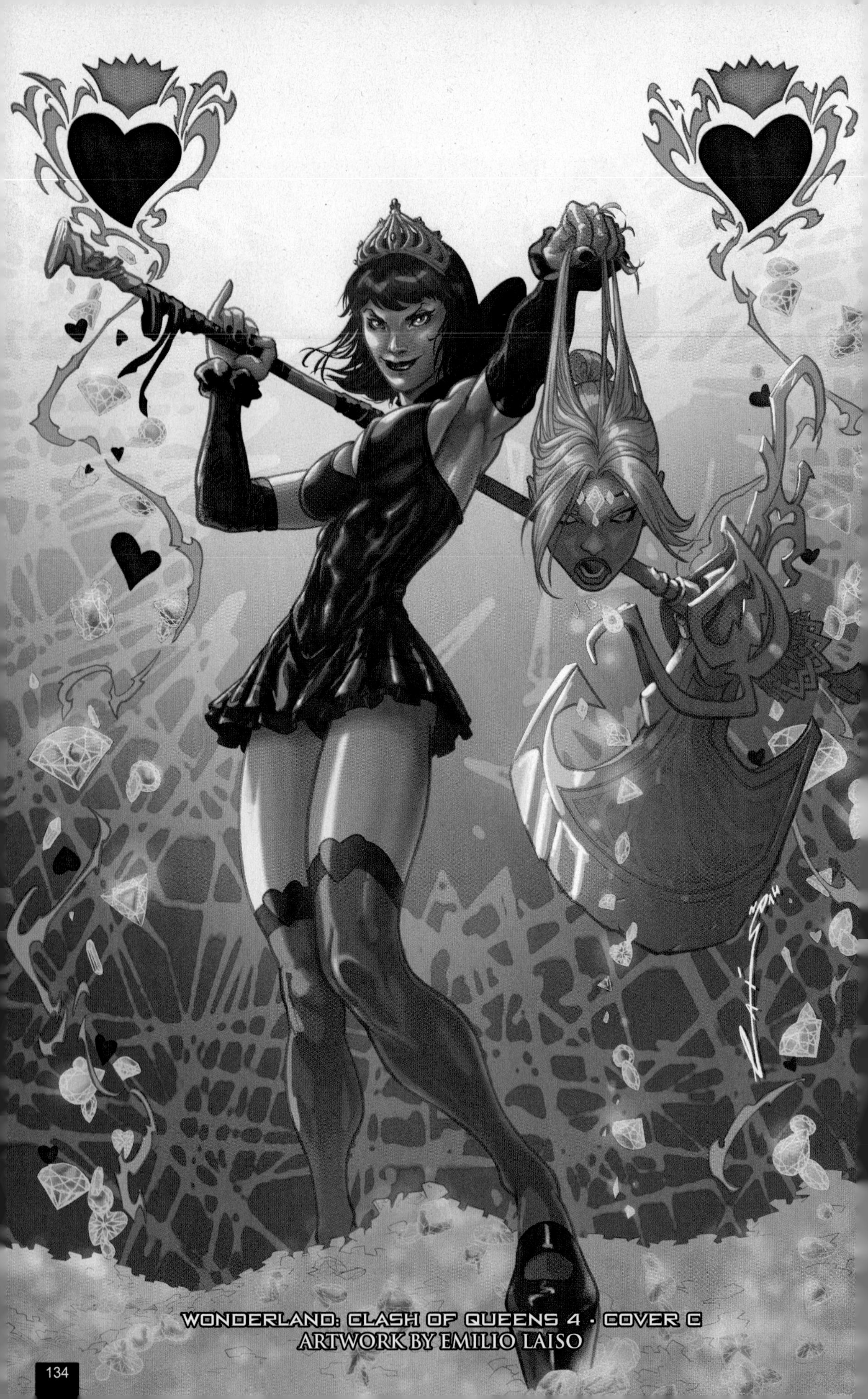

WONDERLAND: CLASH OF QUEENS 4 - COVER C
ARTWORK BY EMILIO LAISO

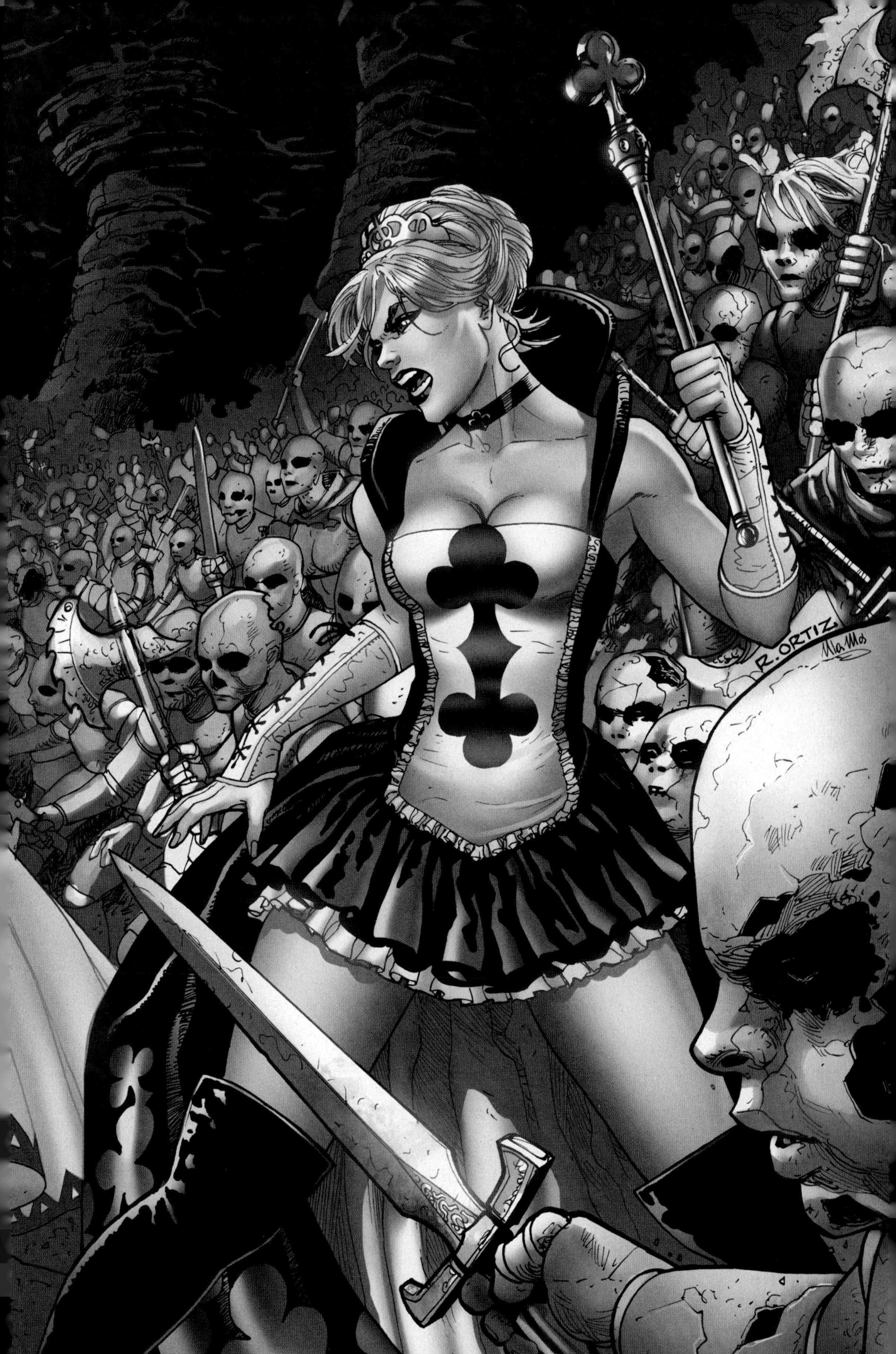
R. ORTIZ
Ula Mos

WONDERLAND: CLASH OF QUEENS 4 • CONNECTING COVER D
ARTWORK BY RICHARD ORTIZ • COLORS BY ULA MOS

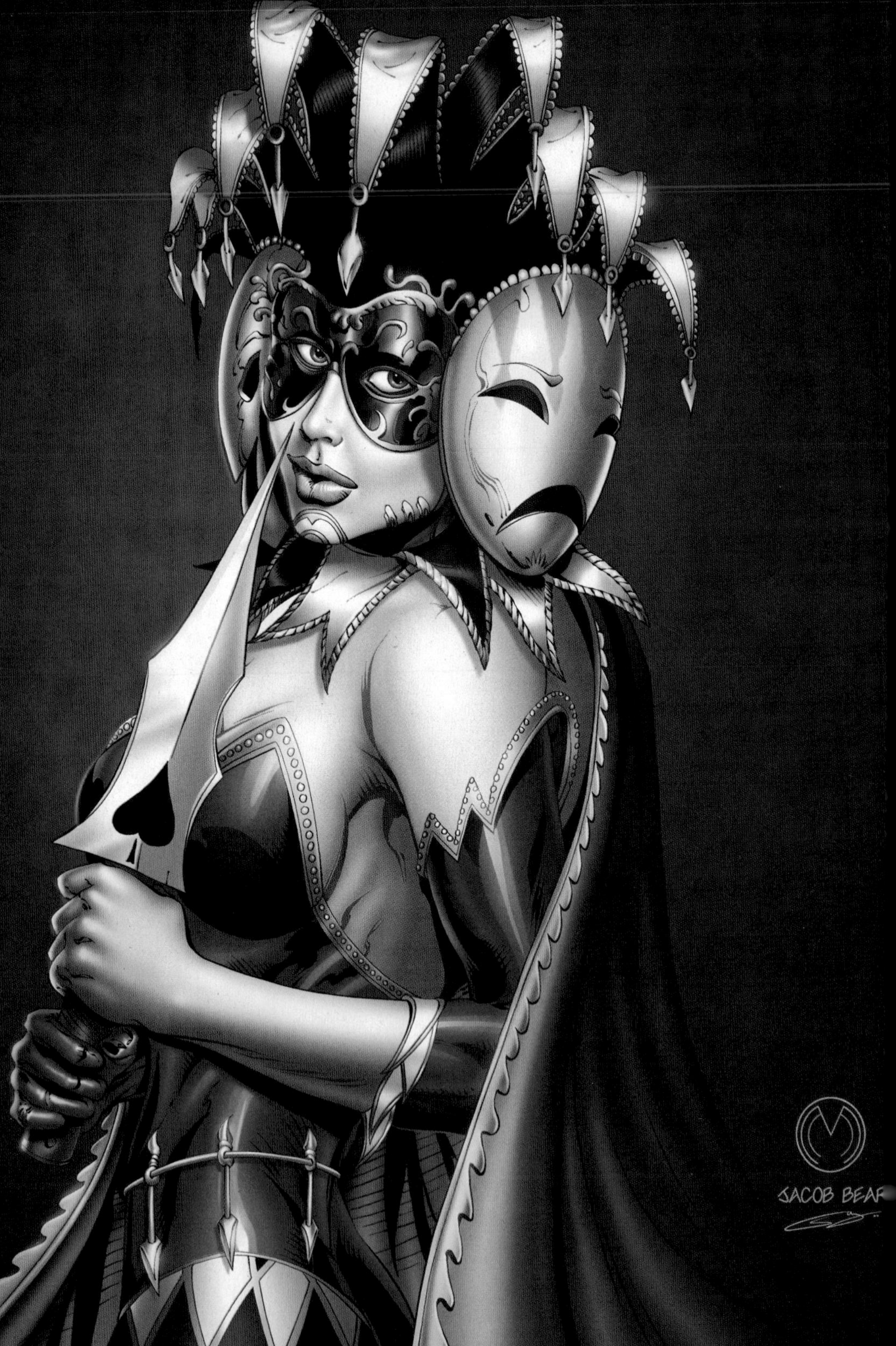
JACOB BEAR

WONDERLAND: CLASH OF QUEENS 5 • COVER A
PENCILS BY MARAT MYCHAELS • INKS BY JACOB BEAR
COLORS BY SANJU NIVANGUNE

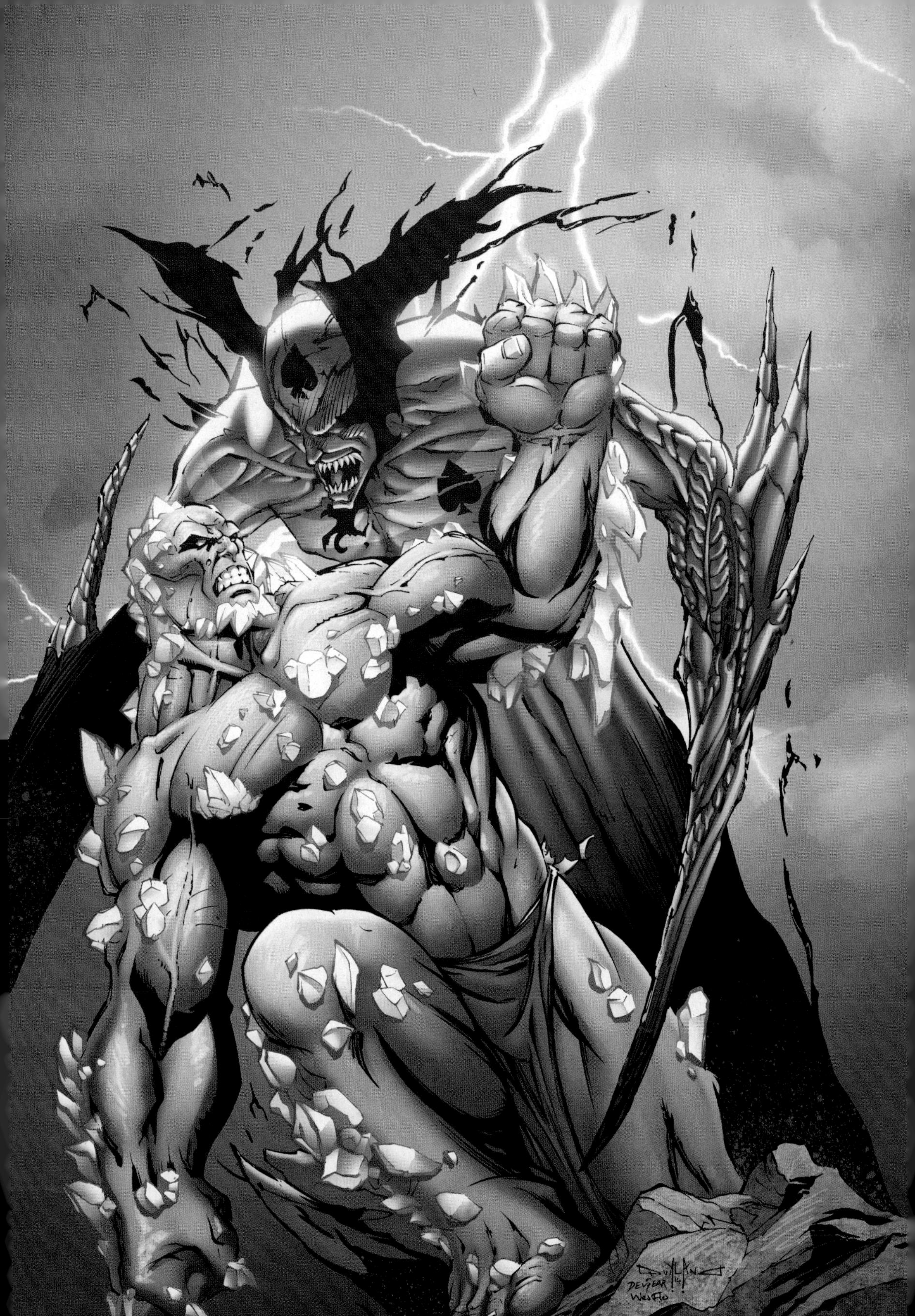

WONDERLAND: CLASH OF QUEENS 5 · COVER B
PENCILS BY PASQUALE QUALANO · INKS BY DEVGEAR
COLORS BY WES HARTMAN

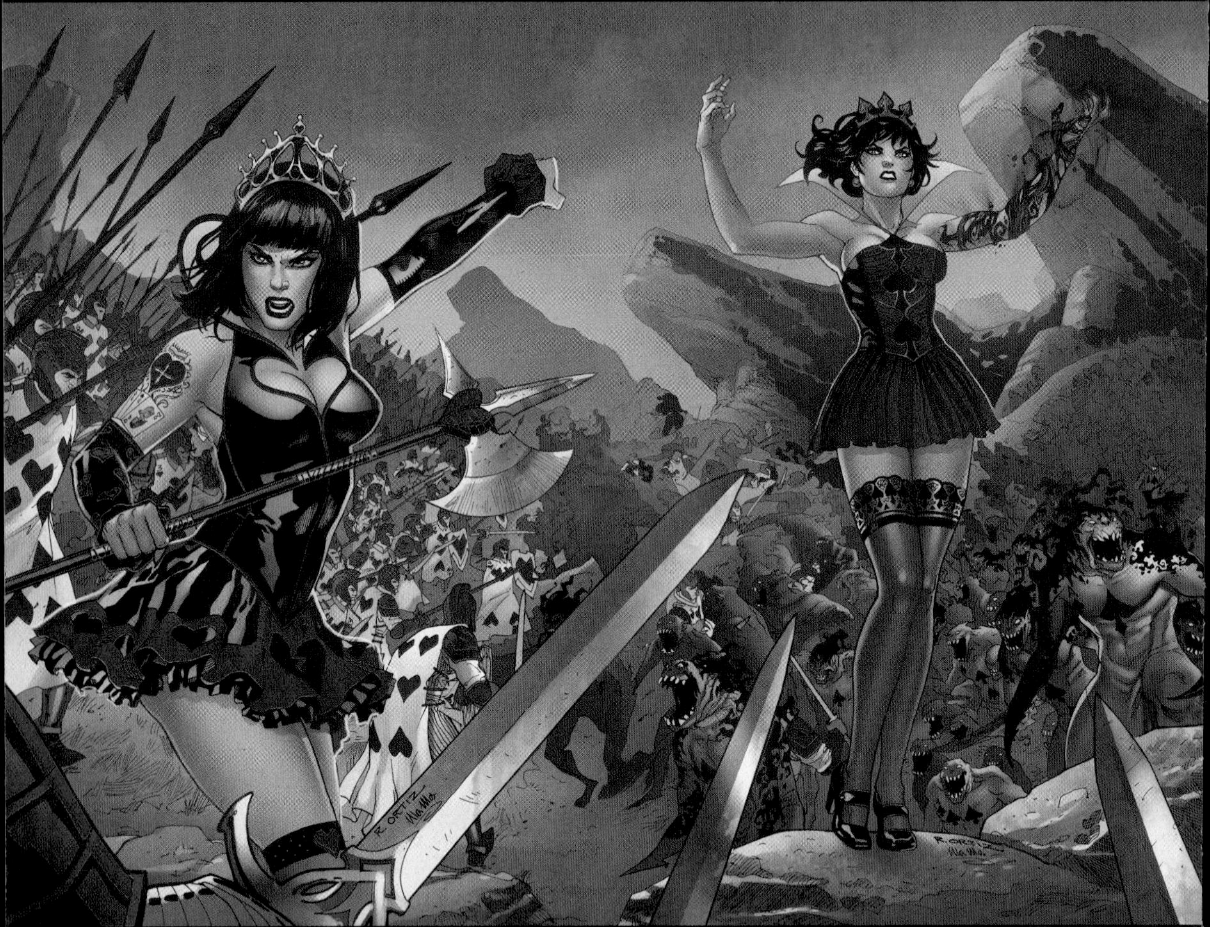

WONDERLAND: CLASH OF QUEENS 5 · GATEFOLD

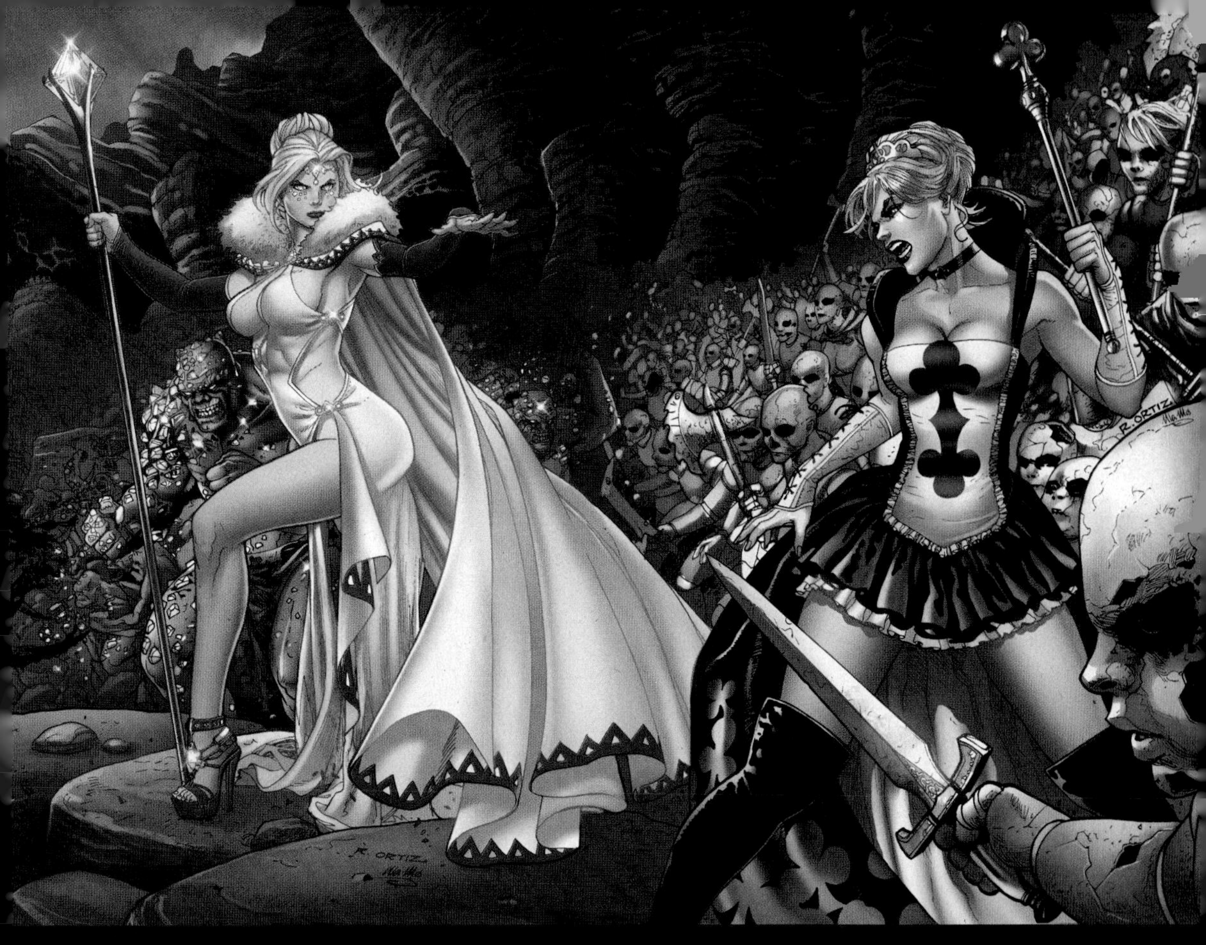
R. ORTIZ
R. ORTIZ

ARTWORK BY RICHARD ORTIZ · COLORS BY ULA MOS

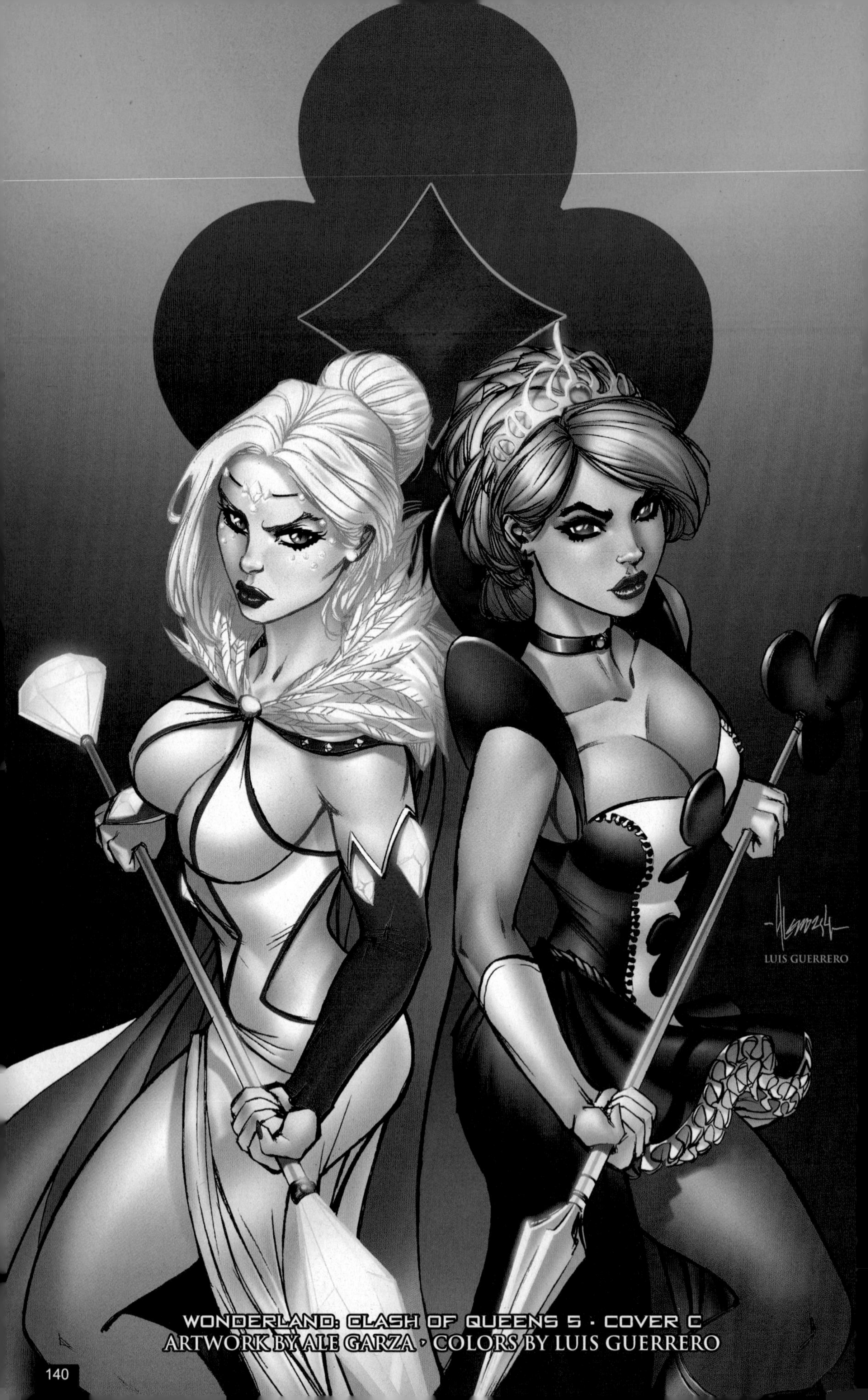
LUIS GUERRERO

WONDERLAND: CLASH OF QUEENS 5 · COVER C
ARTWORK BY ALE GARZA · COLORS BY LUIS GUERRERO

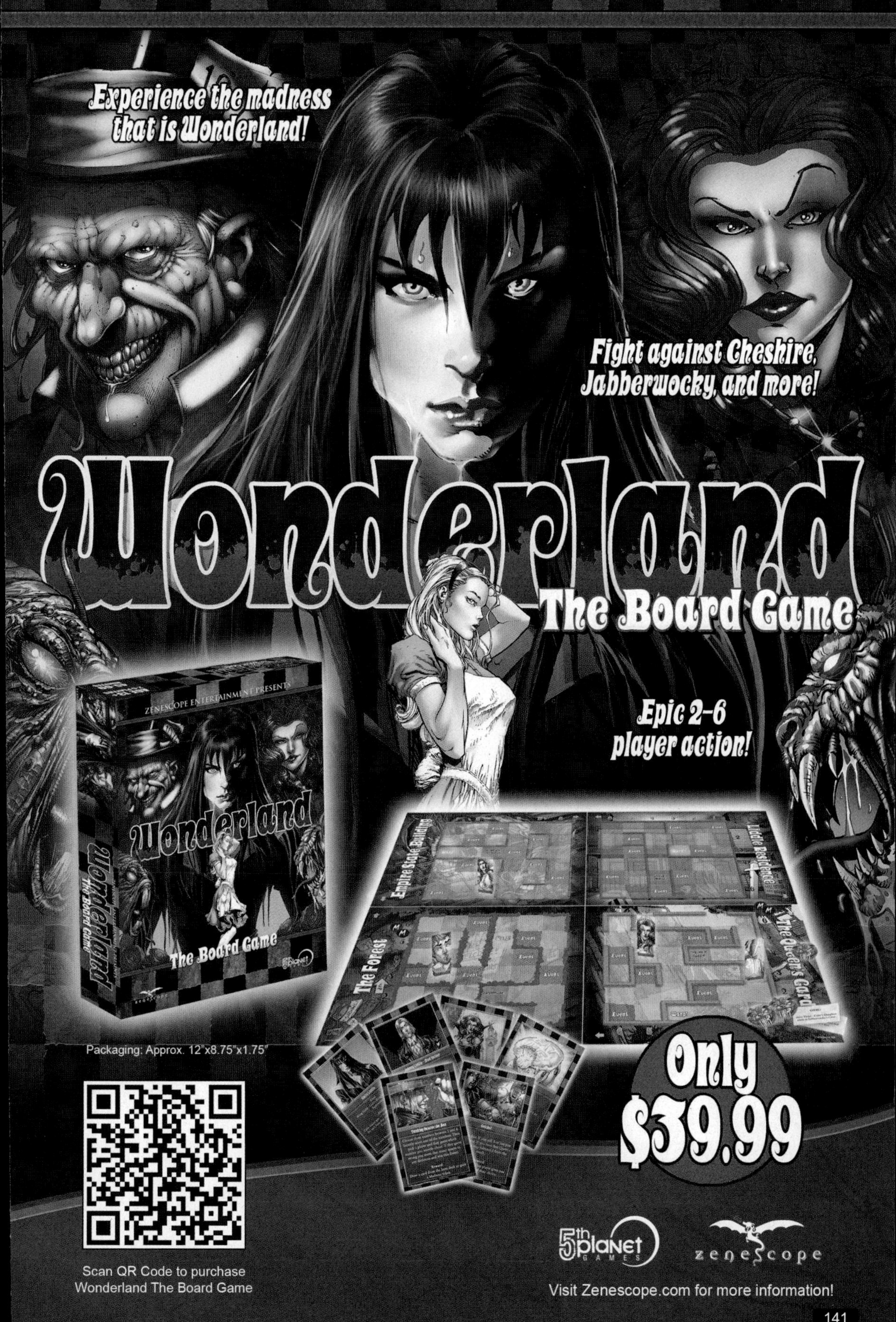
Experience the madness
that is Wonderland!
Fight against Cheshire,
Jabberwocky, and more!
Wonderland
The Board Game
Epic 2-6
player action!
Packaging: Approx. 12"x8.75"x1.75"
Only
$39.99
Scan QR Code to purchase
Wonderland The Board Game
Visit Zenescope.com for more information!

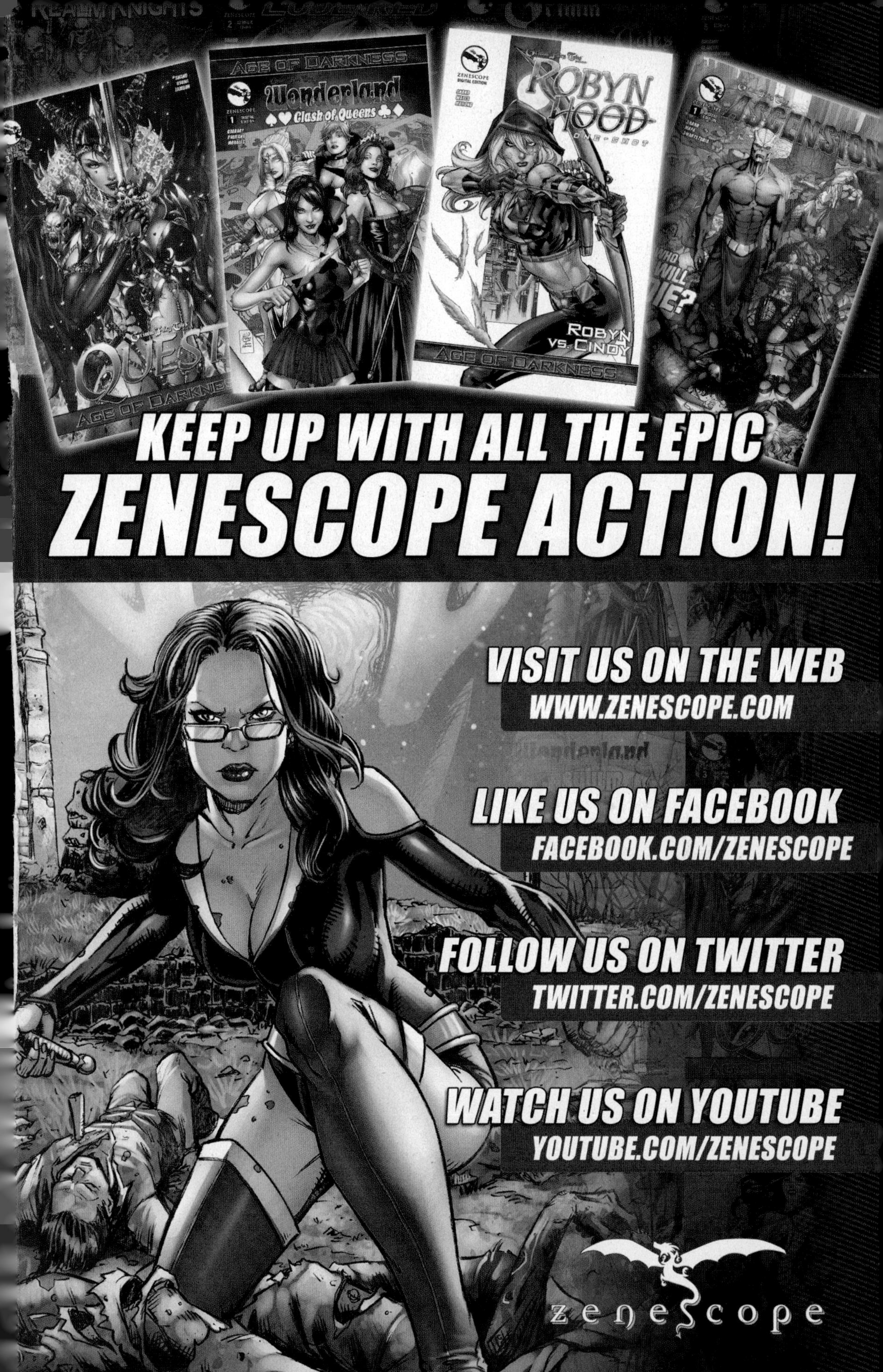
KEEP UP WITH ALL THE EPIC
ZENESCOPE ACTION!
VISIT US ON THE WEB
WWW.ZENESCOPE.COM
LIKE US ON FACEBOOK
FACEBOOK.COM/ZENESCOPE
FOLLOW US ON TWITTER
TWITTER.COM/ZENESCOPE
WATCH US ON YOUTUBE
YOUTUBE.COM/ZENESCOPE
zenescope

Grimm Fairy Tales

Wonderland

♠ ♥ **Clash of Queens** ♣ ♦

AGE OF DARKNESS